# REFUGEE CRISIS IN INTERNATIONAL POLICY

## VOLUME I

### LEGAL AND SOCIAL STATUSES OF REFUGEES

# REFUGEE CRISIS IN INTERNATIONAL POLICY

## VOLUME I

## LEGAL AND SOCIAL STATUSES OF REFUGEES

Edited by

Hasret Çomak, Burak Şakir Şeker, Mehlika Özlem Ultan,
Yaprak Civelek, Çağla Arslan Bozkuş

TRANSNATIONAL PRESS LONDON

2021

MIGRATION SERIES: 27

REFUGEE CRISIS IN INTERNATIONAL POLICY

VOLUME I - LEGAL AND SOCIAL STATUSES OF REFUGEES

Edited by Hasret Çomak, Burak Şakir Şeker, Mehlika Özlem Ultan,

Yaprak Civelek, Çağla Arslan Bozkuş

Copyright © 2021 Transnational Press London

First Published in 2021 by TRANSNATIONAL PRESS LONDON in the United Kingdom, 13 Stamford Place, Sale, M33 3BT, UK.
www.tplondon.com

Transnational Press London® and the logo and its affiliated brands are registered trademarks.

Requests for permission to reproduce material from this work should be sent to: sales@tplondon.com

Paperback
ISBN: 978-1-80135-010-5
Digital
ISBN: 978-1-80135-011-2

Cover Design: Nihal Yazgan
Cover Photo by Julie Ricard on Unsplash.com

www.tplondon.com

# CONTENTS

# PREFACE

Every day, in many parts of the world people are giving the hardest decisions of their lives. With these decisions, they have to leave their homes behind for a better and safer life. Many people in the world, by giving the decision to leave where they grew up, move to a close settlement. Some have to leave their country for a short period of time or for a lifetime.

In many parts of the world, there are many reasons why people try to re-establish their lives in other countries. Some leave their home country to find a job or for education. Others are forced to escape from human rights violations such as inhuman treatment and torture. Millions run away from armed conflicts or violence. These people who do not feel safe; might be targeted due to their characteristics that establish their identity or faith such as their ethnic origin, religious beliefs, gender, and political thoughts.

These journeys that have begun in pursuit of a better future, might be full of danger and fear; some might fall into the trap of human traffickers or other forms of exploitation. Also, some are taken into custody by authorities as soon as they arrive in a country. Many, who settle in a country and start a new life face racism, xenophobia, and discrimination almost every day. They may feel lonely and isolated.

There are many reasons which make it difficult and dangerous for people to stay in their country of origin. Violence, war, hunger, and poverty are the most important ones. Sexual preferences and sexual identity also take an important place. People may also have to leave their home country because of climate change and natural disasters. Mostly, it is possible to encounter many of these difficult conditions all at once.

Fleeing danger is not the only reason people leave their country. Some think of becoming a part of a qualified workforce or gain capital in another country. Moreover, they suppose there is a higher possibility of finding a job in a foreign country. Others seek to live with their relatives and friends currently living abroad. Also, there might be those who aim to begin and continue their education in another country. Therefore, there are many reasons why people might start out to establish a new life in another country.

It is noteworthy to mention the words "refugee", "asylum seeker" and "migrant" in terms of International Law. The refugee is the person who leaves his home country due to the threat of being subjected to grave human rights violations and persecution. These people have to leave their home country and seek asylum in another country due to security threats and threats against their lives. As they have no other choice and they feel their governments cannot or will not protect them against these threats, they are forced to take this decision.

1

According to the provisions of the "United Nations Convention Relating to the Status of Refugees", adopted on 28 July 1951 by the United Nations Conference of Plenipotentiaries on the Status of Refugees and Stateless Persons convened under General Assembly resolution 429 (V) of 14 December 1950 and entered into force on 22 April 1954, refugees have "the right for international protection".

An asylum seeker is a person who has left his home country to seek asylum in another country to be protected from persecution and grave human rights violations. However, in this case, one only has the status of asylum applicants and legally has not yet been accepted as a refugee. Seeking an asylum application is a human right. This means everyone should be given permission to enter a country to seek asylum.

Migrants, on the other hand, are those who live outside their home country thus who are not asylum seekers or refugees. Migrants in general, leave their home countries to work, to have an education, or to live with their family members in another country. Some feel the need to leave their home country for the reasons of poverty, political turmoil, natural disasters, or other difficult conditions.

The issue that should be emphasized here is the situation that many people who do not fit into the "refugee" definition might get be in danger once they are returned to their home country. Even if they may not be escaping from persecution, no matter what their legal status is in the country they established themselves, migrants' human rights must be protected, and these rights must be respected.

States must protect all migrants against violence based on racism and xenophobia, exploitation, and forced labour. Migrants should not be detained without legitimate reasons or forcefully send back to their home country.

Human rights have become both a subject and a legitimate instrument of international politics. Therefore, the human rights of refugees, asylum seekers and migrants must always be protected at the international level. States must fulfill their joint responsibility to protect the rights of refugees, asylum seekers and migrants.

People are not the source of the problem. The main problem is the reasons that force families and individuals to cross borders. Those who cause these reasons have responsibilities. The attitude of authorities who are trying far-sighted and unrealistic approaches matters in the creation of this problem.

States must ensure that refugees, asylum seekers and immigrants are safe, not subject to torture, discrimination and living in poverty. States should assess the applications of asylum seekers according to international rules except for those who;

- has committed a crime against peace, a war crime, or a crime against humanity, as defined in the international instruments drawn up to make provision in respect of such crimes;

- has committed a serious non-political crime outside the country of refuge prior to his admission to that country as a refugee;

- has been guilty or suspicious of acts contrary to the purposes and principles of the United Nations.

The situation of asylum seekers should not be left in a state of uncertainty for years. Unlawful detention practices should not be carried out and the necessary diligence should be taken in this regard. Also, international regulations must be made in order to protect migrants against the exploitation of employers or human traffickers and abuse.

States must take responsibility for and fulfill these responsibilities meticulously for refugees, asylum seekers and immigrants to be able to rebuild their lives safely against serious dangers. Sharing responsibility for global problems is fair in the 21st century.

Welcoming people from other countries might empower host communities by making them more diverse and more flexible in a rapidly changing world. Some of the successful, impactful, and productive people in the field of arts, politics, and technology can be refugees, asylum seekers, or migrants. There are very successful people in the international community who have been given the opportunity to start a new life in another country and become a member of a new community.

In the 21st century, leaders, by showing sufficient political will, should produce and develop new projects to relocate people fleeing conflict and persecution in their countries.

Furthermore, the practice of other safe approaches should be implemented to enable refugees to start a new life. Providing the necessary financial support for refugee families to come to the country and granting them a study or work visa might be considered as an appropriate method for them to establish a new life.

States should not force anybody to return to a country where they might be subjected to human rights violations. Instead, states should ensure a safe place for refugees and asylum seekers, and migrants to live, a job, access to education, and health services.

Refugees, asylum seekers, and immigrants should be treated with dignity without being deprived of their freedom as stated in the United Nations Universal Declaration of Human Rights. Under all the circumstances which require detention and retention, refugees, asylum seekers, and immigrants should be informed about their current rights as well as their fundamental rights. Their detention conditions should comply with international standards in terms of rights and freedoms.

Comprehensive programs should be prepared with the United Nations Member States and the United Nations High Commissioner for Refugees on the provision of social and legal assistance to refugees, asylum seekers and migrants. For this purpose, a valid and secure "country of origin information system" should be established. This system should be targeted to be structured as an "international joint system".

All these developments have revealed the necessity of preparing a multidimensional, original, up-to-date, original and rich content about refugees, asylum seekers and immigrants in the international community and presenting it to science.

This six-volume book series titled "Refugee Crisis in International Politics" are prepared with the aim of clarifying the above-mentioned issues and enriching the content, context, and depth to the field of science.

This first volume offers comprehensive analyses on a variety of topics ranging from legal to social statute of the refugees. The authors and their contributions are as follows: Çağla Arslan Bozkuş "Legal Status of Refugees"; Özkan Gönül and Yunus Karaağaç "Social Rights of Refugees", Hasan Acar and Serhat Bulut "The Political Rights of Refugees"; Gülayşe Ülgen Türedi "Refugees and Human Rights"; Emine Kılıçaslan "Refugee and Cultural Rights of Refugees in the Context of Political Communication"; Cenap Çakmak Clarifying the Legal Status: Distinctions between Refugees, Asylum Seekers and (Irregular) Migrants"; Mehlika Özlem Ultan "Conceptual Framework About Migration"; Akın Kiren "The History of Refugee Movements: A Brief Overview"; Hakan Sezgin Erkan "Development Assistance and Refugee Crisis"; Merve Mamacı "Refugee Well-Being in Work Life"; Saadat Demirci "Integration of Refugees into the Society"; Güneş Koç "Identity Construction of Syrian in their Narratives"; Asena Boztaş "Refugees, Integration and Political-Demographic Concerns in Turkey and the World"; Cemal Kakışım and Ozan Selçuk "Integration Policies of the European Union and Turkey towards Refugees"; and Hekma Wali "The Local Integration of Syrian Refugees in Lebanon, Jordan and Turkey".

We would like to thank all the contributing and researching colleagues who supported us with their research and findings.

We would like to express our gratitude to Prof. Dr. İbrahim SİRKECİ who made the publication of "Refugee Crisis in International Politics" possible.

Special thanks should be given to the staff of Transnational Press London (TPLondon) for their valuable guidance and technical support on this process, for preparing our books for publication, and for designing the covers.

We sincerely hope that the work will be useful and useful to the world of science.

Hasret Çomak, Burak Şakir Şeker, Mehlika Özlem Ultan,

Yaprak Civelek, Çağla Arslan Bozkuş

Istanbul, March 2021

# CHAPTER I

# LEGAL STATUS OF REFUGEES

Çağla Arslan Bozkuş* and Volkan Bozkuş**

It is possible to see the asylum seekers and refugees at 2000s BC at human history. This shows us the importance of this subject once more.[1] The first example of this period is the 30 Years War and forming mass movements; but the basis for today's developments prepared for the forced migration of large masses at the beginning of the 20th century. It begins with the Balkan Wars that gave rise to it. World War I then, with the collapse of the Austro-Hungarian Empire millions of people have to take shelter in various parts of Europe. This dynamism, in the period until the Second World War it continued increasingly, especially with the policies of different regimes. The process reached its peak during and after the Second World War.[2]

To define the "refugee", we can shortly say "They are people who, due to a well-founded fear of persecution, war or violence, have been forced to flee their home country." But the legal definition of the term refugee was set out in the 1951 United Nations Convention on the Status of Refugees. A few years after the II. World War, the leaders of world wanted to ensure that protection for the people those who displaced by war and persecution in international law. The Convention is usually read with the 1967 New York Protocol and when people refer to "the Refugee Convention" we are usually using that as short version for the 1951 Convention and 1967 Protocol together.

The Convention was passed by a United Nations conference on 28 July 1951 and entered into force on 22 April 1954. It was initially backward looking, in the sense that it was limited to protecting European refugees who became refugees before 1 January 1951. The 1967 Protocol gave the Convention new life, forward looking instrument that offered protection on an ongoing basis.

---

* Attorney at Law, Mediator, Arbitrator, Trademark Attorney, Vice President and Founder of the International Law, Arbitration and Mediation Association, Partner/Legal Consultant at Lex Metis International, Owner of Bozars Law Consultancy, Eurpean Union Projects Expert. av.caglaarslan@gmail.com
** Electrical Engineer, MBA, Chairman of The Supervisory Board and Founder of the International Law, Arbitration and Mediation Association, Eurpean Union Projects Expert. volkanbozkus@gmail.com
[1] Tevfik ODMAN (1995), **Mülteci Hukuku,** Ankara, AÜSBF İnsan Hakları Merkezi Press,p..6.
[2] Bülent PEKER, Mithat SANCAR (2001), **Mülteciler ve İltica Hakkı: Yaşamın Kıyısındakilere Hoşgeldin Diyebilmek,** Ankara, İnsan Hakları Derneği Press, p.4-5

The United Nations Convention set out the definition of the 'refugee' as follows:

> "Owing to well-founded fear of being persecuted for reasons of race, religion, nationality, membership of a particular social group or political opinion is outside the country of his nationality and is unable or owing to such fear, is unwilling to avail himself of the protection of that country; or who, not having a nationality and being outside the country of his former habitual residence is unable or, owing to such fear, unwilling to return to it."3

When we check the definition , we can also see that for an asylum seeker, to be recognised as a refugee under the Refugee Convention , they would have to show following conditions :

As said in UN Convention on the Status of Refugees,

"…well-founded fear"

"…of being persecuted…"

"…reasons of race, religion, nationality, membership of a particular social group or political opinion…"

"…is outside the country of his nationality…"

"…is unable or, owing to such fear, unwilling to return to [their country]."4

Refugee Status Determination (RSD) is the legal process by which governments ascertain whether an asylum seeker can be considered a refugee and refugees have to successfully pass through that. Refugee Status Determination, or RSD, is the legal or administrative process by which governments or UNHCR determine whether a person seeking international protection is considered a refugee under international, regional or national law. RSD is often a vital process in helping refugees realize their rights under international law.5

For the UNHCR, refugees and asylum seekers constitute a distinct group of people, because they have left their home in response to serious threats to life and liberty. UNHCR warns against confusing refugees with other groups of migrants who have moved from one country to another for economic or social reasons, while refugees are forced to flee to save their lives or preserve

---

3 The 1951 UN Convention on the Status of Refugees, Definations.Article 1(A).
4 https://helprefugees.org/news/what-is-a-refugee-the-definition-of-refugee-explained/ (Access 10.09.2020)
5 https://helprefugees.org/news/what-is-a-refugee-the-definition-of-refugee-explained/ (Access 14.09.2020)

their freedom.[6]

**Figure 1.** Concept of Refugee[7]

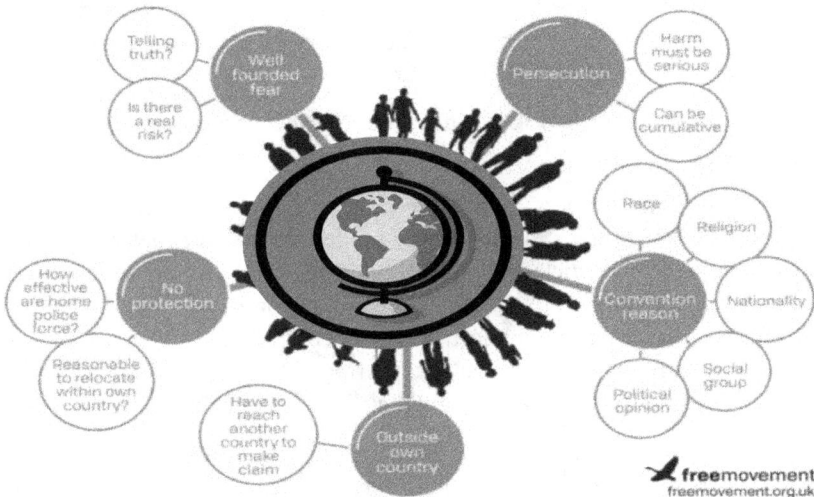

In the media or in daily conversations the "refugee" word is usually used to refer to people fleeing from famine, civil wars, disasters, or conflicts. It is normal calling them "refugees", but they do not necessarily meet the legal definition of a refugee in the Refugee Convention. Also victims of civil wars are not always considered as refugees, if for example they are considered not to have been targeted by either side in the conflict but to have fled the general security situation.[8]

If we explain the term in details;

**Well founded fear:**

Under the Refugee Convention; the refugee must generally show that he or she is telling the truth. If the whole account of what happened is false then usually (but not always) there will be no well founded fear if the person is returned. The level of risk of something bad happening if the refugee is returned must be more than fanciful, otherwise it is not "well founded."

**Being persecuted:**

Meaning of "being persecuted" is not further defined in the Refugee Convention. This is deliberate: it allows the meaning of the word to be

---

[6] UNHCR's Contribution to the Global Forum on Migration and Development, Brussels, 9-11 July 2007
[7] https://www.freemovement.org.uk/what-is-the-legal-meaning-of-refugee/ (Access 14.09.2020)
[8] https://www.freemovement.org.uk/what-is-the-legal-meaning-of-refugee/ (Access 16.09.2020)

flexible and adaptive. This is useful for refugee protection purposes, but it does mean that the student of refugee law will need to look to various other sources and reference points in order to understand the contemporary meaning of the word and how it has evolved. These sources include the views of UNHCR and refugee law academics, other relevant international legal instruments and the domestic and international courts.[9]

The UNHCR Handbook begins its description of persecution as follows at paragraph 55:

> "There is no universally accepted definition of "persecution", and various attempts to formulate such a definition have met with little success. From Article 33 of the 1951 Convention, it may be inferred that a threat to life or freedom on account of race, religion, nationality, political opinion or membership of a particular social group is always persecution. Other serious violations of human rights — for the same reasons — would also constitute persecution."

All Convention reasons mentioned (race, religion, nationality, social group, political opinion ) are very important. Without showing that the future risk is because of one of these reasons, a claim to refugee status will definitely fail. This means, within the legal meaning of the Refugee Convention, some people usually referred to as refugees are not formally refugees. As an example, some who flee from their homes due to famine or flooding or environmental disaster do not fear persecution for any of the UN Convention reasons.

## UNHCR and RSD

UNHCR works closely with states to support and capacitate them in taking over increased responsibility for RSD and with improving their RSD systems and UNHCR Explains the RSD as follows:

> "UNHCR advocates that states establish national RSD systems that are fair, efficient, adaptable, have integrity and that produce quality decisions. Within the broader framework of the Global Compact on Refugees that was adopted by the UN General Assembly on the 17th of December, UNHCR will be establishing an Asylum Capacity Support Group, which will assist states in establishing or strengthening their national asylum systems. In any given year, UNHCR conducts RSD under its mandate in between 50-60 countries, depending on where the applications are received. In 2017, UNHCR registered 252,100 new individual asylum applications, making it the second largest RSD body in the world. In

---

[9] https://www.freemovement.org.uk/what-is-the-legal-meaning-of-refugee/ (Access 14.09.2020)

approximately 20 countries UNHCR conducts RSD jointly with the government pending the state assuming full responsibility for RSD, while in many more countries UNHCR conducts a range of capacity development activities.

In situations where UNHCR conducts RSD under its mandate, UNHCR continues to explore and implement measures to enhance the effectiveness of its RSD response. Where appropriate, UNHCR seeks to identify alternatives to individual RSD under its mandate for select groups of asylum-seekers. UNHCR also uses, and encourages states to use, the most appropriate case processing methodology for a given population, taking into account its characteristics. To this end, UNHCR published in 2017 a glossary of RSD case processing terms that guides the use of case processing methodology in a given situation.

The core standards and best practices to ensure harmonized, efficient and quality RSD procedures, including reception and registration, are presented in the "Procedural Standards for RSD under UNHCR's Mandate." The adoption and implementation of these revised procedural standards is essential to harmonizing RSD and ensuring that persons of concern and the international community continue to have confidence in the fairness, integrity and quality of UNHCR decision-making. Originally published in 2003, the Procedural Standards are in the process of revision to reflect legal and procedural developments.

To assist decision-makers (including state asylum officials, judges and tribunal members, and UNHCR staff) with the assessment of international protection needs, UNHCR issues country-specific policy guidance, in the form of Eligibility Guidelines or International Protection Considerations. These documents contain legal interpretations of the refugee criteria in respect of specific profiles of applicants, on the basis of the human rights and security situation in the country of origin, as well as the social, economic, and humanitarian conditions. UNHCR's assessment of the country conditions is based on in-depth country of origin information research, information provided by UNHCR's global network of field offices and material from independent country specialists, researchers and other sources, rigorously reviewed for reliability."[10]

---

[10] https://www.unhcr.org/refugee-status-determination.html (Access:20.10.2020)

## Country of origin information (COI)

Country of Origin Information (COI) is information which is used in RSD procedures. COI reports collate relevant information on conditions in countries of origin pertinent to the assessment of claims for international protection. To assist decision-makers, UNHCR commissions COI report to independent expert organizations. The Austrian Centre for Country of Origin and Asylum Research and Documentation (ACCORD) maintains a global COI database, which is freely accessible at UNHCR website.[11]

**Figure 2.** Refugees - 2019-2020[12]

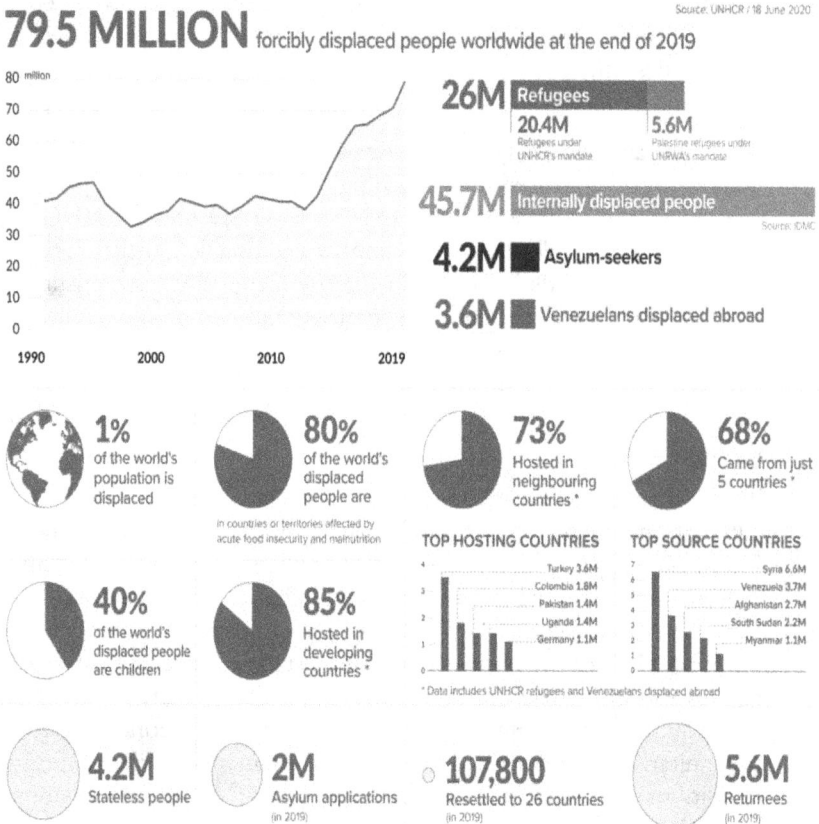

## How many refugees are there around the world?

At least 79.5 million people around the world have been forced to flee

[11] https://www.unhcr.org/refugee-status-determination.html (Access:21.10.2020)
[12] https://www.unhcr.org/figures-at-a-glance.htm (Access : 01.01.2021)

their homes. Among them are nearly 26 million refugees, around half of whom are under the age of 18.There are also millions of stateless people, who have been denied a nationality and lack access to basic rights such as education, health care, employment and freedom of movement. At a time when 1 per cent of the world's population have fled their homes as a result of conflict or persecution.[13]

## Conclusion

There are many different details about legal status of refugees for different countries all around the world. It is possible to see different legal procedures for refugees at each country. Main status might be same but each country applies their own "legal status conditions" to refugees. In this article, we wanted to explain the main term and legal status generally and also we wanted to give information about the system to determine that status.

Refugee numbers are increasing each year because of different reasons and it is becoming more complicated each year to determine their legal status in a right way.

---

[13] https://www.unhcr.org/figures-at-a-glance.html (Access : 26.12.2020)

# CHAPTER 2

## SOCIAL RIGHTS OF REFUGEES

Özkan Gönül* and Yunus Karaağaç**

"For those who starve where they were born…"

### Introduction

As of the written history, it is seen that only 270 years of the last 3000 years did not experience war. This situation reveals the fact that human history is actually the history of wars. The mass wars that took place at the point of sharing lands and scarce resources have been one of the main causes of migration movements, one of the most painful realities of human history. Because the members of the state that lost the war or a society that was tried to be subjected to genocide had to take shelter in another state in the hope of surviving and being safe.

The beginning, development and result of the migration movements that took place is in an interesting position between the life hopes of the individuals who migrated and the responsibility of the states that accepted them. The fact that the rights of immigrants, refugees or asylum seekers and the obligations of states are determined within the scope of international law cannot prevent practical problems. Immigrants cannot benefit from their rights at some points, and states can complain about the heavy cost of their responsibilities. However, this situation does not change the fact that immigrants have fundamental rights.

With the Syrian civil war that broke out in 2011, the migrant and refugee crisis, which rose to the top of the world agenda, has been one of the most up-to-date humanitarian tests faced by the international system. Turkey's proximity to this event, both borderline and humanitarian. It is a topic that is emphasized almost every day in newspapers, news channels and academic writing. But while the topics are being processed; Concepts such as immigration, immigrant, refugee, asylum seeker, stateless have been used interchangeably, intentionally or unintentionally, creating a conceptual confusion. In addition, the content of immigrant, refugee, asylum seeker rights in the context of human rights was conveyed incompletely or incorrectly.

* PhD Candidate, Istanbul Arel University, Political Science and International Relations
** PhD Candidate, Istanbul Arel University, Political Science and International Relations

In this study, first of all, a conceptual framework will be drawn, the basic terms related to migration will be examined, and after a conceptual clarity is revealed, the rights of refugees will be evaluated within the scope of international law. In line with the main topic of the study, the social rights of refugees, content and scope of these rights will constitute the next section. The social rights of Syrian refugees and asylum seekers, which Turkey accepted as of 2011, will constitute the final part of the study as a case study.

## Definitions

### Migration

Migration is a phenomenon as old as human history. People go from their places to another country in order to continue their lives in better conditions, to protect themselves from natural disasters, to ensure their safety due to wars and internal rebellions, it is called migration.

The interdisciplinary aspect of the concept of migration makes it a dynamic, expansionist and social phenomenon. This concept also enables many disciplines to be examined within their own framework and from different angles.[1] Migration has an economic, political, geographical, sociological, psychological and law-legal side. From this point of view, a single disciplinary point of view is not sufficient, and the transition between other disciplines occurs and appears as a phenomenon that needs to be explained.[2] According to the Turkish Language Association, immigration is defined as the country, region and spatial change of individuals or societies due to political, economic and social reasons.[3] From a historical point of view, migration movements in the process up to today create changes and transformations that are much more crystallized in themselves. In this context, new approaches, theories and perspectives are developing.

Migration, which is the subject of change, is a phenomenon that determines a new shaping, the provision of new living spaces and the formation of these living spaces within the time / space relationship, as well as within the framework determined by the conditions.[4]

There are a wide variety of factors that cause people to migrate from one place to another. These reasons are constantly changing throughout the history. The only thing that does not change compared to all these changing

---

[1] Ahmet İçduygu and İbrahim Sirkeci, "Cumhuriyet Dönemi Türkiye'sinde Göç Hareketleri", **75. Yılda Köylerden Şehirlere**, Ed. Oya Baydar, İstanbul, Türkiye İş Bankası Yayınları, 1999, pp.249-267.
[2] Faruk Taşçı, "Bir Sosyal Politika Sorunu Olarak Göç", **Kamu-İş İş Hukuku ve İktisat Dergisi**, Vol:10, No: 4, 2009, pp. 178.
[3] Uluslararası Göç Örgütü, **Göç Terimleri Sözlüğü**, , No:31, 2013, pp.35.
[4] Ayhan Gençler, **Emek Göçü ve Ekonomisi**, İstanbul, Der Yayınları, 2015, pp. 5

reasons is the issue of "a better life".[5] In this context, immigration is formally legal and illegal in two ways. Legal immigration is the fact that people subject to immigration act in accordance with the legal regulations of the country they are transferring to while traveling to other countries.[6] Illegal immigration, on the other hand, refers to people who try to go to other countries by choosing illegal ways contrary to legal rules and norms or who do not leave the country in time by not following the procedures of the country they came from legally.[7] Illegal immigration increases terrorism and crime rates, human, weapon and drug trafficking. Accordingly, countries take severe sanctions and measures against illegal immigrants.

## Immigrant

It is observed that the concept of immigrant and refugee are used synonymously. But the two concepts are different from each other. Immigration is voluntary. People who are mainly due to economic reasons and who leave their country to have a better life are called migrants. From another point of view, they are people who leave their country for many reasons such as political, economic and religious reasons and settle in another country to continue their lives.[8] There is no imposition on immigration. Free will is at the forefront. It is aimed to increase the level of personal and family life by improving financial and social facilities.[9]

## Refugee

The first regulation for refugees is the 1951 Geneva Convention and its successor, the 1967 protocol. States parties to the Convention are obliged to apply the provisions of the Convention to refugees without discrimination based on race, religion or country of origin.[10] UNHCR states that refugees should not be confused with people who have left their country due to economic and social demands, as it regards refugees as a specific group of people who have left their country due to the serious threat to their life rights and freedoms.[11] The collapse of empires after the First World War, the emergence of the nation-state understanding and the widespread spread of nationalism led to the development of the concept of exclusion of the non-self. The violations of rights that took place during the Second World War

---

[5] Mehlika Özlem Ultan, Avrupa Birliği'nde Yasa Dışı Göçün Önlenmesi ve Ülke Uygulamaları, Ankara, Nobel Yayınları, 2016, pp. 11

[6] Ibid.

[7] https://www.yabancilar.org and http://www.calismaizinleri.net/duzensiz-goc (Access: 11.11.2020).

[8] Aydoğan Asar, Türk Yabancılar Mevzuatında Yabancı ve Hakları, Ankara, Emek Ofset, 2004, p.236.

[9] Veli Ağbaba etc. Sınırlar Arasında: İnsanlık Dramından İnsanlık Sınavına, İstanbul, Tekin Yayınevi, 2016, p.28.

[10] Ibid. s.30

[11] Yetişkin Göçmenlerin Dil Entegrasyonu LIAM, https://rm.coe.int/arac-2-multecilerin-haklar-ve-yasal-konumlar-temel-bilgi-ve-terimler-y/1680761f8c (Access: 21.10.2020).

created the need to define the concept of refugee, which turned into a crisis in the international arena as a result of the intensification of population movements as a result of pressure and suffering.[12]

The concept of refugee was defined in the 1951 Convention as follows: "A person who is outside the country of his / her nationality because he/she fears that he will be persecuted because of his/her race, religion, nationality, membership of a certain social group or political thoughts, and who cannot benefit from the protection of that country or who cannot return there".[13]

## Asylum Seeker

The concept of asylum seeker is included in the Turkish law system with some regulations. According to this regulation, the asylum seeker; "Race, religion, nationality, membership of a particular social group or political opinion rightly, because that is where a citizen will be prosecuted because they are afraid the country is located outside the country and unable to benefit from the patronage of a citizen, or who do not want to benefit out of fear, or nationality, or pre-located outside the country of residence if you don't go there, for fear or refers to foreigners who do not want to return" is defined as.[14]

According to Turkey, the feature that distinguishes the refugee from the asylum seeker is defined as those who come from Europe and those who come from outside Europe. He described those from Europe as "refugees" and those from outside Europe as "asylum seekers". Due to their legal status, asylum seekers enjoy minimal social rights compared to refugees.[15] An asylum seeker is a person or persons who, like a refugee, has been subjected to severe persecution and human rights violations in their country and has left their country to protect themselves from these negatives. But those who seek asylum in another country become asylum seekers, while those who receive positive results from their application have refugee status.[16]

## Refugee Rights in The Context of International Law

International law is the law that regulates inter-state relations in general and that nation states must comply with in this context.[17] Not only states but

---

[12] Peter Gatrell, "Europe on the Move: Refugees and World War One", **British Library** https://www.bl.uk/world-war-one/articles/refugees-europe-on-the-move (Access: 01.11.2020).
[13] **Mültecilerin Hukuki Statüsüne İlişkin Sözleşme**, http://www.multeci.org.tr/wp-content/uploads/2016/12/1951-Cenevre-Sozlesmesi-1.pdf (Access:01.11.2020).
[14] 30.11.1994 tarih ve 22127 sayılı Resmi Gazete, p.7, https://www.resmigazete.gov.tr/arsiv/22127.pdf (Erişim Tarihi: 02.11.2020).
[15] Eda Bozbeyoğlu, Mülteciler ve İnsan Hakları, **Moment Dergisi,** 2015, Vol:2, No:1, p.65.
[16] Uluslararası Af Örgütü, Mülteci Hakları, https://www.amnesty.org.tr/icerik/multeci-haklari (Access: 07.09.2020).
[17] Philip Allott, "The Concept of International Law", **European Journal of International Law**, Vol:10,

also international organizations and non-governmental organizations must abide by the rules and responsibilities set out by international law.[18] In this context, refugees also have fundamental rights guaranteed under international law. The legal agreements and protocols prepared by the United Nations and the European Union for refugees are the most important milestones that determine the migration movements and the refugee asylum-seeker relationship within the framework of international law.

## United Nations and Refugee Rights

The severe destruction caused by the Second World War brought concepts such as international peace and human dignity to the fore, and the United Nations was established on October 24, 1945 to prevent wars and ensure lasting peace.[19] On 10 December 1948, the United Nations declared the Universal Declaration of Human Rights, declaring that all people were born free, equal in dignity and rights.

According to this declaration, everyone has fundamental rights and freedoms without any discrimination of race, color, sex, language, religion, political. Life, security, freedom, education, health, thought, conscience, civil rights and freedoms are guaranteed by the member states of the United Nations. No group, organization or state can violate these human rights or violate freedoms.[20]

In Article 13 of the United Nations Universal Declaration of Human Rights "Everyone has the right to freedom of movement and residence within the borders of each State. Everyone has the right to leave any country, including his/her own country, and to return to his country", the phrase is included.[21]

But the displaced people are waiting for a long process full of negativity. These negativities are sometimes caused by the displaced persons themselves, and sometimes by the difficult conditions they have recently encountered and do not know anything about. For this reason, with the Geneva Convention on the Legal Status of Refugees dated 1951 and the protocol dated 1967, some regulations were made regarding how refugees should be treated in the

---

1999, pp.31-50.

[18] Rüdiger Wolfrum, "International Law", **Max Planck Encyclopedias of International Law**, https://opil.ouplaw.com/view/10.1093/law:epil/9780199231690/law-9780199231690-e142 (Access 09.10.2020).

[19] Thomas G. Weiss, "The United Nations: Before, During and After 1945", **International Affairs**, Vol:91, No:6, 2015, pp.1221-1235.

[20] United Nations, "Universal Declaration of Human Rights", https://www.un.org/en/universal-declaration-human-rights (Access 10.10.2020).

[21] Ibid; Mehmet Semih Gemalmaz, Ulusalüstü İnsan Hakları Hukukunun Genel Teorisine Giriş (Introduction to the General Theory of Supranational Human Rights Law), Istanbul, Legal Publishing, p.351.

countries they visited.[22]

The 1951 Geneva Convention entered into force on April 22, 1954. However, while this contract was limited to people in Europe who escaped from the events that took place before January 1, 1951 after the Second World War, the said geographical and temporal limitations were removed with the additional protocol dated 1967, and the contract regulating the rights and freedoms of refugees reached a universal dimension.[23]

The 1951 Geneva Convention Relating to the Status of Refugees consists of 7 chapters and 46 articles. According to Article 3 of the Convention, States parties are obliged to apply the provisions of the Convention to refugees without discrimination based on race, religion or country of origin. At the same time, it is stated in Article 2 that refugees must comply with the laws, regulations and public order of the country where they are located.[24]

According to the 1951 Convention, as a result of the events that occurred before January 1, 1951; Refugees are people who are outside the country of their citizenship and cannot benefit from the protection of this country because of their race, religion, nationality, membership of a certain social group or political ideas, and who are justly afraid of being persecuted. [25]

According to the Geneva Convention, refugees;

The right to live their religion and beliefs in their country of residence without any restrictions (Article 4),

- Right to purchase movable property and real estate (Article 13),

- The right to establish professional unions and associations (Article 15),

- Right to freely apply to civil courts (Article 16),

- Right to work in a paid profession (Article 17),

- The right to open their own businesses in the fields of art, trade,

---

[22] Murat Urk, Göç Olgusu Bağlamında Mülteciler, Sığınmacılar ve İnsan Hakları (Refugees, Asylum Seekers and Human Rights in The Context Of The Migration Phenomenon), Istanbul Maltepe University, Master Thesis, 2010.

[23] United Nations High Commissioner for Refugees (UNHCR), **Convention and Protocol: Relating to the Status of Refugees,** Geneva, Switzerland, 2011, p.2, https://cms.emergency.unhcr.org (Access 11.10.2020).

[24] United Nations Conference of Plenipotentiaries on The Status of Refugees and Stateless Persons, **Final Act and Convention Relating to The Status of Refugees,** Geneva, Switzerland, 1951, p.17, https://treaties.un.org/doc/Treaties/1954/04/19540422%2000-23%20AM/Ch_V_2p.pdf (Access 10.10.2020).

[25] Ersan Barkın, "1951 Tarihli Mülteciliğin Önlenmesi Sözleşmesi", **Ankara Barosu Dergisi, Vol**:1, 2014, p.338.

agriculture, industry (Article 18),

The right to continue basic and university education without interruption (Article 22),

- The right to receive social assistance (Article 23),

- Has the right to travel and reside freely (Article 26).[26]

Therefore, when a general classification of refugees is made; We see that they have fundamental rights and freedoms such as freedom of thought, freedom of religion and conscience, economic and legal rights, the right to education and work, and social rights.

Considering that the Convention on the Legal Status of Refugees, signed in Geneva on July 28, 1951, only covers individuals who became refugees as a result of events that occurred before January 1, 1951, the New York Protocol dated 1967 was adopted.[27] The most important regulation introduced by the 1967 Protocol to the convention was the removal of temporal and geographical restrictions by removing the expressions 'as a result of events occurring before 1 January 1951' and 'within Europe' contained in the refugee definition in the convention.[28]

The 1967 Protocol Concerning the Legal Status of Refugees consists of 11 articles. Turkey became a party to the United Nations Geneva Convention of 1951 on the legal status of refugees in 1961 and joined the New York protocol of 1967, which expanded the scope of the convention, in 1968. However, while Turkey became a party to the convention, it placed a comment on geographical restrictions and maintained this limitation until today.[29]

## European Union and Refugee Rights

Europe is experiencing more and more intensity on immigration every

---

[26] **Final Act and Convention Relating to The Status of Refugees**, Geneva, Switzerland, 1951, https://treaties.un.org/doc/Treaties/1954/04/19540422%2000-23%20AM/Ch_V_2p.pdf (Access 11.10.2020).
[27] UNHCR, **Handbook on Procedures and Criteria for Determining Refugee Status and Guidelines on International Protection**, Geneva, 2019,https://www.unhcr.org/publications/legal/5ddfcdc47/handbook-procedures-criteria-determining-refugee-status-under-1951-convention.html?query=1967 (Access 11.10.2020).
[28] UNHCR, Implementation of the 1951 Convention and the 1967 Protocol Relating to the Status of Refugees EC/SCP/54, 07 July 1989, https://www.unhcr.org/excom/scip/3ae68cbe4/implementation-1951-convention-1967-protocol-relating-status-refugees.html (Access 11.10.2020).
[29] T. C. Başbakanlık Kanunlar ve Kararlar Tetkik Dairesi, "Cenevre'de 1951 tarihinde imzalanmış olan Mültecilerin Hukuki Durumuna dair Sözleşmenin tasdiki hakkında kanun tasarısı ve Dışişleri Komisyonu raporu (1/125)", 05.05.1961, https://www.tbmm.gov.tr/tutanaklar/TUTANAK/KM__/d00/c002/km__00002024ss0053.pdf (Access 12.10.2020); T. C. Resmi Gazete, "Kararnameler", 05.08.1968, https://www.resmigazete.gov.tr/arsiv/12968.pdf (Access 12.10.2020).

day. Especially, the increase, which started after the Cold War, needed commonality in regulating the process of change and adaptation. The process that started with Maastricht continued with the Amsterdam Treaty, and very important steps were taken in migration and refugee issues.

With the Maastricht Treaty, which entered into force on 1 November 1993, the European community's three-block starting point was determined; common foreign policy, security and justice issues are gathered under one heading. The Maastricht Treaty caused the policies of the member states to take a holistic form with a common target. At this point, basic issues such as threat perceptions of the EU, defense and human rights have been revised again. Especially with the transitions to Western Europe and the formation of a common market, migration and asylum issues have also made cooperation obligatory.[30]

The Maastricht Treaty is based on five main objectives. Economic unity is the expansion of social relations among members of the union, common foreign policy and security, strengthening of the legitimacy of institutions and increasing the efficiency of institutions. Under the title of Cooperation in Justice and Home Affairs, it was decided to establish a European Police Office (EUROPOL), which envisages the union members to act together on immigration or political asylum.[31] The Maastricht Agreement, which entered into force on 1 November 1993, has an important place in terms of ensuring that immigration policies are included in the EU agenda. With this agreement, it was aimed to ensure the control of migration movements and to regulate the coordinated functioning of immigration legislation.[32]

After the Cold War, as a result of the dissolution of the USSR, the disintegration of Yugoslavia and the tensions in the Balkans, serious immigration movements towards EU countries took place. The high increase in the demand for asylum seekers led to the signing of the Dublin Convention, which is based on determining the areas of responsibility of the EU countries. The Dublin Convention is a contract that provides a legal framework for the procedures and principles of the requests of asylum seekers and includes explanations on the determination of the responsible country.[33]

---

[30] Yunus Karaağaç ve Eren Akgün, "Entegrasyonun Çözülüşü Mü?: Post-pandeminin Muhtemel Senaryosu, **EURO Politika Dergisi**, Vol:4, No:2, 2020, pp.308-310; **TUIC Akademi,** "Maastricht Antlaşması ODGP Sütunu", 2012, http://www.tuicakademi.org/maastricht-antlasmasi-odgp-sutunu/ (Access: 15.11.2020).

[31] Antlaşmalar, "**Maastricht Antlaşması**", https://antlasmalar.com/maastricht antlasmasi/#Maastricht_ Antlasmasinin_5_Temel_Hedefi (Access: 15.11.2020).

[32] Murat Koca, "AB Ülkelerinde Göç, Mülteciler ve Yabancı Uyrukluların İstihdamı", **Türk İdare Dergisi**, p.101.

[33] Mehmet Duruel, "Avrupa Birliği Göç Politikası ve Kitlesel Göç Akınları Karşısındaki Durumu", **Uluslararası Politik Araştırmalar Dergisi**, Vol:3, No:3, 2017, s.3-4.

The Dublin Agreement, which was signed in Dublin, the capital of Ireland on 15 June 1990 and entered into force on 1 September 1997, was signed by 12 European countries. Later, Austria and Sweden joined Finland in 1998. The Dublin Convention aims at identifying and transferring asylum seekers to the EU country they entered into, as well as preventing asylum seeking in more than one EU country.[34] The Dublin convention was later extended to Dublin II (17.03.2003) and Dublin III (19.07.2013).[35]

The regulation of the European Parliament and the EU Council, dated 26.06.2013 and numbered 604/2013, also empowers the EU member states to assess asylum requests from third country nationals or stateless candidates. With Dublin III, the right to asylum and the asylum process have been expanded and strengthened. Unlike the Dublin II Convention, the Dublin III Convention has taken into account the Fundamental Conditions of the European Court of Human Rights and the European Court of Justice. Likewise, with the EURODAC application, the police and other security personnel can access the stored data, thus keeping the asylum process under control.[36] In the Dublin III Regulation, the procedures and principles of determination of the country responsible for the asylum application for which international protection has been requested by stateless persons or by the third state in one of the member countries is determined.[37]

With the Amsterdam Treaty, which was signed on October 2, 1997 and entered into force on May 1, 1999, it was aimed to establish a common asylum system. The titles related to asylum and immigration in the Maastricht Treaty were transferred to the first column, which is the community column, with the name "Visa, Asylum, Immigration and Other Policies Related to the Free Movement of Persons".[38] In this way, the issue of asylum and immigration has been moved to the first pillar of international relations.[39]

With the Amsterdam Treaty, arrangements have been envisaged that will lead the EU to achieve more successful results in a wide range of issues from refugees and immigrants to procedural principles in decision-making processes.[40] In addition, the following issues related to asylum and refugees

---

[34] Anadolu Ajansı, **"Sığınmacı Krizi Dublin Sözleşmesi'ni Askıya Aldırdı"**, https://www.aa.com.tr/ tr/dunya/siginmaci-krizi-dublin-sozlesmesini-askiya-aldirdi/12842 (Access: 15.11.2020).

[35] Oktay Hekimler, "Üstesinden Gelebilir(mi)yiz: Federal Almanya'nın Yeni Sığınmacı Politikası ve Yansımaları", **Ulisa: Journal of International Studies**, Vol:2, No:1, 2018, p.23

[36] Ibid.

[37] Şebnem Çakran and Veysel Eren, "Mülteci Politikası: Avrupa Birliği ve Türkiye Karşılaştırması", **Mustafa Kemal University Journal of Social Sciences Institute**, Vol:14, No:39, 2017, p.16

[38] Nurcan Özgür and Yeşim Özer, **Türkiye'de Sığınma Sisteminin Avrupalılaştırılması**, Derin Yayınları, İstanbul, 2010, p. 25.

[39] Satvinder Singh Juss, "The Decline and Decay of European Refugee Policy", **Oxford Journal of Legal Studies**, Vol:25, No:4, 2005, p. 754.

[40] Verda Canbey Özgüler, Avrupa Birliği ve Türkiye İşgücü Piyasalarının Karşılaştırmalı Analizi, Cinius Yayınları, İstanbul, 2013, p. 86.

were also emphasized.

Criteria and mechanisms for determining which member state is responsible for examining an asylum application lodged by a third-state citizen in a member state,

- Minimum standards for the admission of asylum seekers in the member states,

- Standards for the recognition and recovery of refugee status in member states,

- Minimum criteria for third country nationals to qualify for refugee status,

Besides, if it concerns refugees and displaced persons;

- The minimum required standards for the people who were displaced from third countries who can not return to their home country provided temporary protection to persons who otherwise need international protection for other reasons,

- Important articles such as supporting a balanced effort between member states in the admission of refugees and displaced persons and taking on the consequences of this, measures in their fields are included in the 63. article of the agreement.[41]

With the influx of refugees in the wave of immigration after the Syrian crisis, restrictions on social rights are increasing in EU countries. Some of the countries under the EU umbrella have left the Schengen system by drawing wire fences on their borders. Asylum seekers who come to Europe in different ways, struggle to survive in camps that are formed spontaneously on the border of countries that close their borders with wire fences. The Calais camp in France is an example. The increase in infectious diseases, lack of treatment and impossibilities in the camp fuel mafia practices and human trafficking.[42] Another example is the Idomeni camp, which is located on the Greek border with Macedonia, under bad conditions such as Calais camp. In this camp, which has 12 thousand people at the beginning, people struggle to survive by their own means.[43]

---

[41] Cenk Bolayır, "Amsterdam Anlaşması: Bütünleştirilmiş Haliyle Avrupa Birliği Korucu Anlaşmaları", **İKV** İstanbul, No:162, 2000, p. 18.
[42] Zehra Hopyar, "Avrupa'nın Mülteci Politikası", **Uluslararası Politik Araştırmalar Dergisi**, Vol:2, No:3, 2016, p.62-65.
[43] Ibid.

## Social rights of refugees

Social rights; are the rights necessary for full participation in social life. It primarily includes the rights to life, health, education, to found and maintain a family (civil), to housing and to protection from discrimination. All states must protect the social rights of their citizens and fulfill their responsibilities. In addition, refugees have social rights just like state citizens. Admissions and measures for human rights must be compatible with refugees.[44] In addition, states that have signed the International Convention on Economic, Social and Cultural Rights (ICESCR), which was adopted on December 16, 1966 and entered into force on January 3, 1976, are obliged to meet the social rights of refugees.[45] The right to life, the right to health, the right to shelter, the right to protection and non-discrimination, the right to work, the right to participate in cultural life, the right to civil and education, constitute the fundamental social rights that refugees have.

## The right to life

According to Article 3 of the Universal Declaration of Human Rights, all people have the right to live freely and in safety. The refugee status of individuals whose right to life is endangered due to their race, religion and political affiliation, who are persecuted or who think they will be persecuted, is guaranteed by international law.

## The right to health

According to Article 25 of the Universal Declaration of Human Rights, everyone has the right to live well, to protect their health and to be healthy. Medical care and hospital procedures are one of the fundamental rights of refugees like all people. The level of humanitarian health standards that states are for their own citizens, should be applied at the same level for refugees in that country. In addition, health services for asylum seekers and refugees vary from country to country, but are not at the desired level, including developed countries. Refugees face serious problems in counseling, basic health and preventive services, diagnosis, treatment opportunities and access to medicine worldwide.[46]

---

[44] Rosa da Costa, "Rights of Refugees in the Context of Integration: Legal Standards and Recommendations", **Legal and Protection Policy Research Series**, UNHCR (United Nations High Commissioner for Refugees), Switzerland, 2006, https://www.unhcr.org/44bb90882.pdf (Access 11.10.2020).

[45] Bobana Ugarkovic, "A Comparative Study of Social and Economic Rights of Asylum Seekers and Refugees in the United States and the United Kingdom", **Georgia Journal of International and Comparative Law**, Vol:32, No:2, 2004, p.551; United Nations Human Rights, "**International Covenant on Economic, Social and Cultural Rights**", https://www.ohchr.org/Documents/Professionalinterest/cescr.pdf (Access 13.10.2020).

[46] World Health Organization, **Health of Refugees and Migrants**, WHO European Region, 2018, p.9-

## The right to shelter

Article 11 of the International Covenant on Economic, Social and Cultural Rights includes adequate nutrition, clothing, shelter and continuous improvement of living conditions. Therefore, refugees also have the right to shelter and nutrition within certain humanitarian measures.[47] Refugees have the right to adequate shelter in which they can live and hide their belongings, protect their privacy and security. The shelter is a closed living space that provides a safe and healthy environment for privacy, comfort and emotional support, as well as protection from the elements, living and storage areas. Housing programs often include a mix of housing solutions such as kits, plastic covers, tents and cash assistance.[48]

## The right to protection and non-discrimination

According to Article 7 of the Universal Declaration of Human Rights and Article 2 of the International Convention on Economic, Social and Cultural Rights, every human being has the right to equal protection against discrimination and discriminatory incitement. Accordingly, it is prohibited under international law for refugees to be subjected to any kind of discrimination in their country of residence.[49] Protecting refugees is the primary responsibility of States. All countries that have signed the 1951 Convention have to protect refugees within their borders and treat them in accordance with international standards. Non-discrimination is the fundamental principle of international law and all humanity.[50] However, parameters such as the prejudiced and discriminatory attitudes of the citizens of the country towards refugees, mass lynch attempts, and inhumane discourse of the media are among the main threats against the rights of refugees to non-discrimination and protection.

---

12, https://www.who.int/migrants/publications/EURO-report.pdf?ua=1 (Access 12.10.2020); Özge Karadağ and Kerim Hakan Altıntaş, "Refugees and Health", **TAF Preventive Medicine Bulletin**, Vol:9, No:1, 2010, p.56

[47] United Nations Human Rights, "**International Covenant on Economic, Social and Cultural Rights**", https://www.ohchr.org/Documents/Professionalinterest/cescr.pdf (Access 13.10.2020).

[48] The UN Refugee Agency, **Emergency Handbook-Shelter Solutions**, p.1-2, https://emergency.unhcr.org/entry/60043 (Access 13.10.2020); Better Shelter, **A Home Away From Home**, https://www.bettershelter.org/wp-content/uploads/2015/12/About_Better-Shelter.pdf (Acces 13.10.2020).

[49] Nana Charles Nguindip, "The Right to Non-Discrimination and The Protection of Refugee Status Under Cameroonian Law", **International Journal of Law**, Vol:3, Issue:5, 2017, pp.83-92.

[50] Frances Nicholson and Judith Kumin, "A guide to international refugee protection and building state asylum systems", **Handbook for Parliamentarians**, No:27, 2017, p.201, https://www.unhcr.org/3d4aba564.pdf (Access 13.10.2020); The UN Refugee Agency **Mültecileri Korumak: Kıbrıs**, UNHCR Cyprus Office, 2017, p.4, https://www.unhcr.org/cy/wp-content/uploads/sites/41/2018/05/UNHCR_Brochure_TR.pdf (Access 13.10.2020).

## The right to work

According to Article 23 of the Universal Declaration of Human Rights and Article 6 of the International Convention on Economic, Social and Cultural Rights, States Parties recognize the right of everyone to work and take the necessary measures to protect this right. The right to work includes the right of everyone to have the opportunity to earn a living by working in a job of their choosing and entering.[51]

Refugee work rights are laws and policies that protect refugees as they enter and participate in the labour economy. Work rights of refugees; It ensures their legal work without discrimination, protects them from exploitation or wage theft, ensures that they earn a fair wage and work in a safe environment.[52] In the practical reflection of the subject, it is seen that a restrictive approach to refugees' right to work prevails. The majority of refugees work informally and are exploited under conditions below humanitarian standards.[53]

## The right to participate in cultural life

According to Article 27 of the Universal Declaration of Human Rights and Article 15 of the International Convention on Economic, Social and Cultural Rights, everyone has the right to freely participate in cultural life, to benefit from arts and to participate in scientific developments.[54] Asylum-seekers and refugees have the necessary conditions for the protection of their interests in any literary, scientific and artistic work they have created within the framework of their own cultural understanding, habits, etc.[55] In addition to access to fundamental rights, the social and cultural relations that refugees establish with other refugees or members of the community they migrate to are one of the necessary and important factors for the integration of refugees.[56] However, the concerns of the citizens of the country that the social and cultural situation will be weakened and changed by the refugees constitutes one of the most active obstacles in reaching the cultural rights of

---

[51] Canan Öykü Dönmez Kara, "The Right to Work of Foreigners in Turkey: Syrians Situation in The Labour Market", **Üsküdar University Journal of Social Sciences**, Issue:2, p. 155-156.
[52] Asylum Access, "Refugee Work Rights", https://asylumaccess.org/global-initatives/refugee-work-rights (Access 13.10.2020).
[53] Roger Zetter and Héloïse Ruaudel, "Refugees' Right to Work and Access to Labour Markets-An Assessment", **KNOMAD Working Paper and Study Series**, September 2016, p.iii, https://www.knomad.org (Access 13.10.2020).
[54] United Nations Human Rights, **The Economic, Social and Cultural Rights of Migrants in an Irregular Situation**, Geneva, United Nations Publications, 2014, p.33-36, https://www.ohchr.org/Documents/Publications/HR-PUB-14-1_en.pdf (Access 13.10.2020).
[55] Murat Urk, Göç Olgusu Bağlamında Mülteciler, Sığınmacılar ve İnsan Hakları (Refugees, Asylum Seekers and Human Rights in The Context Of The Migration Phenomenon), Istanbul Maltepe University, Master Thesis, 2010.
[56] Doğuş Şimşek, "Refugee Integration, Migration Policies and Social Class: The Case of Syrian Refugees in Turkey", **Journal of Social Policy Studies**, 2018, p.373, https://doi.org/10.21560/spcd.vi.446153

refugees.[57]

## The civil rights

Civil rights; protection against arbitrary detention, presumed innocent until the court decides to be guilty, voting, marriage-divorce, inheritance-release, property and debt relations, as well as the rights that prevent arbitrary practices within the legal and political system.[58] The civil rights of refugees are guaranteed under international law. For example, refugees have the right to freely and easily apply to courts of law, to transfer their property to the country, to enter into official marriage after obtaining a residence permit. However, refugees do not have the right to vote in countries where they do not have citizenship.[59]

## The right to education

According to Article 22 of the 1951 Geneva Convention, States Parties are obliged to provide basic education to refugees. In addition, States parties must treat refugees in education other than basic education, recognition of educational certificates from foreign schools, university diplomas and degrees, exemptions from fees and study grants, not less than those granted to foreigners under the same conditions.[60]

Education is recognized as a universal human right:

- Article 26 of the Universal Declaration of Human Rights;

- Article 13 of the Economic, Social and Cultural International Convention;

- Article 28 of the Convention on the Rights of the Child;

- Article 12 of the American Declaration of Human Rights and Duties;

- Article 9 of the Cairo Declaration of Human Rights in Islam;

Underlines that education is a fundamental and universal right for all

---

[57] Yılmaz Demirhan and Seyfettin Aslan, "Trans-Border Migration Policies and Administration of Turkey", **Birey ve Toplum**, Vol:5, No:9, 2015, p. 9.
[58] Rosa da Costa, "Rights of Refugees in the Context of Integration: Legal Standards and Recommendations", **Legal and Protection Policy Research Series**, UNHCR (United Nations High Commissioner for Refugees), Switzerland, 2006, https://www.unhcr.org/44bb90882.pdf (Access 13.10.2020).
[59] Vera Gowlland-Debbas, **The Problem of Refugees in The Light of Contemporary International Law Issues**, Office of The United Nations High Commissioner for Refugees, Geneva, 1994, https://www.corteidh.or.cr/tablas/30218.pdf (Access 13.10.2020).
[60] United Nations High Commissioner for Refugees (UNHCR), **Convention and Protocol: Relating to the Status of Refugees**, Geneva, Switzerland, 2011, p.24, https://cms.emergency.unhcr.org (Access 13.10.2020).

children, boys and girls, with disabilities, including refugee and asylum-seeking children.[61]

### Case Study: Social Rights of Syrian Refugees and Asylum Seekers in Turkey

Turkey is a region that is experiencing very intense population movement due to the geographic location of each period. However, in terms of refugee law, despite the 1951 United Nations Geneva Convention on the Legal Status of Refugees and the additional protocol dated 1967, it could not make a general regulation in terms of domestic law. Unification studies on legislation started during the EU accession process. 11.04.2013 Date institution established in the Immigration Administration, entry to foreigners in Turkey, the stay and downs and held principles to-do about protecting requested next to it.[62]

The regulation on social assistance for refugees in the 1951 Geneva convention is stated in Article 23. In Turkey, the Law No. 6458, "to those in need of international protection have contacts with people from the applicant has provided access to social assistance and services", are arranged in.[63]

Turkey has made reservations to the Geneva Convention depending on geographical conditions. In this context, it does not grant refugee status to non-Europeans. Therefore, Syrians in Turkey have been granted "temporary protection" as an international protection status, since those who fled en masse are expected to return if the war or crisis is over when the Syrian internal turmoil has taken a state of war.[64]

Turkey, Syria after the crisis for the living population movements "open door" policy was followed. In this direction, it applies the provisions regulated within the framework of the Temporary Protection Regulation, which entered into force in October 2014, and is approached within the framework of the "Temporary Protection and Return Policy". According to the same regulation, nobody can be tortured and inhumane treatment. No one; provides protection to persons with temporary protection status, with the statement that they cannot be sent to a place where their life and freedom will be threatened according to their race, religious and political belief.[65]

---

[61] David Nosworthy, "International Legal Standards", **Action for the Rights of Children**, p.37-38, https://www.unhcr.org/3e37e5ba7.pdf, (Access 14.10.2020).
[62] 11.04.2013 tarih ve 28615 sayılı Resmi Gazete, "**6458 Sayılı Yabancılar ve Uluslararası Koruma kanunu**", s 27, https://www.resmigazete.gov.tr/eskiler/2013/04/20130411.pdf (Access: 02.11.2020).
[63] 11.04.2013 tarih ve 28615 sayılı Resmi Gazete, "**6458 Sayılı Yabancılar ve Uluslararası Koruma kanunu**", s 89, https://www.resmigazete.gov.tr/eskiler/2013/04/20130411.pdf (Access: 02.11.2020).
[64] Murat Erdoğan, "Türkiye'deki Suriyeli Mülteciler", **Konrad Adenauer Stiftung**, 2019, p.3
[65] Heinrich Böll Stiftung Türkiye, Türkiye'deki Sığınma Mevzuatı ve Politikalarına İlişkin Rapor, 2019, p. 13-16.

Assistance for refugees and asylum seekers in Turkey is provided by provincial and District Social Assistance and Solidarity Foundations in the form of shelter, health, clothing, food and financial assistance under certain conditions. The needs of refugees and asylum seekers are met by AFAD and the Red Crescent until March 2018, and after that date the General Directorate of Migration Administration has started to be met.[66]

A report published by the Middle East Strategic Research centre (ORSAM) in 2014 compared the camps established in Turkey with the camps created by other countries for Syrian refugees and asylum seekers and evaluated the status of the camps in Turkey. In the report, it was stated that 3 thousand teachers were allocated within the framework of the training provided for refugees staying in the camps, 22 schools with a total of 850 classrooms served and 69 thousand students were educated. In addition, 273 adult courses were created, in which 21 thousand people received training. 21 health centres consisting of 399 health personnel have been established in order for Syrian refugees and asylum seekers to benefit from health services.[67]

Ministry of National Education announced on November 1, 2020 that the number of Syrian students studying at state universities between 2018-2020 was 73,570. In the statement dated June 30, 2020, it was stated that 35.553 students were educated in Kindergarten, 338.807 in Primary School, 222.703 in Secondary School and 89.518 in High School. According to the statement made by the Ministry of Family, Labour and Social Services on 31 March 2019, the number of Syrians granted work permits in Turkey is 31,185 people.[68]

According to the report of the Parliamentary Sub-Commission on Refugee Rights, organized in 2018 the largest share of spending for refugees in Syrian refugees in Turkey are included. Some of these expenditures can be documented, while some cannot be documented. Until this period, the amount of indirect and direct spending made to Syrian refugees was 30 billion dollars. According to OECD data, the annual education expenses of a student in Turkey is $ 3,000. Health expenditure is $ 1000. Education and health expenditure of 3 million Syrians and 600,000 students reached $ 19.2 billion.[69]

The Turkish Red Crescent delivers assistance from national and

[66] Erkan Savar, Umut Kedikli, "Türkiye'de Mülteci ve Sığınmacılara Sağlanan İmkânlar ve Uyum Sorunları: Çankırı Örneği", Uluslararası Yönetim İktisat ve İşletme Dergisi, Vol:15, No:4, 2019, p.1129-1130.
[67] ORSAM, Suriye'ye Komşu Ülkelerde Suriyeli Mültecilerin Durumu: Bulgular, Sonuçlar ve Öneriler, , Report No:189, April 2014, https://www.orsam.org.tr/d_hbanaliz/201452_189tur.pdf (Access: 03.11.2020).
[68] Ibid.
[69] TBMM Mülteci Hakları Alt Komisyonu, Göç ve Uyum Raporu, 2018, p.269-270. https://www.tbmm.gov.tr/komisyon/insanhaklari/docs/2018/goc_ve_uyum_raporu.pdf (Access 14.11.2020).

international aid organizations to Syrians at 14 border aid points along the Syrian border line. The Turkish Red Crescent distributes the list of needs determined by the Governorships to Syrian refugees, in line with the supervision and observation of the International Observation Committee, with the donations and aids provided by the Turkish Red Crescent. Between August 2012 and September 2020, 3,410,210,798.26 TL and 974,251,930.24 kg/piece/lt material shipments were made.[70]

**Table 1.** The Number of Registered Syrians in Turkey as of October 21, 2020[71]

| AGE RANGE | MEN | WOMEN | TOTAL |
|---|---|---|---|
| 0-4 | 255. 900 | 247.400 | 503.300 |
| 5-9 | 282.601 | 259.721 | 542.322 |
| 10-14 | 203.410 | 184.596 | 388.006 |
| 15-18 | 142.058 | 118.556 | 260.614 |
| 19-24 | 286.703 | 212.812 | 499.515 |
| 25-29 | 203.103 | 148.213 | 351.316 |
| 30-34 | 159.210 | 116.003 | 275.213 |
| 35-39 | 119.421 | 97.213 | 216.634 |
| 40-44 | 84.812 | 76.034 | 160.846 |
| 45-49 | 60. 622 | 57.407 | 118.29 |
| 50-54 | 49.814 | 48.956 | 98.770 |
| 55-59 | 38.213 | 38.279 | 76.492 |
| 60-64 | 28.606 | 29.416 | 58.22 |
| 65-69 | 20.366 | 20.795 | 41.161 |
| 70-74 | 7.785 | 8.775 | 16.560 |
| 75+ | 7.723 | 9.994 | 17.717 |
| TOTAL | 1.950.347 | 1.674.170 | 3.624.517 |

Source: https://multeciler.org.tr/turkiyedeki-suriyeli-sayisi (Accessed: 11.11.2020)

In the wave of migration during the Syrian crisis, the most important problem for refugees in Turkey was at the point of shelter. At the first stage, the lack of camps caused by the intensity of the migration wave inevitably affected the creation of new ones. Failures in the camps and difficulties in control caused refugees to leave the camps and spread to cities and live in adverse conditions. It is difficult to find housing in places where Syrian refugees are staying, especially in border cities, with an increase in demand for key issues such as house rents and food, inflation pressure has been created that exceeds the Turkish average.[72]

---

[70] Türk Kızılay, Suriye İnsani Yardım Operasyonu, 2020, p.15-17. https://www.kizilay.org.tr/Upload/Dokuman/Dosya/eylul-2020-suriye-krizi-insani-yardim-operasyonu-raporu-02-11-2020-44797141.pdf (Access 14.11.2020).

[71] Mülteciler Derneği, "Türkiye'deki Suriyeli Sayısı", https://multeciler.org.tr/turkiyedeki-suriyeli-sayisi/ (Access: 11.11.2020)

[72] Tuğba Yıldız and İbrahim Yıldız, "Suriyelilerin Türkiye Ekonomisinde Kayıt Dışı İstihdama Etkileri ve Bunun Yansıması Olarak Türkiye'ye Maliyetleri Üzerine Bir İnceleme", **İktisadi İdari ve Siyasal Araştırmalar Dergisi**, Vol:2, No:3, 2017, p.43.

**Table 2.** Border Assistance Shipment Based on Material Sector

| | Total AMOUNT | Total PRICE (TL) |
|---|---|---|
| **SHELTER** | **126.536,00** | **129.787.709,80** |
| SHELTER OTHER | 16.975,00 | 15.501.123,38 |
| TENT | 109.561,00 | 114.286.586,42 |
| **EDUCATION** | **3.594.767,00** | **22.633.455,29** |
| EDUCATIONAL MATERIAL | 3.594.767,00 | 22.633.455,29 |
| **FOOD** | **670.719.924,63** | **1.306.754.640,55** |
| BREAD | 108.528.893,00 | 25.669.828,10 |
| FOOD OTHER | 134.725.763,58 | 312.274.312,05 |
| FOOD BOX | 7.722.874,0 0 | 448.184.503,96 |
| STORES | 29.420.458,50 | 59.919.803,00 |
| WATER | 37.917.668,00 | 13.980.187,05 |
| SUGAR | 1.916.655,55 | 4.562.349,03 |
| FLOUR | 350.487.612,00 | 442.163.657,35 |
| **NON-FOOD MATERIAL** | **106.987.516,68** | **1.224.476.559,30** |
| BLANKET | 3.558.200,00 | 72.358.116,11 |
| ENERGY MATERIAL | 21.792.61100 | 37.048.483,88 |
| NON-FOOD MATERIAL OTHER | 21.813.993,68 | 175.551.608,14 |
| CLOTHING | 58.977.111,00 | 902.177.964,14 |
| BED | 845.601,00 | 37.340.387,02 |
| **LOGISTICS** | **120,00** | **8.408.581,74** |
| VEHICLE | 120,00 | 8.408.581,74 |
| **HEALTH** | **165.474.296,90** | **576.567.956,00** |
| AMBULANCE | 523,00 | 30.041.348,00 |
| MEDICINE VARIOUS | 99.947.547,60 | 314.620.273,97 |
| VARIOUS MEDICAL DEVICES | 209.584,00 | 42.878.835,85 |
| MEDICAL CONSUMABLES | 65.316.642,30 | 189.027.498,18 |
| **WATER, SANITATION, HYGIENE** | **27.348.769,04** | **141.581.895,59** |
| HYGIENE KIT | 2.769.616,00 | 72.275.687,03 |
| WATER, SANITATION, HYGIENE OTHER | 24.579.153,04 | 69.306.208,55 |
| **General Total** | **974.251.930,24** | **3.410.210.798,26 TL** |

## Conclusion

Individuals in the world try to rebuild their lives in other countries for many reasons. They leave their homeland for economic, political and security reasons. In these journeys that seek a better future and life, they encounter numerous difficulties. Turkey is the host of forced migration movements from the Middle East, Eurasia and Central Asia after 1980 and is the transit route to Europe. Due to the instability, internal conflicts, wars and social problems caused by failed states and social movements, the wave of migration in the region creates continuity and intensity. In a country, people have transferred all their rights other than freedom and life rights to the state through a social contract. In this sense, the state determines the regulatory rules within the framework of law for people to live together.

Within the phenomenon of migration, the concepts of refugee and asylum are due to the most sacred of human being, "life" and "security". At this point, the displacement brings with it political, economic, social and environmental security problems. The concept of human rights is seen as the whole of people's language, religion, race and social status. It is evaluated within the framework of basic rights and universal values such as equality and having common values that result from being a mere human. In the light of universal principles of human rights, the rights of refugees and asylum seekers are regulated within the framework of international law.

At the beginning of the problems that refugees and asylum seekers face most in the countries where they go, violations of social rights occur. All people have the right to education, health, food, security, shelter, social security and coexistence. In this sense, as stated in Article 2 of the Universal Declaration of Human Rights, the statement "every human being has all the rights in this declaration without discrimination on behalf of color, language, sex, religion, social origin or any status"[73] is the most basic approach.

At this point, what is essential is the application of the rights and gains that states apply to their own citizens in the implementation of the titles subject to social rights to refugees and asylum seekers without discrimination. However, those who go to other countries as refugees or asylum seekers are also obliged to comply with the domestic law of the country they live in and not to disturb the social order. Holy is the right to life. In this sense, states have to protect the lives of refugees and asylum seekers and meet their vital needs.

---

[73] İnsan Hakları Evrensel Beyannamesi, Madde 2: https://www.tbmm.gov.tr/komisyon/insanhaklaripdf 01/203-208.pdf (Access 15.11.2020).

# CHAPTER 3

# POLITICAL RIGHTS OF REFUGEES

Hasan Acar* and Serhat Bulut**

## Introduction

The worldwide refugee population rose from 10,4 million in 2011 to 26,0 million by the end of 2020. In this context, the world has witnessed an extraordinary increase in the number of people with refugee and refugee status over the past nine years. According to the United Nations High Commissioner for Refugees (UNHCR) data, people in refugee status more than half of Syria, Venezuela, Afghanistan, and comes from southern Sudan and in turn the global refugee of 90 percent of the southern hemisphere countries host population even as, Turkey is like 3,6 million in numbers, the world is one of the countries hosting refugees. Although Turkey and Lebanon also follow Uganda, unprecedented in European countries such as Germany and Sweden form of the refugee population continues to increase.[1]

While this is the global rise of the refugee population, public debates also include issues regarding the political, social, economic and security aspects of the refugees' country of asylum. Refugees, who have to go to a better and safer environment than their own countries by being subjected to persecution, violence, conflicts, political and ideological pressures, offer opportunities to rebuild their lives in security and stability. It is, of course, no coincidence that public debates are in this direction in terms of their settlement, adaptation and integration into the environment.

The problems related to political rights and participation in political activities as well as the political pressures suffered by refugees who leave their countries due to persecution, violence, conflict and political pressure are largely ignored. In this context, while the debates continue what kind of political activities refugees can participate in and what political rights they have in the country of asylum, most of the refugees are seen as individuals in need of humanitarian aid and precautions in the asylum country. While refugees may be perceived as a threat in domestic practices, especially in political activities, negative attitudes are displayed regarding their

* Ph.D., Gendarmerie and Coast Guard Academy, Işıklar Gendarmerie Petty Officer Vocational School, ORCID: 0000-0001-8956-7836, e-mail: hasanacar.uludag@gmail.com
** Kırıkkale University, Faculty of Economics and Administrative Sciences, Department of International Relations, ORCID: 0000-0002-2286-5916, e-mail: serhatbulut65@gmail.com
[1] Global Trends: Forced Displacement in 2019, UNHCR, Geneva, 2019, p. 1-3.

involvement in political issues. In our opinion, refugees are among the most marginal groups of the international community in this regard. As a matter of fact, the refugees' forced to leave their homeland due to pressure can be seen as a possible tool for them to have their voices heard in the country of asylum through political and political means and internationally. In this context, refugees are people who have the potential to become bilateral political actors as a part of the country of asylum while maintaining ties with their homeland.

Therefore, it is the main purpose of this article to research and analyzes the political rights of refugees in their country of asylum and their country of origin, to what extent they can exercise these political rights. In the literature review on refugees' exercise of their political rights and participation in political activities, the main element is the need for states to protect their citizens. In this context, the article seeks answers to the following questions:

1. What political rights do refugees have in the country of asylum?

2. Do refugees have the right to vote out of the country in their homeland?

3. Can refugees vote in their country of asylum?

4. Do refugees have the right to freedom of expression, freedom of assembly, freedom of movement, freedom of association, and membership in institutions and organizations that do not have political or political aims in the country of asylum?

This study was conducted from a realist perspective, issues related to the political rights of refugees were analyzed from international organizations and actor levels. While conducting the study, it was focused on defining the concept of refugee first. Second, the political rights of refugees guaranteed in international law are analyzed. Finally, the discussions on the political rights of refugees and their participation in political activities in the country of asylum were analyzed through case studies.

## The refugee concept

As Confucius said: *"If the names are not correct, the addresses will not be correct."*[2] As it can be understood from this, it would be correct to explain the concept of refugee at the beginning of the study by staying true to the integrity of the subject.

It should be known that the concept of the refugee has a history as long as human history. It can be understood that the concepts of asylum and refugee have a history as long as the history of humanity when considering

---

[2] Ersan Barkın, "1951 Tarihli Mülteciliğin Önlenmesi Sözleşmesi", **Ankara Barosu Dergisi**, Cilt 1, Sayı 1, 2014, p. 1.

the reasons that drive people from their lands. The phenomenon of refugee existence has been continuing since the 2000s before Christ when the borders were not clearly defined. It is known that many different civilizations have traces of the concept of refugee in inscriptions, inscriptions (for example, Aztec Principles)[3], sacred and religious books.[4] For example, King Urchi-Teshup, who was the Hittite King in the 14th century BC, was deposed by his uncle and sent to Egypt as a refugee.[5] Similar examples are similar to this, as in the Ancient Greek Site States, Medieval Europe, the refugee in Abyssinia due to the pressure on the first believers of the history of Islam, the Jews fleeing from Spain and obtaining asylum in the Ottoman Empire, and the concept of the refugee has not yet been defined. It is frequently encountered even in periods when the foundations of the law were not laid.

The foundations of the phenomenon of refugee and refugee law were laid after the mass migration movements that started after the international conflicts caused by the First and Second World Wars in the 20th century. After the First World War, a High Commissioner was established based on the League of Nations regarding the refugee phenomenon. However, the United Nations High Commissioner for Refugees was established after the Second World War due to the inadequate results regarding the refugee phenomenon and the refugee problem. With the establishment of the United Nations High Commissioner for Refugees, international definitions regarding the phenomenon of refugees have been made and important steps have been taken regarding the status of refugees in the international arena.

In this context, with the signing of the 1951 United Nations Convention on the Legal Status of Refugees, which can be considered as the constitution of refugees or the Magna Carta of refugees, the first international definitions regarding the concept of refugee have been made. According to Article 1 of the convention, the refugee was defined as:[6]

"He/she is located outside his country of origin, because he/she is rightly afraid that he/she will be prosecuted as a result of the events that took place before January 1, 1951, and because of his/her race, religion, nationality, membership of a certain social group or political convictions, and benefit from the protection of this country is defined as a person who cannot or does not want to benefit due to fear, or does not have a nationality and if he/she is located outside

---

[3] İdil Ege Taşdelen, Türkiye'de Mültecilerin Hukuki Durumları ve İzmir'e İlişkin Bir Araştırma, İzmir, Dokuz Eylül Üniversitesi, 2011, p. 14.
[4] Tevfik Odman, **Mülteci Hukuk**, Ankara, İnsan Hakları Merkezi Yayınları, 1995, pp. 5-6.
[5] Odman, ibid., pp. 6-7.
[6] Cenevre'de 1951 Tarihinde İmzalanmış olan Mültecilerin Hukuki Durumuna dair Sözleşmenin Tasdiki hakkında kanun tasarısı ve Dışişleri Komisyonu Raporu, T.C Kanunlar ve Kararlar Tetkik Dairesi, Ankara, 1961, p. 6.

the country where he/she previously resided as a result of the mentioned incidents, cannot return there or does not want to return due to the aforementioned fear."

As seen in the definition of the concept of refugee made in the convention, there is a time limit regarding the refugee phenomenon with the phrase "events that occurred before January 1, 1951". However, besides this time limitation, the definition in the contract included the events that took place in Europe before 1951. For this reason, the Convention on the Legal Status of Refugees dated 1951, with the New York Protocol[7] signed in 1967, is a regulation that makes the definition of the phenomenon of refuge valid for all peoples of the world, because it does not cover individuals who have to leave their homeland due to persecution, violence, conflict or pressure outside Europe has been subjected.

Besides some Regional Refugee Conventions deal with the definitions of the refugee phenomenon more broadly. The Convention Regulating Special Aspects of Refugee Problems of the Organization of African Unity, signed in 1969, is one of these sources. According to the convention, the concept of a refugee was defined as: *"any person whose country of origin or a part or whole of the country of which he is a citizen has to leave their country of residence as a result of foreign attack, occupation, foreign sovereignty or events that seriously disrupt public order."*[8] In addition to the concept of refugee defined in the Convention on the Status of Refugees of 1951 and the New York Protocol of 1967 in the Cartegena Declaration, widespread violence, incidents stemming from internal conflicts have included those whose life, security and freedom are threatened as a result of human rights violations into refugee status. The Council of Europe's Declaration of Territorial Asylum of 1977 also referred to the 1951 Convention on the Status of Refugees, preventing the granting of asylum to refugees for humanitarian reasons, as well as criteria such as religion, language, race, nationality, membership of a particular social group, persecution, and political beliefs. has seen.

In the Universal Declaration of Human Rights, against the absence of any definition of a refugee phenomenon, article 14/1 states: *"Everyone has the right to take refuge in other countries in the face of persecution and to be treated as a refugee against these countries."*[9] declared that everyone has the right to seek asylum in

---

[7] The 1951 Convention Relating to the Legal Status of Refugees and the New York Protocol of 1967 removed the expressions "as a result of the events occurred before January 1, 1951" and "as a result of these events" in the definition of the concept of refugee, declaring that every person included in the definition of the concept of refugee in the convention will accept refugee status.

[8] Parlamenterler İçin El Kitabı, "Mültecilerin Korunması: Uluslararası Mülteci Hukuku Rehberi", **Birleşmiş Milletler Mülteciler Yüksek Komiserliği**, No.2, 2001, pp. 9-10., https://www.refworld.org/ cgi-bin/texis/vtx/rwmain/opendocpdf.pdf?reldoc=y&docid=55fa659a4 (Access 25.11.2020).

[9] Lawyer Prof. Dr. Hüseyin Pazarcı made the definition of a refugee as follows: "It is when a person gets

the face of persecution and declared that the right to asylum is a fundamental human right.

As a result, the following definition can be made based on international and regional conventions regarding the refugee phenomenon. Refugees are individuals who leave their country and have to leave their country as a result of fear of being subjected to violence due to their race, religion, nationality, membership of a certain social group and political thoughts. At the same time, every person who has to leave his country of origin or the country of his citizenship due to foreign attacks, occupation, foreign sovereignty, internal conflicts, serious events that disrupt public order and humanitarian reasons can be defined within the framework of the definition of a refugee.

As seen above in the definitions of a refugee, people who have to leave their homeland as a result of reasons such as race, religion, nationality, membership of any social group, political opinions, internal conflicts, serious events that disrupt public order and humanitarian reasons, against the country of origin in the country of asylum and/or discussions continue today about what their political rights and participation in political activities are, which they can make their voices heard in the country of asylum for the reasons mentioned above. In this context, international law rules will show us what the political rights refugees can obtain in their country of asylum and their country of origin.

## The political rights of refugees guaranteed in international law

### The 1951 convention relating to the status of refugees

The Convention on the Legal Status of Refugees dated 1951, considered as the Constitution of Refugees or Magna Carta, outlines the status of refugees in the international arena. It determines and regulates the rights of the persons who have applied for asylum before the international community and the duties of the states granting the right to an asylum with the reasons in the definition of refugee specified in Article 1 of the Convention.

When the rights of refugees specified in the agreement are examined, it is seen that there is no provision regarding the political rights of refugees in their country of origin and asylum. However, Article 2 of the convention states: "The refugee has obligations that require him to comply with the laws of the country he is in and the measures are taken to protect the public order." inscription is available. As a matter of fact, when this provision is evaluated

---

the assurance of the state he wants to take refuge in as a result of escaping from the pressure and legal proceedings against him by his state or another foreign state by entering the country of any foreign country, consulate buildings, warships or state aircraft." For detailed information, see more at: Hüseyin Pazarcı, **Uluslararası Hukuk**, Ankara, Turhan Kitapevi, 2007, 5. Baskı, pp. 153.

in terms of refugees, it indicates the rights and obligations of refugees when they came under the sovereignty of the country of asylum.[10] It is also the case in the states where refugees come under their sovereignty on their way to the country of asylum.

The 1951 Convention Relating to the Status of Refugees also includes regulations on the treatment of refugees. Only one of these regulations has an important place in terms of the political rights of refugees. In this context, Article 26 of the convention states that "Refugees who reside legally in the state will be given the right to choose the place of residence provided to other foreign citizens and to travel freely." refugees are granted the right to move freely within the country. For matters other than freedom of movement, the contract 7/1. Article is applied.

"The Contracting States will apply to refugees the same treatment as foreigners in general." Thanks to this provision in the agreement, refugees will generally be able to obtain the rights of other foreign citizens in the country of asylum.[11] However, it should be noted that this provision is not explicit in terms of political rights. For this reason, 7/1 of the contract. It would be wrong to interpret the article in line with political rights. 7/3 of the contract. According to the article, after the contract entered into force, the gains of the rights arising from the regulation of the domestic law rules of the states parties to the convention are guaranteed. Nevertheless, the political rights that refugees can obtain based on the domestic law of the country of asylum depend on the consent of the country of asylum. In this context, it will be possible and correct to say that the articles that can be considered as political rights[12] in the contract refer to International Human Rights Law, since there is no specific provision in terms of political rights in the contract.

### Regional refugee agreements

In the regional refugee conventions, when the African Union Organization Convention Regulating Special Aspects of Refugee Problems, which deals with the definition of refugee in the first broad framework, is examined in terms of political rights and participation in political activities, the first striking fact is that the 1951 Convention on the Legal Status of Refugees, as in the Convention on the legal status of refugees, and states that it must comply with the rules regarding the protection of public order. However, in Articles 3/1 and 3/2 of the convention, refugees: "Avoiding

---

[10] **Political Rights of Refugees**, PPLA, Cenevre, 2003, p. 1.
[11] Regarding the enjoyment of the rights specified in Article 7/1 of the Refugee Convention, it is subject to Article 3, which prohibits any discrimination specific to race, religion and their own countries.
[12] Article 15 of the Convention grants refugees rights to join associations and unions that do not have political purposes. As a result of the provision given on the condition that it does not carry a political purpose, it is not evaluated in terms of the political rights given to refugees.

destructive action against any of the member states of the Organization of African Union and avoiding behaviors that may cause tension between member states through the press or radio"[13] highlight the need. As a matter of fact, there is no explanation in the contract about the actions that can cause "destructive" and "tension".

Therefore, when we evaluate this situation in terms of the political rights of refugees, it is possible to evaluate it positively in line with the rules of Human Rights Law. However, when we consider the rights of refugees arising from the contract in the African Union Organization in the context of the domestic law rules, it is possible to address the 3/1 and 3/2 articles of the agreement as the refugees do not have political rights and their participation in political activities. As a matter of fact, in the second statement, there is evidence that the states of the Organization of African Unity have a strictly negative attitude towards the political rights of the refugees. In this context, the participation of refugees in political activities, especially in Ethiopia, can be considered as a behavior against the security and stability of the refugee's country of origin. Likewise, in Zimbabwe, the refugees' expressing their political views and criticizing the political regime in the context of political rights can be considered as a destructive and tense action and may lead to the deportation of refugees from the asylum country.[14]

In the context of regional conventions, the Cartagena Refugee Statement does not contain any provision regarding the political rights of refugees. It should be noted that the Cartagena Declaration is not binding. Also based on the provisions of the American Convention on Human Rights, the Declaration of Cartegena prescribes that "minimum standards"[15] should be established for refugees and treatment should be displayed towards these standards.[16] In this context, if it is considered that the Cartegena Declaration refers to the Civil and Political Rights Convention, it is revealed that the Cartegena Declaration does not have a positive and/or negative effect on the political rights of refugees and their participation in political activities.

### Human Rights Law

Human rights law is fed by moral values. In this context, it has had a magnificent effect on the rise of the status of refugees in international law since its emergence. In this context, it does not make any discrimination

---

[13] http://madde14.org/index.php?title=Afrika_Birli%C4%9Fi_%C3%96rg%C3%BCt%C3%BC_M%C3%BClteci_Sorunlar%C4%B1n%C4%B1n_%C3%96zel_Y%C3%B6nlerini_D%C3%BCzenleyen_S%C3%B6zle%C5%9Fme (Access 27.11.2020).

[14] Political Rights of Refugees, ibid., p. 20.

[15] In international law, "minimum standards" are addressed in the treatment of foreigners. While there is no clear provision on what the minimum standards are, the issue of how to handle the minimum standards is still controversial.

[16] **Cartagena Mülteciler Deklerasyonu**, Cartagena de Indias, 1984, pp. 1-4.

between foreigners, refugees and local citizens, as human rights law is nurtured by moral values.[17] However, there are several of exceptions regarding the political rights of refugees. These exceptions belong to the right to elect and be elected, which is a precondition for refugees to determine their future.

### The Right to Vote and be Elected in the Country of Asylum

Article 25/b. of the International Covenant on Civil and Political Rights states: "Every citizen has the right to vote and to be elected, and to exercise public duty, with general and equal voting rights in periodic elections."[18] With the phrase, every citizen is given the right to elect and be elected. Considering this situation in terms of refugees in the country of asylum, refugees are not given the right to elect and be elected according to the rules of international law. Because the right to elect and be elected is a situation related to citizenship. Not surprisingly, regional human rights treaties are in the same position. For example, Article 13 of the African Convention on Human Rights and Article 23 of the American Convention on Human Rights support this situation.[19]

When the right to vote and be elected is considered in terms of refugees, states do not have an obligation to give foreigners and refugees the right to vote. However, in some exceptional cases, permission is given to participate in elections in line with the consent of the state, in accordance with the rules of domestic law. For example, in Sweden, foreigners and refugees within the country have the right to vote in regional and provincial elections and to be a candidate in elections. Besides the European Convention on the Participation of Foreigners in Life at the Public Level; *"Every foreigner residing under legal conditions five years before the elections undertakes the right to vote and to support his election in local government elections."*[20] grants foreigners in the country the right to vote in elections. However, it should be noted again that refugees' voting in elections in the country of asylum depends on the consent of the asylum state.

### The Right to Choose and be Elected in the Country of Origin

When it comes to the right of refugees to vote in their own countries, the International Covenant on Civil and Political Rights also comes into play. In this context, it states that, by the above-mentioned article of the contract, every citizen has the right to elect and be elected within the scope of certain

[17] Kemal Gözler, **İnsan Hakları Hukuku**, Bursa, Ekin Basım Yayın Dağıtım, 2. Baskı, 2018, s. 1.
[18] TBMM İnsan Hakları İnceleme Komisyonu Raporu; Kişisel ve Siyasal Haklar Sözleşmesi, TBMM, Ankara, 2000, p. 63.
[19] Political Rights of Refugees, ibid., pp. 3-4.
[20] http://debis.deu.edu.tr/DEUWeb/Icerik/Icerik.php?KOD=10468 (Access. 28.11.2020).

conditions. A general provision regarding the right to vote and be elected is the condition of residence.

As a matter of fact, this situation can be regarded as a justified article since citizens who do not live in their own country have a small share in their thoughts and wishes about the political future of their country. However, considering the special situation of refugees, unlike expatriates, refugees did not leave their country voluntarily. In this respect, this special situation of refugees should be taken into account when considering the refugees' leaving their homeland due to reasons such as pressure, persecution and conflict. Considering that refugees are willing to return to their country of origin in the short term, it can be thought that it depends on their voting against their country of origin by the remote voting system in the country of asylum. In this context, while there are regulations regarding the participation of refugees in the political activities of their countries of origin through the remote voting system, in most countries there are no regulations regarding refugees voting.

Considering that states generally limit voting to citizens residing in their territories, a special arrangement should be made for refugees. It should not be forgotten that the asylum state requires diplomatic contact with the countries of origin of the refugees to obtain the right to vote remotely, which may cause a diplomatic crisis for refugees and their countries in every sense.

## Freedom of Expression

Freedom of expression is a right granted to all individuals by International Human Rights Law. When considered in a political context, freedom of expression and thought is at the centre of individuals' attitudes or participation in political activities. In this context, Article 19/1 of the Covenant on Civil and Political Rights guarantees freedom of expression for all world citizens.

"Everyone has the right to get the opinion they want and to express them. This right; It includes the freedom to research, acquire and share all kinds of information and ideas, verbally, written or printed, in any way of their choice, regardless of national boundaries." The exercise of freedom of expression is not a fully unlimited right like other rights. Following Article 19/3 of the same contract, respecting the rights of others is subject to restrictions in terms of public order, public health, national security and protection of social general morality. These restrictions are not a restriction on individuals' thoughts. Restrictions imposed in this context have been introduced to protect the interests of states in the international community. Therefore, refugees do not have absolute freedom to express their opinions, whether in their own country or the country of asylum. However, it should be noted that there are no restrictions on any kind of political opinion that does not violate public order, public health, national security and public morality.

However, Article 20 of the Covenant on Civil and Political Rights states that "war propaganda, provoking against national, racial and religious discrimination, hostility or violence" and absolute and absolute forms are prohibited. When commenting on this article, it is clear that the activities of the individual organization or political organization established by refugees in the refugee countries will be prevented if they include behaviors as described in the article. In this context, it is possible to say that political organizations established by refugees in the country of asylum will not be prevented from their political activities within the scope of not including the behaviors mentioned in Article 20. This comment should not be evaluated in terms of the attitude of the asylum state towards refugees.

It is worth mentioning the attitude of the European Court of Human Rights on freedom of expression. In this context, Article 10 of the European Convention on Human Rights: "guarantees the freedom of expression of the people in the regions subject to the necessary restrictions for the economic welfare of the country, without the intervention of public institutions and authorities and regardless of the borders of the country."[21] in the form. However, Article 16 of the European Convention on Human Rights "None of the provisions of Articles 10, 11 and 14 can be considered as prohibiting the participation of foreigners in political activities." expressions are included. When we look at Articles 10 and 16 of the convention, it can be interpreted that there are no restrictions on the participation of refugees and foreigners in all kinds of political thoughts and activities of a political nature. However, the European Court of Human Rights drew attention to the fact that the articles specified in the contract are in contradiction with Articles 1 and 14 of the convention. In this context, especially Article 16 of the European Convention on Human Rights can be interpreted narrowly.

As a result, the European Court of Human Rights or the Covenant on Civil and Political Rights has guaranteed that foreigners and refugees have political freedom of expression without destructive action.

### Freedom of Assembly

In the context of political rights, freedom of assembly is a prerequisite for individuals to communicate their views, ideas and thoughts to each other or to carry out their marches, actions and campaigns for whatever reason. In this context, Article 21 of the Covenant on Civil and Political Rights; "Peaceful assembly right is recognized by law. No other restrictions can be

---

[21] Avrupa İnsan Hakları Sözleşmesi: Avrupa Antlaşmaları Serisi, Fransa, Avrupa Konseyi Yayınları, 2010, pp. 11-12.

imposed on this use, except for the necessary restrictions on public safety, public order, public health, or the protection of public morals." in the form. Therefore, any collection that does not endanger public health, public order, public morals and public safety is legal for refugees. As a result of peaceful demonstrations, whether for political activity or individual reasons, refugees have the right to enjoy the freedom of assembly.

As mentioned above, in terms of refugees and foreigners, Article 16 of the European Convention on Human Rights also imposes certain restrictions on the right of collection under Article 11. In this context, considering that the effect of Article 11 of the European Convention on Human Rights is limited, it is strictly forbidden to apply arbitrary restrictions by the countries of asylum and origin within the scope of the decision taken by the European Courts of Human Rights in the context of organizing legal and peaceful demonstrations.[22]

### Freedom of Association

Like all citizens, the guarantee of freedom of association in Article 22 of the Covenant on Political and Civil Rights gives refugees the right to establish political organizations.

The functioning of established political organizations can be restricted for the same reasons as in Article 21. For this reason, it is a legal justification to ban a refugee organization that contains hate speech against a particular political group in the country of asylum when it poses a risk to public order. Likewise, refugees have the right to join organizations that peacefully act against their country of origin for political regime change, and this is protected by Article 22. In the European Convention on Human Rights, the freedom of association given in Article 11 of the refugees is considered within the scope of freedom of assembly.

### Freedom of Movement

Refugees have the right to move freely within the state under their sovereignty with Article 12 of the Covenant on Civil and Political Rights, which is consistent with national security, public order, public health, public morality and restrictions taken to protect the rights and freedoms of other persons and others. In this context, every person who is legally a refugee in the country of asylum will be deemed to have freedom of movement within the country.

---

[22] Political Rights of Refugees, ibid., pp. 7-8.

## Interpretation of Refugees' Political Activity Types

As can be seen as a result of the analyzes made above, a refugee's political rights and ability to carry out political activities probably fall into one of three categories:

- Activities that the Asylum State has to permit within the framework of International Law and Human Rights Law

- Activities permitted by the State of Asylum subject to its consent

- Activities that the Asylum State is obliged to prevent within the framework of International Law and Human Rights Law

In this context, it would be appropriate to evaluate these rights individually and examine the attitudes of the asylum states regarding these rights, as we categorize the rights of refugees as guaranteed in international law.

## Participation in Political Elections

As mentioned above, refugees do not have any rights arising from international law regarding the participation of states of asylum in elections. However, depending on the rules of international law, the countries of asylum may grant refugees and foreign citizens the right to choose, depending on their consent regarding domestic law regulations. Approximately 45 countries give voting rights to refugees and foreign citizens[23] in local elections. Nevertheless, most countries advocate for refugees and foreign citizens to acquire citizenship as a precondition for voting and/or participating in elections. In this context, it would be correct to consider the criteria of citizenship right, which is a precondition for refugees and foreign citizens to participate in the elections in the countries of asylum, from the perspective of refugees.

## Citizenship

Article 34 of the 1951 Convention on the Legal Status of Refugees; "It will make it easier to absorb and naturalize refugees to any extent possible. It will make special efforts to expedite naturalization procedures and to reduce the costs of these procedures to any extent " in the form. Similarly, the Global Compact on Refugees refers to the granting of citizenship and permanent residence to refugees. [24] In this context, the naturalization of refugees in the

---

[23] David C. Earnest, The Enfranchisement of Resident Aliens: Variations and Explanations, **Democratization**, Vol.22, No.5, 2015, pp. 861-883.; Luciy Pedroza, The Democratic Potential of Enfranchising Residen Migrants, **International Migration**, Vol.53, No.3, 2015, pp. 22-35.

[24] https://www.unhcr.org/protection/basic/3b66c2aa10/convention-protocol-relating-status-refugees.html (Access 28.11.2020).

country of asylum is the only element that is legally required to obtain political rights. It does not mean that refugees can exercise their political rights fully and equally like the local people, even if they acquire citizenship in the country of asylum. While the right of citizenship does not eliminate the problem of repatriation for refugees to their country of origin, it is the only status that allows permanent settlement in the country of asylum. For this reason, within the framework of freedom of movement arising from international law, the right to free movement is seen as an incentive for refugees to be naturalized.

In obtaining the right to citizenship, states generally apply several procedures determined by nationality laws. From the perspective of refugees, this means looking at the citizenship exams made by the states, their economic status and the duration of residence within the country.[25] Given a worse scenario during the naturalization phase and the discrimination against refugees, some countries make it difficult for refugees who want to acquire citizenship to obtain citizenship. In return, following Article 34 of the above-mentioned convention, refugees should be facilitated in acquiring citizenship.

There is another secondary aspect of facilitating refugees in terms of citizenship, together with the rights arising from the contract. Despite the reduction of the residence requirement in the countries of asylum or the abolition of the residence requirement, refugees are asked to renounce their citizenship of their country of origin. In this context, the practices for refugees to acquire citizenship rights are implemented as a dual preference system.

For example, when we look at the German citizenship laws, refugees need to have a permanent residence permit for 6 years, they must live in Germany without social assistance or unemployment benefits, have a good command of German, successfully pass the citizenship exams, and have no convictions for any crime.[26] Besides Germany does not recognize dual citizenship rights for immigrants who are not members of the European Union. In this context, as we mentioned above, any refugee who applies for German citizenship will have to give up the citizenship of their country of origin during the naturalization process.

As in the case of Germany, the process of naturalization of refugees in the country of asylum is at the discretion of the country. While international law provides facilitation on the right to citizenship as a permanent solution to the problems of refugees, asylum countries take stricter and harsh

---

[25] Roger Zetter, More Labels, Fewer Refugees: Remaking the Regufee Label in an Era of Globalization, **Journal of Refugee Studies**, Vol.20, No.2, 2007, pp. 172-192.
[26] Kay Hailbronner, EUDO Citizenship Observator Country Report: Germany, European Universitiy Institue, Robert Schuman Center for Advanced Studies, 2010, pp. 3-10.

measures for the right to citizenship creates problems in the context of the political rights of refugees. In this context, refugees are generally seen as a burden for the countries of asylum and they are sent by the country of asylum to their country of origin, not citizenship.[27] Also, the tightening of the status of refugees by the international community day by day creates a problem regarding the citizenship of the refugee country and the use of their political rights. It is for this reason that the asylum countries are reluctant to expand the political rights of refugees.

### Participation in Elections and Political Organizations

Exercising the right to vote and be elected in political activities is of course not the only way of political participation where refugees can have their voices heard in the country of asylum. However, participation in elections is both an important component of citizenship and the building block of a democratic system.[28]

As mentioned above, the inclusion of refugees in elections depends on citizenship. Some countries regulate their domestic law and encourage refugees to participate in elections without obtaining citizenship. In this context, for example; Sweden is the only state that gives refugees the right to vote and stand as a candidate in regional municipal elections. However, the Swedish Regional Election Law requires refugees to reside in the region where the election will be held for three years before the election. In 1976, it was argued that refugees living in Sweden would increase their political qualities, interests and self-confidence, and the right to elect and be elected for the elections held in municipalities and provinces was expanded. With these extended rights granted to refugees in Sweden, it has encouraged the equal participation and political participation of refugees with the local community.

Considering the refugees who are given the right to vote and be elected, having the right to vote and to be a candidate does not mean that the refugees will participate in the election phase. As a matter of fact, according to the analyzed data, the actual participation of refugees in the selection phase is very low compared to the local community. Unfortunately, data on the electoral behavior of refugees are not available, as data in states where refugees have the right to vote are not disaggregated into refugee-based voters and local-based voters. However, it is known that refugees are ineffective in practice exercising their right to vote and be elected. The behaviors of refugees regarding the exercise of the right to vote and be

---

[27] B.S Chimni, From Resettlement to Involuntary Repatriation: Towards a Critical History of Durable Solutions to Refugee Problems, **Refugee Survey Quarterly**, Vol.23, No.3, 2004, p. 67.
[28] Armend Bekaj and Line Antara, **Political Participation of Refugees: Bridging the Gaps**, Stockholm, International IDEA Publications, 2018, p. 35.

elected vary according to their education level, gender, age and class.[29] In this context, their situation in practicing the right to vote and be elected, given to refugees; deficiencies in how democratic rights can be exercised for refugees from authoritarian regimes, as well as the refusal of women from male-dominant peoples to exercise their right to vote and be elected by their spouses, their negative attitudes towards the right to vote in the country of asylum, the ineffectiveness of refugees in actually exercising the right to vote and be elected. constitute. Also the political experiences of refugees in their country of origin regarding their reluctance to participate in political life in the country of asylum may also create reluctance. In this context, refugees may have had negative political experiences in their homeland and have been forced to leave their homeland, subject to the oppression of the political regime. Therefore, his willingness to participate in political life in the country of asylum will be low.

Despite legal restrictions on refugees 'right to vote and be elected in the country of asylum, as we have already explained in most countries, membership of political parties and political parties can be seen as an intermediary for refugees' participation in political activities in the country of asylum. The rules of domestic law regulating the membership rules for political parties may differ from country to country. In this context, Germany allows refugees to become members regardless of their legal status at the stage of joining political parties in Sweden and the UK. It is in countries like Turkey and Lebanon citizenship participation in the next stage of the political parties are being sought.

In this context, regarding the political rights of refugees, citizenship is required for refugees to exercise their right to vote and be elected in most countries of asylum. Likewise, the right of citizenship is sought in most of the asylum states at the stage of political party membership or establishing a political party. However, given the particular situation of refugees, they can't return to their country of origin soon. For them to be included in the local society by taking cultural, social and political aspects in the countries of asylum, especially the extension of the domestic law of the asylum countries in terms of refugees will relax the refugees in social and psychological terms. In this context, the exercise of the political rights of refugees can be seen as an exit for refugees.

Apart from the participation of refugees in political parties, they can become active in political life with different organizations. Indeed, their participation in organizations conducting peaceful political activities can be seen as a chance-enhancing factor for refugees to organize demonstrations and grabs for change in their country of origin. In general, as we have

---

[29] Bekaj and Antara, ibid., p. 37.

mentioned before, the right to participate in peaceful organizations is guaranteed by human rights, especially the right to expression and association. It has the right to organize several activities including the participation of refugees in peaceful political organizations, announcing their views through the media, organizing peaceful demonstrations and sending representatives to highlight their problems in the context of international organizations. In this context, the asylum state's tolerance and support of such organizations and such organizations by the refugees will not put the asylum state in a difficult position against the refugee's country of origin. However, refugees should have the right to participate in institutions related to domestic politics in the states of asylum. The fact that refugees today do not have the right to vote and be elected in most countries does not mean that they do not have the right to express their views about themselves or socially alarming issues in the country of asylum.

## Rights Granted to Refugees by the States of Asylum

### Lebanon

Lebanon is one of the countries with the highest number of Syrian refugees per capita globally. In Lebanon, when looking at the political rights of Syrian refugees, the Lebanese government is reluctant to keep Syrian refugees in their country for the long term. This situation restricts the political rights and political activities that Syrian refugees can use in Lebanon. For this reason, Syrian refugees face obstacles in Lebanon regarding the right to citizenship, the right to vote and be elected, or participation in peaceful political organizations. Although there are restrictions for Syrian refugees in Lebanon in the context of non-governmental organizations, Syrian refugees operate informally within the framework of non-governmental organizations.

As for the right to vote for Syrian refugees in the context of their country of origin regarding the exercise of the right to vote and be elected, Lebanon was one of the few states in Syria that gave remote voting rights in the 2014 elections. However, since the majority of the votes cast through the remote voting system supported President Assad, the Lebanese government adopted restrictive policies in the context of the right to vote. At the same time, the inability of Syrian refugees to meet their basic needs for survival in Lebanon and the precarious legal status of most refugees in Lebanon creates an unwillingness to participate in international political activities aimed at influencing the building of democracy in Syria.[30]

---

[30] Zeina El-Helou, **Political Participation of Refugees: The Case of Syrian Refugees in Lebanon**, International IDEA Publication, Stockholm, 2018, pp. 11-12.

## Turkey

Turkey is the country with the most refugees in Syria over the world. When considering the fact that Turkey is bordered by Syria to be a large number of Syrian refugees in Turkey is not surprising.

In Turkey, when viewed Syrian refugees' political rights that are available, change in the status of Turkey's asylum system in the context of Syrian refugees in Turkey is impossible. In this regard, there are no voting rights for Syrian refugees in Turkey for failing to meet the conditions of the refugees on the front of Turkish citizenship law.

Besides Syrian refugees in Turkey, are reluctant to participate in political elections in Syria. The reason for this is that they think that elections held with the remote voting system cannot be held freely and fairly. They state that if the elections held through this remote voting system meet the demands of Syrian refugees, they will exercise their right to vote for the Syrian Refugee countries. Indeed, when it comes to Syrian refugees in Turkey to citizenship, if they reside in Turkey will gain in 5 years. But in this case as an exception, if Turkey refugees are believed to survive under temporary protection status for the Syrian refugees will not exceed a Turkish citizen.[31]

## Germany

Germany is the second-largest country in Europe for Afghan and Syrian refugees. There are legal restrictions on the participation of refugees in political activities in Germany by the German Government. In this context, especially considering the legal status of refugees in Germany and the negative effects of the refugee discourse in society, there are major obstacles and problems regarding the use of the political rights of Afghan and Syrian refugees.

In this context, since the political participation of refugees in Germany is a legal framework that is directly taken with the right to citizenship, there are problems regarding the participation of refugees in political activities. Considering the participation of refugees in the elections of their country of origin through a remote voting system in Germany, there is no legal regulation in terms of using a remote voting system for refugees in Germany. However, in Germany, non-governmental organizations are used very effectively for Syrian and Afghan refugees, and the role of non-governmental organizations in the context of international activities for refugees to continue their struggle for democracy in the context of their country of origin from Germany. However, although civil society organizations for refugees in

---

[31] Ezra Mannix, **Political Participation of Refugees: The Case of Syrian Refugees in Turkey,** International IDEA Publication, Stockholm, 2018, pp. 14-15.

Germany are seen as an important factor in the demand for peace and democracy-building processes, it does not seem like a situation that refugees can solve on their own in terms of long-term crises.

Syrian and Somali refugees constitute the largest refugee group in Sweden. Both refugee groups can use their political activities and political rights without obtaining citizenship in Sweden. As we have mentioned before, they have the right to vote and to be elected in municipal elections, to join political parties, to organize protests, to establish associations and to join non-governmental organizations.

### United Kingdom (UK)

Afghan refugees live in the majority in the UK. In this context, looking at the political rights of Afghan refugees in the UK, refugees do not have the right to vote and be elected for their country of origin both within the UK and through a remote voting system. Afghan refugees must obtain British citizenship to participate in political activities in the UK. In this context, under the British citizenship law, at least 7 years of residence in the UK is required. However, refugees have the right to be members of British political parties and non-governmental organizations to have their voices heard in the UK. In this context, refugees can participate in political activities without obtaining citizenship in the UK. Also this situation is an important element in terms of the integration of refugees with British society.

In this respect, although it seems possible for Afghan citizens in the UK to carry out their political activities with various institutions and organizations such as non-governmental organizations, parties, associations, especially their participation in political life in Afghanistan is not realized due to the lack of remote voting regulations. In this context, the issues related to the political movements of Afghanistan are handled by the refugees generally through non-governmental organizations, associations and different institutions and organizations. However, although this may seem like an opportunity for Afghan refugees to make their voices heard in an international arena, it can be seen as a factor that harms on the resolution of political crises in the long run. Finally, the good use of social media by young Afghan refugees plays an important role in following the political developments in Afghanistan and participating in political debates both in the UK and Afghanistan.[32]

### Conclusion

The phenomenon of the refugees is as old as human history. It is possible to talk about the existence of the phenomenon of refugee even in periods

---

[32] Shoaib Sharifi, Political Participation of Refugees: The Case of Afghan Refugees in the United Kingdom, International IDEA Publication, Stockholm, 2018, pp. 10-15.

when the borders are not sharply and clearly defined in the historical process. As a result of the mass migration movements that started after the First and Second World Wars, the phenomenon of refugees has emerged as a big problem in the face of humanity. In this context, the international status of the refugees was determined with the Convention on the Legal Status of Refugees dated 1951, which is considered as the constitution of refugees including the United Nations High Commissioner. As a matter of fact, with the emergence of Human Rights Law, the status of refugees in the international arena has increased.

In this context, most of the refugee agreements made so far refer to the Human Rights Law and refer to the rights of refugees. In addition to the personal rights of the refugees, no clear steps have been taken as to what their political rights are, which is still a matter of debate today. Most of the political rights of refugees arising from the Human Rights Law have been left to the consent of the country where the refugees took refuge. For this reason, refugees are seen as a burden in most countries of asylum. In this context, it has been stated within the framework of the analyzes that there are some obstacles to refugees from exercising their political rights as well as their rights. However, it should be noted that the exercise of certain political rights by refugees is an essential element, especially for human dignity.

In the context of the political rights of refugees, the absence of the right to elect and be elected in the asylum states is not seen as an obstacle in terms of participating in political activities by exercising their universal rights such as freedom of thought, freedom of movement, freedom of association, and freedom of assembly. These universal rights of refugees can also be blocked by some states. In this context, although they cannot use them legally, in most countries, refugees can use these rights that Human Rights Law has committed to all humanity by informal means. While most countries do not grant political rights to refugees by their refugee policies, in exceptional cases, as we mentioned in the Swedish example, refugees may have the same rights as local citizens.

Citizenship, which is an important element in terms of the integration of refugees with the local society in the country of asylum, is often given difficult conditions against refugees under legal procedures. In this context, there are deficiencies in the integration of refugees with the local society in the country of asylum and refugees are exposed to discrimination following state policies. The fact that refugees' countries of asylum do not have remote voting regulations against their country of origin keeps them away from the politics of their country of origin. For this reason, even if the refugees want to return to their country of origin in the short term, they cannot make political decisions and cannot participate in the peaceful solution of their country of origin, as the remote voting system is not regulated in most countries.

53

Although most of the refugee citizens cannot use their legal political rights within the asylum country, they continue to participate in political activities with the rights granted by the Human Rights Law informally. As we mentioned at the beginning of the study, in our opinion, refugees are people who have the potential to become bilateral political actors if their internal political rights are fully recognized. They will both actively participate in political activities in the country of asylum and request to carry out some activities for the political future of their country of origin. In other words, refugees are people who have the potential to have a say in the interests of their country of origin while protecting the interests of their country of asylum. However, as a result of the analysis made in the context of asylum countries, refugees are seen as people who need to return to their countries, especially in the short term. This is why, while imposing difficult conditions regarding the political rights of refugees to recognize the rights granted to the consent of the states to refugees, they display a negative attitude towards the long-term presence of refugees in their country.

It should be noted here that in the countries of asylum, there is a collective attitude taken by the society against all refugees as a result of the involvement of any of the refugee citizens in illegal activities. As a matter of fact, while all refugees suffer from this situation as a result of the negative activity of a person in the society, it causes the legal restrictions and policies regarding refugee rights by the state to be hardened.

# CHAPTER 4

# REFUGEES AND HUMAN RIGHTS

## Gülayşe Ülgen Türedi *

"The continued gross violations of human rights, ethnic cleansing and forcible return of refugees and displaced persons underline the importance of a firm commitment by all parties to human rights and humanitarian principles"

(Sadako Ogato, United Nations High Commissioner for Refugees 1991-2000)

## Introduction

Human rights are the main sources of refugee rights as refugee rights are born because of human rights violations. To be more specific, refugee flows happen because of human rights violations. In the beginning the violations start in the country of origin; people leave their country because of human rights violations and they become refugees. Then most of the times same or another kind of violations continue during the "journey" to third party countries where the refugees try to apply for asylum. Finally, when the refugees arrive to third countries, they have to wait under different temporary status, and not always the best status for human rights, based on the migration law of third countries. *In other* words, the human rights of refugees are violated gradually between their country of origin and the asylum country. However; as it is mentioned by UN Office of the High Commissioner for Human Rights (OHCHR) the refugees' rights should be respected prior to, during and after the process of seeking asylum.[1] Hence the refugee rights codification started firstly in the framework of human rights protection with asylum right in Article 14 of Universal Declaration of Human Rights (1948):

"(1) Everyone has the right to seek and to enjoy in other countries asylum from persecution.

(2) This right may not be invoked in the case of prosecutions genuinely arising from non-political crimes or from acts contrary to

---

* Dr. Research Assistant, Kırklareli University, Faculty of Economics and Administrative Sciences, International Relations Department, Political History, gululgen@gmail.com.
[1] **UN Office of the High Commissioner for Human Rights (OHCHR)**, "Fact Sheet, Human Rights and Refugees", No. 20, July 1993, p. 2.

the purposes and principles of the United Nations".[2]

The field of human rights and refugee rights have developed simultaneously as a result of the political conjuncture after the Second World War. But according to Frelick, there is a neat line between human rights and refugee rights which depends on international borders.[3] The main concern of human rights is to prevent the violations of rights of citizens by their own governments or by active non-governmental parties within the borders of their own states. Meanwhile refugee is a concept which is used for persons seeking protection abroad, that is beyond the borders of their country. This neat line was created within the framework of UN's two main documents, Universal Declaration of Human Rights (1948) and UN Convention Relating to the Status of Refugees (1951).[4]

In this chapter, the relationship between human rights and refugee rights has been addressed within the context of their interdependent nature. The protection of refugee rights is dependent on the prevention of the abuses of people' rights in their own country, on the road and at the host country. Firstly, the chapter explains the causes of refugee flows based on definition of the term "refugee". Additionally, the journeys of refugees from their country of origin to third countries for seeking asylum has been evaluated by taking into account innate, inalienable and inviolable rights of humankind. Then the relative slow evolution of migration law despite the growing number of refugees in the world has been discussed. At the end of the chapter the simultaneous evolution of the field of human rights and refugee rights has been discussed.

## The Reasons of Refugee Rights

The 1951 UN Refugee Convention defines the concept of refugee as:

> "Someone who is unable or unwilling to return to their country of origin owing to a well-founded fear of being persecuted for reasons of race, religion, nationality, membership of a particular social group, or political opinion".[5]

The persecution for reasons of race, religion, nationality, membership of particular social group and political opinion is accepted as the main rule of

---

[2] **Universal Declaration of Human Rights,** United Nations, 1948, https://www.un.org/en/universal-declaration-human-rights/#:~:text=Article%2014.,principles%20of%20the%20United%20Nations, (Access 10.10.2020)

[3] Bill Frelick, "Refugee Rights: The New Frontier of Human Rights Protection", **Buffalo Human Rights Law Review**, Vol. 4, No. 261, 1998, p. 261.

[4] Ibid.

[5] **UN Convention Relating to the Status of Refugees,** Art. 1a, 1951, https://www.unhcr.org/about-us/background/4ec262df9/1951-convention-relating-status-refugees-its-1967-protocol.html, (Access 12.10.2020).

being accepted as refugee. This is related to the political conditions of the time in which the Refugee Convention was declared; that is post Second World War. Due to "incidents" during the Second World War, the primary concern was to protect persons who become refugees" as a result of events occurring before 1 January 1951". However as refugee flows had been proven not to be temporary, the 1967 Protocol relating to the Status of Refugees removed this restrictive temporal clause for applying Convention universally.[6]

Hathaway interprets the notion of persecution in the definition of refugee as "sustained or systemic violation of basic human rights demonstrative failure of state protection".[7] This human rights-based interpretation of persecution is also acknowledged by European Union via Qualification Directive. The Directive sorts the acts of persecution in Article 9 as:

"a) be sufficiently serious by their nature or repetition as to constitute a severe violation of basic human rights, in particular the rights from which derogation cannot be made under Article 15(2) of the European Convention for the Protection of Human Right and Fundamental Freedoms; or,

(b) be an accumulation of various measures, including violations of human rights which is sufficiently severe as to affect an individual in a similar manner as mentioned in (a)".[8]

According to Chetail, this human rights-based approach is not limited with the notion of persecution, the other distinctive features of the refugee definition make references to other rights of human expressed in Universal Declaration of Human Rights (UDHR) and the International Covenant on Civil and Political Rights (ICCPR).[9] The persecution for reasons of religion and political opinion can be accepted as the violation of freedom of thought, conscience and religion cited in Art. 18 of UDHR and ICCPR. It is also related to the violation of the freedom of opinion and expression in Art. 19 of UDHR and ICCPR. Additionally, the rule of non-discrimination should be taken into account during the investigation of violations regarding race,

---

[6] **1967 Protocol Relating to the Status of Refugees**, Art. 1, 1948, https://www.ohchr.org/EN/ProfessionalInterest/Pages/ProtocolStatusOfRefugees.aspx, (Access 12.10.2020)

[7] James C. Hathaway, **The Rights of Refugees under International Law**, Cambridge University Press, New York, 2005, pp. 305-306.

[8] **European Council Directive 2004/83/EC L 304/17**, "Minimum standards for the qualification and status of third country nationals or stateless persons as refugees or as persons who otherwise need international protection and the content of he protection granted", 29 April 2004, https://eur-lex.europa.eu/legal-content/EN/TXT/PDF/?uri=CELEX:32004L0083&from=EN, (Access 12.10.2020).

[9] Vincent Chetail, "Are Refugee Rights Human Rights? An Unorthodox Questioning of the Relations between Refugee Law and Human Rights Law", **Human Rights and Immigration**, Ruth Rubio-Marín (Ed.), 2014, p. 27.

nationality and membership of a particular social group.[10]

It is already affirmed in the Preamble of the Refugee Convention that "human beings shall enjoy fundamental rights and freedoms without discrimination". Thereby the human rights of refugees are guaranteed in the Preamble of the Refugee Convention.[11] In other words the rights of people which are violated by their country of origin, pave the way for the status of "refugee" and the protection of related rights.

The most common cause of refugee flows is all kinds of persecution which can be political, racial, religious and social. Most of the refugees still escapes from the conditions of war in the world. According to UNHCR 1 per cent of the world's population have to leave their homes because of conflict or persecution.[12] Poverty, food insecurity, climate change and other environmental disasters are the other reasons which push people to move in search of new horizons. These latter "unorthodox" reasons clearly indicate that the violation of social and economic rights may produce refugee flows as well. The right to work (Art. 6), the right to an adequate standard of living including food, clothing, and housing (Art.11), the right to physical and mental health (Art.12), the right to social security (Art. 9), the right to a healthy environment and the right to education (Art. 13) of refugees are also violated.[13]

These violations do not end after people leave their country of origin, on contrary they continue in different forms during the migration; be it legal or illegal; to third countries. Despite that fact, there is a tendency in the international community to ignore innate, inalienable and inviolable rights of humankind when considering the conditions of refugees. States' restrictive migration and border policies leave refugees vulnerable in between their country of origin and their destination. People who leave their country because of human rights violations, are deprived of basic rights because their ambiguous status between asylum seeker, illegal immigrant and refugee.

## On the Road to Becoming A Refugee

The rights of people; even the fundamental rights like "right to life", "right to freedom of movement", "right to food", "right to asylum", "rights to health"; are also violated during the process of seeking asylum. These rights are the ones which people can have simply as human beings regardless of nationality, sex, national or ethnic origin, color, religion, language, or any

---

[10] Ibid.
[11] Niraj Nathwani, **Rethinking Refugee Law,** Martinus Nijhoff Publishers, 2003, Boston, p. 18.
[12] **United Nations Refugee Agency (UNHCR),** https://www.unhcr.org/figures-at-a-glance.html (Access 15.10.2020)
[13] **International Covenant on Economic, Social and Cultural Rights,** 1966, https://www.ohchr.org/en/professionalinterest/pages/cescr.aspx, (Access 15.10.2020)

other status like being refugee.[14] The principle of universality and inalienability of human rights can be ignored during the refugees' process of asylum seeking as the countries prefer to apply restrictive measures for blocking refugees' entry to their territories. Arendt called this ignorance as "the paradox of human rights" in her book, the Origins of Totalitarianism. She explains the paradox as:

> "Since the Rights of Man were proclaimed to be "inalienable," irreducible to and undeducible from other rights or laws, no authority was invoked for their establishment… The Rights of Man, after all, had been defined as "inalienable" because they were supposed to be independent of all governments; but it turned out that the moment human beings lacked their own government and had to fall back upon their minimum rights, no authority was left to protect them and no institution was willing to guarantee them."[15]

As Arendt points out, the lack of any authority and institution willing to protect refugees' rights leave them rightless and stateless in limbo. Weis describes this rightless of refugees with the absence of any protection by a state. According to him the status of refugee can be described by this absence; in fact he offers to use the term of "a vessel on the open sea not sailing under any flag" for refugees instead of *de facto* or *de jure* unprotected persons.[16] The existence of human rights conventions and committees with judiciary organs established in the context of these mechanisms cannot hinder the restrictive measures taken by third countries.[17] These restrictive measures may take different forms such as more complicated than usual visa requirements, refoulement at airports and borders, the forcible return of asylum-seekers to the countries of origin, the detention of asylum-seekers for extended periods without legitimate reasons, harsh interrogation procedures, establishing refugee camps and push-back operations.[18]

The mass migration became a problematic issue for Europe Union (EU) since 2015. Its political and humanitarian aspects of the topic cause internal and external criticism for the organization. In one hand EU has tried to assure solidarity within the organization by strict border controls; on the other hand,

[14] **United Nations Human Rights Office of the High Commissioner,** https://www.ohchr.org/en/issues/pages/whatarehumanrights.aspx, (Access 16.10.2020)
[15] Hannah Arendt, **The Origins of Totalitarinism**, Harvest Book Harcourt Brace & Company, 1973, Orlando, pp. 291-292.
[16] Paul Weis, "Human Rights and Refugees", **Israel Yearbook on Human Rights,** Vol. 1, January-April 1972, p. 20.
[17] Sibel Yılmaz, "Modern Yurttaşlığın İstisnaları: Hannah Arendt ve Giorgio Agamben'in Görüşleri Çerçevesinde İnsan Haklarının Eleştirisinde Mülteciler ve Kamplar", **Ankara Üniversitesi SBF Dergisi,** Vol. 73, No. 3, 2018, p. 768.
[18] UN Office of the High Commissioner for Human Rights (OHCHR), "Fact Sheet, Human Rights and Refugees", p. 10.

it conducts an externalization policy which depends on cooperation with non-EU neighbouring countries. EU New Pact on Migration and Asylum which was agreed upon and codified on 23 September 2020, reflects the combination of internal and external aspect of organization's migration policy. According to European Union Vice President Margaritis Schinas, this pact is a building with three floors; first is the external dimension depending on cooperation with non-EU neighbouring countries, the second is robust management of external borders based on restrictive measures, and the final floor is to apply firm but fair internal rules for assuring solidarity within the organization.[19] All floors of this building demonstrate the rightness status of refugees. EU wants to deal with the refugee issue on securitization grounds, it does not possess a human rights-based or humanitarian approach.

The establishment of refugee camps by international community on temporary basis is an urgent solution to unexpected problem. The temporary nature of this solution requires providing basic humanitarian needs of refugees. When camps are transformed from temporary solutions to permanent settlement areas, settlers of these camps are destitute of fundamental rights like right to healthy environment, right to work, right to education, right to freedom of movement as most of the host countries are not willing to let the refugees create a life outside the camp.[20]

The European centre for Constitutional and Human Rights defines push back operations as:

> "set of state measures by which refugees and migrants are forced back over a border – generally immediately after they crossed it – without consideration of their individual circumstances and without any possibility to apply for asylum or to put forward arguments against the measures taken. Push-backs violate – among other laws – the prohibition of collective expulsions stipulated in the European Convention on Human Rights."[21]

The right which is violated directly with push-back operations is "right to asylum"; however, "right to life" is also violated indirectly because operations can provoke undesirable results. But the most fundamental right of non-refoulement which is guaranteed by human rights, refugee humanitarian and

---

[19] **European Commission**, Speech by Vice-President Schinas on the New Pact on Migration and Asylum, https://ec.europa.eu/commission/presscorner/detail/en/speech_20_1736, (Access 20.10.2020).

[20] Christele Harrouk, "Refugee Camps: From Temporary Settlements to Permanent Dwellings", https://www.archdaily.com/940384/refugee-camps-from-temporary-settlements-to-permanent-dwellings, (Access 20.10.2020).

[21] **European Center for Constitutional and Human Rights,** https://www.ecchr.eu/en/glossary/pushback/#:~:text=Push%2Dbacks%20are%20a%20set,arguments%20against%20the%20measures%20taken., (Access 21.10.2020).

customary law, is not respected under push-back operations. Recently, allegations about the complicity of European Border and Coast Guard Agency (FRONTEX) in Greece's illegal push back operations to Turkey were revealed. The Agency which is supposed to be upholder of the rule of law at EU borders; passes over the illegal actions of one-member state.[22] The value-based foundation of EU is on stake in recent years because of refugee crisis. The Rights cited in Charter of Fundamental Rights of the European Union are just valid for European Union citizens; and as Arendt points out, it is the paradox of human rights. The human rights are not universal and inalienable enough to embrace refugees. As a result, refugee' rights continue to be violated under different forms after the process of seeking asylum.

## The Final Stage

The refugees who can arrive in third countries safely and apply for asylum, do not experience a better treatment in terms of human rights, as human rights violations continue in different forms like periods of detention or interrogation, temporary status for refugees, xenophobic and racist aggression.

A good example in case is Hungary adopting a new detention law on March 7, 2017. This law depended on mandatory detention of all asylum seekers, including children for the entire length of asylum procedure.[23] The conditions of detention were explained as shipping containers surrounded by high razor wire fence at the border for extended periods of time in the UN press briefing. The UN press briefing pointed out that detention of refugees and asylum seekers could be possible on limited grounds if it is "necessary, reasonable and proportionate". In other words restrictions on the exercise of some rights can be justified when they have a legal basis, are necessary and proportionate; the three divine principles in human rights restrictions are also taken into consideration for the protection of refugee rights. As a result, all these detention sites were declared illegal by the Court of Justice of the European Union on 14 May 2020.[24] Even if Hungary adhered to the decision, he initiated a new asylum system in the context of emergency powers of pandemic. This system requires a "statement of intent" at the Hungarian embassy in Belgrade or Kyiv from people for seeking asylum in Hungary. The applicants which are accepted, will be detained in Hungary for one

---

[22] Matina Stevis-Gridneff, "E.U. Border Agency Accused of Covering Up Migrant Pushback in Greece", **New York Times,** 26.11.2020, (Access 27.11.2020).
[23] United Nations High Commissioner for Refugees(UNHCR), "UNHCR deeply concerned by Hungary plans to detain all asylum seekers", 07 March 2017, https://www.unhcr.org/news/briefing/2017/3/58be80454/unhcr-deeply-concerned-hungary-plans-detain-asylum-seekers.html, (Access 25.10.2020).
[24] Court of Justice of the European Union, "Judgment in Joined Cases C-924/19 PPU and C-925/19 PPU", 14.05.2020, https://curia.europa.eu/jcms/upload/docs/application/pdf/2020-05/cp200060en.pdf, (Access 26.10.2020).

month.[25] The EU Commission declared that it would open infringement procedures by sending a letter of formal notice to Hungary on the incorrect application of EU asylum legislation. The Commission considers that new asylum procedures created by Hungary are in breach of EU law, in particular the Asylum Procedures Directive envisaged in the framework of the Charter of Fundamental Rights of the European Union.26

The measures which were taken by Hungary were not limited with these types of physical barriers, it also applied legislative and politic obstacles to enter the country and to apply for asylum.[27] Hungary announced as the entrance country that it would suspend the acceptance of asylum seekers transferred back from other countries under the Dublin Regulation for an indefinite term on June 23, 2015 even it took it back after two days.[28] Because the Hungary suggested that Dublin regulation, the European Union law which establishes the first point of irregular entry within the EU as responsible Member State for the examination of the asylum application, overburdened the country at the Western Balkans borders of EU.

Asylum-seekers who are granted asylum, are not accepted as refugees in the regulations of some countries. They have to live with the temporary status without same rights as citizens have. Turkey is an example in case because of her geographical reservation on Turkey's protection obligation under the 1951 Refugee Convention. She accepts people originating from Europe as refugees according to the Law on Foreigners and International Protection. Turkey's asylum and international protection legislation is codified with this law. Turkey, the host of the largest number of refugees, (3,6 million Syrians) created a temporary status under temporary protection regime apart from three status on the Law (refugee, conditional refugee, subsidiary protection).[29] This regime provides right to health, right to education, right to social assistance, and right to work. But right to work was granted with work permits to a small number of Syrians, 27,930 between 1 January 2016 – 30 September 2018. Turkey officials use always the term of "guest" for Syrians so the status which was created for them fits to this narrative. But this status blocks any chances of citizenship for people staying in Turkey for 10 years

---

[25] https://www.globaldetentionproject.org/countries/europe/hungary, (Access 26.10.2020).

[26] EU Commission, "October infringements package: key decisions", 30.10.2020, https://ec.europa.eu/commission/presscorner/detail/en/inf_20_1687, (Access 31.10.2020).

[27] Ved P. Vanda, "Migrants and Refugees Are Routinely Denied the Protection of International Human Rights: What does the Future Hold", **Denver Journal of International Law &Policy,** Vol. 45, No. 3, 2017, p. 307.

[28] European Council of Refugees and Exiles(ECRE), "Hungary reverses suspension of Dublin Regulation", 26.06.2015, https://www.ecre.org/hungary-reverses-suspension-of-dublin-regulation/#:~: text=Hungary%20announced%2C%20on%2023%20June,its%20decision%20the%20next%20day, (Access 26.10.2020).

[29] Turkey Law on Foreigners and International Protection, No. 6458, Art.91, 2013, https://www.mevzuat.gov.tr/MevzuatMetin/1.5.6458.pdf, (Access 30.20.2020).

and leaves them in limbo without rights equal to citizens. Syrian refugees have protection in Turkey but not legally obtained but *de facto* protection with limited rights.

Thirdly, refugees become target of xenophobic and racist attacks in recent years; increasing in parallel with the number of refugees. Furthermore, they are instrumentalized by politicians in domestic politics; resulting in the rise of right wing nationalist and populist parties.

The rights of refugees that are constantly violated reflects the lack of protection for people without a state protection. The whole international human rights and refugee protection regime depend on voluntary contribution of states. The increase in refugee numbers, the deteriorative economic conditions because of the pandemic, the rise of far-right nationalist parties worldwide are not promising facts for the future of refugee rights. But without human rights, we cannot talk about refugee rights, latter's evolution is strictly related to the former's expansion of space. Both of them already has gained momentum together since the end of Second World War. If the first relational dimension of human and refugee rights is violation, the second one is simultaneous evolution.

## Simultaneous Evolution of Human and Refugee Rights

The neat line between human rights and refugee rights was created after a specific Refugee Convention was accepted in 1951. But the second relational dimension between human and refugee rights which is simultaneous evolution, reflects the interaction between human rights law and refugee law. The Refugee Convention cannot be interpreted or applied without the text and jurisprudence of human rights treaties.[30] According to Cherem, the Refugee Convention has been interpreted in the context of human rights.[31]

Edwards explains the relation between human rights and refugee rights as supplementary. She elabourates that human rights law has been resorted generally for filling in the grey areas of refugee protection like explaining the terms "persecution" and "social group" within the refugee definition, expanding the rights of refugees with Covenants like Covenant on Civil and Political Rights (ICCPR), Covenant on Economic, Social and Cultural Rights (ICESCR), determining appropriate asylum procedures.[32]

---

[30] Tom Clark and François Crépeau, "Mainstreaming Refugee Rights: The 1951 Refugee Convention and International Human Rights Law, **Netherlands Quarterly of Human Rights,** Vol. 17, No. 4, 1999, p. 389.

[31] Max Cherem, "Refugee **Rights**: Against Expanding the Definition of a "Refugee" and Unilateral Protection Elsewhere", **The Journal of Political Philosophy** , Vol. 24, No. 2, 2016, p. 185.

[32] Alice Edwards, "Human Rights, Refugees, and The Right to Enjoy Asylum", **International Journal**

The most fundamental right of the refugee law, the principle of *non-refoulement* is appropriated by human rights law. It is codified universally in the 1984 Convention against Torture (Art. 3) and the 2006 UN International Convention for the Protection of All Persons from Enforced Disappearance (Art. 16). The several regional human rights treaties also acknowledge the principle of *non-refoulement*, like the 1969 American Convention of Human Rights (Art.22), the 1985 Inter-American Convention to Prevent and Punish Torture (Art. 13), the 2000 Charter of Fundamental Rights of the European Union (Art. 19).[33] The normative base of this principle is the same for both of the branches of law, which is to prevent the expel of people to their state of origin. Even if both branches envisage this principle and right to asylum for refugees, they have reluctant to oblige states to provide asylum. This dichotomy contradicts with the universality of human rights and the founding principles of refugee protection regime.

As the scope of human rights law expands, the rights of refugees which should be protected expands as well. For example, the protection of environmental rights as a part of the third generation human rights is on the agenda of the world; consequently the rights of the "climate refugees" have started to be discussed. In other words, the second relational dimension between human rights and refugees puts forward the interdependent nature of their relation.

## Conclusion

The relation between human rights and refugee rights has two dimensions. The first relational dimension bases on cause-and-effect relationship, and its main argument is that the human rights violations are the main causes of the emergence of refugee rights. But this cause-and-effect relationship continues after the refugee rights were codified in 1951 Convention; the rights of refugees are violated in every stage of their journey; prior to, during and after the process of seeking asylum. Even if the abuser and the forms of violations changes, the permanent situation of violation stays the same. The universality principle of human rights does not provide the necessary framework for people without rights and protection because the third states in which the refugees apply for asylum, prefer to protect their borders in the context of migration policies based on securitization.

The second relational dimension depends on simultaneous evolution of human rights law and refugee law. It is also related to the cause-and-effect relationship because the refugee law can develop as a result of the occurrence of human rights treaties. After all the normative scope of human rights law

---

of **Refugee Law**, Vol. 17, No. 2, 2005, p. 295.
[33] Vincent Chetail, op. cit., p. 34.

and refugee law are similar; the rights that rank among the articles of human rights treaties, are the ones which the refugees need most during their asylum seeking process. Consequently the scopes of both branches of law expand together. The extension of the list of human rights is direct result of the changing and increasing needs of humankind so the needs of refugees also changes according to contemporary political, social and economic conditions. To the extent that human rights are recognized as universal, refugee protection regimes may develop. They have a common destiny.

# CHAPTER 5

# REFUGEE AND CULTURAL RIGHTS OF REFUGEES IN THE CONTEXT OF POLITICAL COMMUNICATION

## Emine Kılıçaslan[*]

### Introduction

From past to present people have left their country and taken shelter in another for various reasons. Information is to be found concerning refugees even in some documents dating back to ancient time. Regulations have been found in historic aztec documents as to how to protect from immigration. Similar regulations were also present in Roman Empire and Medieval Europe.

When the factors leading to the problem of immigration are inspected, it can be noticed that they involve many issues like invasions, civil wars and changes in political system. In addition to these, there are problems relating to the rights of minority groups as to their race, religious choices or sexual preferences. The involuntary displacement of people due the aforementioned reasons sharply quickened in the 20th century and still keeps its pace.

Particularly after 1980s, the direction of immigration at a global scale has been towards Europe and the USA. After 1990s, the policies of the USA with regard to Afghanistan, the invasion of Iraq, and the Bosnia-Herzegovinan civil war intensified the immigration and defection problems. Besides, in the Syrian civial that started on the 15 March 2011, about 400 thousand people died; 3 million people got injured; and 1 million people have been crippled in seven years. Further, millions of people have been forced to immigrate to other countries and historical places have been demolished.[1]

This situation in Syria, which is still ongoing, has turned the problems of immigration, defection and asylum seeking into a messy balls-up for Europe and Turkey especially. Furthermore, the fact that the problem originates from the Middle East and Afghanistan has worsened the situation for Europe. As for Turkey, which is the most important transition path for immigrating masses, it has been the country that has faced the problem in the most tragic way. As well-known, Turkey is one of the coutries among those experiencing irregular flows of immigration. Turkey is a country that immigrants perefer

* Dr. Aydın Adnan Menderes Universty, emine.kilicaslan@adu.edu.tr.
[1] NTV news, 2018; https://www.ntv.com.tr/galeri/dunya/suriye-7-yilda-ic-savasla-nasil-coktu, (Access 25.09.2020).

as a transition path to those countries that promise hopes for them. However, there are to many immigrants living in the camps in Turkey. The European Union in particular apply certain policies to Turkey in order prevent immigrants from arriving in their countries. One of these policies is to treat Turkey as a buffer country for immigrants.

Especially in the period of the Syrian civil war that started in 2011 the emerging chaotic situation has led immigrants to come to Turkey and go to Europe from there and this, in turn, has created many problems for Turkey and Europe. In Syria, the population of which was 22.4 million then, almost 500 thousand people lost their lives in 8.5 years. Besides, 6-7 million people had to flee to other countries as refugees. According to the data of UNHCR, as a result of this most important flow of immigration that the humanity has ever seen the number of those who have taken shelter and been recorded is 5.626.914, 3.643.870 of which are in Turkey. Only one million of those managed to go to the USA, Canada or Europe.[2]

The problem of immigration should be examined in terms of human rights. Immigrants bring their cultures with themselves to the countries they move to. This should be considered as a problem both for the immigrated country and for immigrants and should be solved taking human rights into consideration. The notion of refugee comes to the fore in discussions concerning these matters. Assuming that they wish to be conceptually consistent, liberal democracies like the USA and Europe are expected not to behave against the principles of freedom and equality. Immigrants leaving their countries mainly due to the policies of dominant countries and moving to the West for a better life are still forced to leave in non-humanitarian circumstances in the countries they have settled in. The Office of the United Nations High Commissioner for Human Rights (OHCHR) stipulates that human rights should be secured when restraining immigration and solving the problems of immigrants.[3]

In this study, the cultural rights of immigrants are examined in terms of the basic rights of immigrants and the imperialistic policies of dominant countries from the point of view of political communication.

**Immigration and Being Immigrant in the Historical Process**

In the simplest sense, 'immigration' is defined as taking shelter in a foreign country. It has been experienced from past to present in each phase of human history for various reasons. It is recorded orally and in writing for human beings to prefer to leave where they are situated and move to a different place

---

[2] https://www.kas.de/documents, (Access 25.09.2020).
[3] http://cenevreofisi.dt.mfa.gov.tr/Mission/ShowInfoNote/353799, (Access 30.09.2020).

due to disasters or security concerns. Information concerning immigration is found in the ancient inscriptions in these records. According to Odman, the Aztecs had regulations in order to protect immigrants. Likewise, a Hittite king made a treaty with the governors of another nation that an immigrant coming from the other party is not to be sent back. Another Hittite king, King Urhi-Teshup, was detrhoned by his uncle and sent to Egytp as an immigrant.[4] Events of immigration were frequent in ancient Greece, Rome and medieval Europe.

Immigration and immigrants have not fallen off the agenda even in the 20th and 21st centuries. On the contrary, the problem keeps growing particulary in the 21st century. Among the major reasons of immigration are social, political, economic and environmental problems, epidemic illnesses, and food and water shortages. What underlies these reasons are cross-national wars, civil wars, invasions, oppression, environmental and climatic catastrophes, and other life-threatening dangers. In particular, starvation, poverty and security concerns are the main triggers of immigration. In addition, people immigrate today to increase their life standards and receive better education, too.

There are nuances between being immigrant and migrating. Being immigrant differs from immigration in that it corresponds to the case where individuals or groups of individuals ask asylum from a foreign government due to religious, political or other reasons. For this reason, the definition of asylum and being immigrant is determined in accordance with the regulation made by international institutions. The issue of asylum and being immigrant turned to a very complicated problem for humanity, particularly in the 20th century. After the First and Second World Wars, people preferred to immigrate and live in a new country due to the reasons like civil wars, starvation, poverty, and unemployment. For this reason, the office of the United Nations High Commissioner for Refugees (UNHCR) was created in 1950, during the aftermath of the Second World War by the United Nations General Assembly, resolution 428 (V) of 14 Aralık 1950.[5]

The issue of international immigration and asylum has taken new dimensions after the adoption of the 1951 Geneva Convention. The Geneva Convention, considered the Magna Carta of this issue takes two constraints as premises. These constraints presuppose spatio-temporal factors. The Geneva Convention entered into force on 22 April 1954.

According to the International Organization for Migration (IOM) report, immigration has risen up because of the so-called globalization process. It

---

[4] Odman, M.T. **Refugee Law**, Ankara: Human Rights center Faculty of Political Sciences, 1995, pp. 5-6.
[5] https://www.unhcr.org/tr/wpcontent/uploads/sites/14/2017/02/indekiler.pdf, (Access 27.09. 2020).

has come to a peak in the 21st century. In addition to the aforementioned reasons, it is worth touching upon the role of the media in this event. Especially, the US media companies propagandize the Western culture with all its products. News programs, cartoons, serials, movies, and documentaries glorify the Western culture. Almost in all these programs, the main discourse of political communication shapes around the expressions of "country of freedom", "peace", "democracy", and "human rights". In an even seemingly innocent cartoon, such as He-Man, the hero is blonde. He is attributed the title the "master of the universe". Besides, he carries the sign of the cross on his costume. In short, the USA and Europe have promised the people of the third world "hope", "prosperity", "beauty", "freedom" and, most crucially, "democracy". Hence, the issue of being immigrant and asylum has acquired a new dimension in the 21st century. This is a covert factor in the process.

In this regard, the most important factor underlying the immigration process seems to be economic. Immigrants aim to get a socially and economically better life. Further, if they are oppressed where they originally live, escape form oppression becomes another reason for people to immigrate. Thus, immigrants say they were minorities and were oppressed for political, religious, cultural or other reasons in their own countries. Millions of people leave their birth places each year and hope to create a new life in new places because of wars, starvation, poverty, unemployment and misgovernment. The number of immigrants and refugees reached 173 million in 2000 and 222 million in 2010. According to the data of immigration provided by the International Organization for Migration, this number became 248 million in 2018.[6]

Partcicularly, the Occupation of Iraq, the Civil War in Afghanistan, and wars taking place in the Middle-East in 1990s turned the direction of immigration toward Europe to a greater extent. This situation triggers various political, economic, and social problems for European countries. These countries have difficulties in solving these problems. Similarly, those illegally immigrating to a European country are considered to be immigrants. These immigrants face various problems in the countries they have moved to. Immigrants get exposed to inhumane conditions in the out-of-town refugee camps in the countries where they have migrated with big hopes. The United Nations usually become the leading actor to solve such problems. The 1951 Convention Relating to the Status of Refugees set up several regulations under the leadership of the United Nations in order to deal with the world-wide problems of refugees. However, these regulations cannot be put into force due mainly to economic reasons.

If the 1951 Convention Relating to the Status of Refugees is examined, it

---

[6] http://gocvakfi.org/iom- (Access 16.09. 2018).

is seen that the convention is grounded in the Universal Declaration of human rights and the principle of non-discrimination. These principles determine a status to the problem of immigrant from the perspective of Western states. According to these states, there are some conditions for becoming a refugee. These conditions are listed below:

Being a Foreigner: An asylum seeker lives in a country other than his/her own.

Statelessness: Those who do not have any nationality or connection to any state are defined as stateless. Statelessness turns out to be the case when an individual is not taken to be a citizen of any state. Even though stateless individuals can also be refugees, the two notions are different and the concern of UNHCR covers both.

Being Oppressed: The notion of oppression, widely used for legal, religious, ethical etc. cases, is defined as "placing one somewhere s/he does not belong to."[7] The notion of oppression covers cases of harming, hurting, exploiting, unfairly treating someone. When the notion of being immigrant is in question, oppression also covers violations of religious, ethnical, and political rights.[8]

In conclusion, immigration has been a big problem in all phases of the history for countries and keeps being so. The feeling of insecurity, oppression, or the feeling of it are naturally the main reasons behind immigration. Furthermore, experiencing such problems due to racial, religious, or political reasons is considered as discrimination. In fact, moving from the homeland to another country without an intention or hope to return in order create a new life results out of desperation.

As pointed out above, the media factor should be added to those factors leading to immigration. The globalization process turning the world into a village due to the rapid developments in communication technologies and the hope with which dominant countries inflict people with public diplomacy and political communication performed by means of the media instruments they own cause people to go after the hopes promised by those creating problems in their homelands. Nonetheless, those people still keep the hope to create a happy and prosperous life after migrating to Europe or the USA trying various tough ways.

## Cultural and Cultural Rights As An Ideology

Culture is defined as every thing that humanity produces abstractly and concretely to maintain its own existence biologically and socially. Man is born

---

[7] https://islamansiklopedisi.org.tr, (Access 20.09.2020).
[8] https://www.unhcr.org/tr/vatansiz-kisiler. (Access 20.09.2020).

and shaped within culture. Everyperson is a social product of the culture in which he lives. In this context, it thinks, shapes and lives in line with what culture has taught itself. The Latin dictionary meaning of the concept of culture comes from the root Word "colere", which is "to reside, to grow, to protect". The concept of culture was used especially for agricultural activities at the first point of exit.[9]

Developments in social sciences have made the concept of culture available to this fiield and social sciences. Afterwards, the concept became rich and widespread by gaining abstract meanings in the field of social sciences. The concept was first included in the Dictionnaire de l'Academie Française in 1718. Culture has often been used with complements such as "art culture", "literary culture", "culture of science".[10]

The concept of culture was also used with abstract concepts after the 20th century. Durkheim implied that social phenomena have a cultural dimension because of their symbolic structure. Durkheim rarely used the concept of culture and translated the English Word "culture" into "civilization".[11] With the enrichment of social sciences literatüre, the concept of culture began to emerge as an important element of this field. In this context, everything related to spiritual life is within the scope of culture except the material civilizations that people created in the historical process. For example, if you want to use many elements such as traditions, customs, habits, language, beliefs, value systems, are covered by the concept of culture. In the same way, these elements have been identified as the field of study of some areas in their social science. Because people are born into culture and the cultural mind directs thier lives both in the natural flow of life and at the most critical moments of life. The religion, ethics and legal rules created by the culture also lay down the rules for people tol ive in harmony in the collective life spaces.

Addressing culture with the social, political and economic dimension of life directly reveals the ideological dimension of culture. When we look at the concept of ideology based on the concept of culture, it seen that societies create their own thought systems with the cultures they create. It is note that they act within this thought system with the culture created. The name of this system of thought is ideology. Marx brought a materialistic perspective to this situation. The ideology created by culture affects the way people perceive the

---

[9] Williams, R., **Keywords: The Vocaturism of Culture and Society**. Istanbul: Communication Publications, 2005.
[10] Galley, C. C., Cultural policy, cultural heritage and regional development. Yayımlanmamış yüksek lisans tezi, The State University of New Jersey, New Jersey, 2001.
[11] Alexander, J. C., "Culture and political crisis", J. C. Alexander, & J. C. Alexander (Ed.), in **Durkheimian Sociology: Cultural Studies** (pp. 187-224). Cambridge: Cambridge University Press, 1988.

world. It is an important claim of socialist ideology that these ideologies serve the interests of the ruling class by hiding social contradictions in various ways.

In short, when we look at the relationship between culture and ideology, it is seen that the roots of the concept of ideology date back to the Medieval. The traditional beliefs and behaviors that shaped the mental World of the Middle Ages, the rituals, are the cultural shaping of that period. Habermas (1970), sad that "ideologies as new world views of humanity emerge from the criticism of traditional interpretations of the World" to the relationship between culture and ideology.[12] As a result, ideology is an illusion that social reality creates through cultural codes in the perception of subjects. These illusions are also called false consciousness. This consciousness is encoded in the mind of the individual through culture.

The concept of cultural rights should be looked at in terms of culture and ideology relationship. One should not ignore the concept of "liberal democracy", the basic political communication slogan of Western ideology. In this context, the person who gets up from his own country and emigrates to another country and is a refugee there goes there with his own cultural codes. However, it is not very possible for immigrants tol ive with their own cultural codes where they migrate. The conflicts and crises in the destination reval the importance of adapting. The path to this harmony is in the United Nations Declaration of Human Rights "which allows refugees to participate in cultural life where they are. Therefore, cultural rights are tried to be protected and promoted especially through education, science and arts. In particular, the right to benefit from fine arts and to participate in and benefit from scientific developments and the protection of materil and moral interests arising from these are bound by international conventions and laws. Based on this, the rights of refugees arising from culture have been taken under protection.

## In the Context of Political Communication Refugees and Cultural Rights

From the point of view of concepts, all people expressed with the concepts of "Refugee", "Migrant", "Asylum Seeker" actually share the same fate. As is known, the United Nations convention defines the status of being a refugee with certain conditions. These conditions are; he explained as those who were persecuted or would suffer because of their religion, sect, race or political thoughts. In addition, refugees are people who live outside their own country and do not want to benefit from the protection of this country. Refugees, anyone who is outside the country of residence where they used

---

[12] Jürgen, Habermas, "Toward a Theory of Communicative Competence", (ed) Drietzel, H.P. in **Recent Sociology**, New York McMillan, 1970.

tol ive, cannot return there or do not want to return because of the fear in question.[13]

In order to become refugees, the United Nations cares that people are subjected to distinctions such as race, religion, gender and nationality in their home country. In addition, the fear experienced by people for these reasons is seen as the main determining reason for becoming a refugee. Following World War II, the United Nations Human Rights Commission was established in 1946. The United Nations, the Human Rights Commission, signed a United Nations treaty in 1951 setting out the status of refugees in the countries they go to. This agreement determines the minimum living standards of refugees in the countries they go to. It is also includes work, life, identity belonging, freedom of travel. Most importantly, it includes the freedom of refugees to transfer their presence in their own country to the country they are going to. Under this agreement, refugees cannot be forcibly returned or deported.

Globally, it has become a major problem, especially, for European countries today. In this context, the title "refugees" caused the Universal Declaration of Human Rights to address human rights in a whole way. In this way, the distinction between civil and political rights and economic and social rights in the Declaration is tried to be eliminated. However, it is drawn according to certain standards by law; economic, social and cultural rights are still secondary. In fact, the most important reasons underlying this situation are economic reasons. The need for economic resources causes social and cultural rights to be ignored. This actually leads to a human rights violation for European countries, which are strongholds of liberal democracies. Under their own rules, European states do not benefit refugees from social and cultural rights. That's how they commit crimes. For this reason, the idea of protecting human rights struggles with political rights and equal protection of social and cultural rights.

What is this social and cultural rights is listed among articles 22-27 of the Universal Declaration of Human Rights. Economic and Social Rights below;

- Right to Social Security

- Work

- Choosing Your Job Freely

- Working in Fair and Favorable Conditions

- Protection against unport charges

---

[13] https://search.un.org/, (Access 25.09.2020).

—   Equal Pay for Equal Work

—   A Fair and Favorable Wage

—   Right to Be a Member of Union and union

—   Right to Take Paid Leave

—   Food, Clothing, Housing Rights

—   Right to adequate standard of living

—   Including Medical Care and Social Services

—   Right to Education

—   Free Participation in Cultural Life

—   Right to Enjoy Fine Arts

—   Right to Participate in Scientific Development and Benefit from It

—   The right to the protection of material and moral interests arising from literary and artistic products.[14]

When economic, cultural and social rights are evaluated, it is clearly seen that these rights are directly related to the economic standards of the country where refugees are located and their perspective towards foreigners. As it is known in this context, refugees are treated as secondary in the countries they go to. They also often do not benefit.

Therefore, it is important that economic, social and cultural rights are equally accepted as other civil and political rights. Because this situation is among the most important problems of refugees today. Today, although these rights are considered equal as civil and political rights, there are still big problems in practice. Accordingly, ensuring and protecting economic, social and cultural rights is equal to ensuring and protecting civil and political rights. Vienna Declaration and Programme of Action .[15]

Especially the most basic elements of humane living; the right to food, health and housing is very important refugees. As is known, it is against basic human rights to live without feeling safe in the worst conditions in the countries whre they emigrated with very high hopes.

They contradict the concepts of political communication such as "hope", "freedom", "equality", "peace", "human rights", "democracy" that the West defends globally. Refugees do not have their basic socio-economic and

---

[14] https://www.un.org/en/universal-declaration-human-rights/, (Access 30.11.2020).
[15] https://www.refworld.org/docid/3ae6b39ec.htm), (Access 29.09.2020).

cultural rights in Europe, where they go with high hopes. In this context, other basic concepts such as freedom of expression, freedom of religion and conscience mean nothing to refugees.

### Cultural Rights and Cultural Rights in Turkey

On August 15, 2000, the Republic of Turkey signed the United Nations Convention on "Economic Social and Cultural Rights" on refugees. In particular, the contract is not in section third article emphasizes the equal provision of all economic, social and cultural rights specified in the convention to men and women. According to artcile third, "states parties to this agreement are obliged to provide equal rights between men and women in the use of all economic, social and cultural rights set forth in this Agreement.[16]

The convention's right to participate in cultural life is shaped by the following four articles. Accordingly, the first article, the right to participate in cultural life, is also limited to three articles. These items are listed below;

1. The right to participate in cultural life.

2. Participating in cultural life.

3. Benefiting from the blessing and results of scientific developments

4. To benefit from the protection of material and spiritual interests arising from the scientific, literary and artistic products he created.

5. There are measures to be taken by the states that are parties to the convention to fully exercise the right to participate in cultural life. These should include the necessary measures fort he preservation, development and dissemination of science and culture.

6. States parties to this convention are committed to respecting freedom, which is mandatory for scientific research and creative activities.

7. States parties to this convention agree to promote and improve international relations and cooperation in scientific and cultural fields. They recognize the interests to be derived from the contract.[17]

---

[16] http://www.unicankara.org.tr/doc_pdf/metin134.pdf, (Access 29.10.2020).
[17] https://turkey.un.org/, (Access 30.11.2020).

## Conclusion

As a result, it is important to look at the refugee problem from todays window. In this context, it is seen that the changing World balances after the 1990s played a very important role in the emergence of this problem. The new smaller states that emerged with the disintegration of the Soviet Union have docked in the Western bloc, which appears to be only superpower. This new process has revealed new conflicts, crises and problems.

One of the most important problems created by the new process is the phenomenon of migrating and becoming a refugee for a better life. Refugees are from their own land; civil war is separated by the invasion of another country or illegal terrorist organizations (DAESH, Boko Haram, PKK). One of the most important problems created by the new process is the phenomenon of migrating and becoming a refugee for a better life. In addition, many other causes of persecution, economic, political or social causes that people see are other reasons for migration. People who are willing to emigrate, women, men and children are on their way, dreaming of starting new lives for themselves in another country with great hope. This journey ends either with death on the way or poverty and contempt in refugee camps where reached.

After World War II, transnational organizations such as the United Nations on migration, asylum and refugees began to do various studies. These studies have mainly been on improving the living conditions of refugees. There have been great difficulties in the implementation of what has been written on these issues until today. These troubles are particularly economical. In the context of cultural rights, the refusal of the countries where refugees take refuge to spend money for them pushes the refugees to live in very harsh conditions in the countries they pass. According to Arendt, "even in one of the most developed people's regimes in the world, refugees and asylum seekers still find themselves in semi criminal status.[18]

Looking at the back side of the refugee problem, which is a global problem, it will be seen that it is the result of the imperialist policies of Western countries. However countries such as the United States and Europe states through the media that this problem is due to lack of democracy in the countries of refugees. Western states, through the media, stress "human rights", "democracy", "freedom" and "peace" through the media. These concepts are of ideological importance to Western states. Through the political messages of these concepts, it blacks out the essence of the problem eperienced by refugees. It removes the problem from the truth.

---

[18] Agamben, G. (1994). We refugees (trans. M. Rocke). http://www.egs.edu/faculty/agamben/agamben-we-refugees.html (Access 04.09.2020).

Likewise, through the media, "World human advocacy, the slogans of bringing peace and democracy to the World are also basic concepts of western ideology. These concepts can also be added to the image of the protector of environmental disaster, the countries of prosperity, wealth, freedom and hope". In this way, the way of migration and becoming refugees is opened for children, young people, women and men of countries where there are problems.

CHAPTER 6

CLARIFYING THE LEGAL STATUS: DISTINCTIONS
BETWEEN REFUGEES, ASYLUM SEEKERS AND
(IRREGULAR) MIGRANTS

Cenap Çakmak*

## Introduction

The mobilization of people has been attracting attention in the media and
policy circles as a major development that is affecting the conduct of
international politics.[1] A number of national institutions and international
agencies are focusing on the issues the mobilized people are facing in an
attempt to address their needs, as well as to avert any potential security or
humanitarian threats associated with the huge wave of mobilization. People
who leave their original homes or places of settlement are motivated by
different factors, including building a brighter economic future for
themselves and for their household, escaping persecution, finding a safe place
after experiencing bloodshed in a civil war or seeking refuge due to fear of
life-threatening conditions. In the vast majority cases of the mobilization of
the people, a certain degree of distress is observable. Only a very small
portion of the people who leave their homelands do not experience any sort
of repression or security threat. Therefore, it will be safe to argue that the
emerging wave of mobilization as one of the new facts of international
politics is at least partially due to the instability and insecurity in the
international political order which has been traditionally concerned with the
survival and protection of the state and its interest, thus often disregarding
the betterment of the ordinary people.

This is why recent decades have witnessed a growing interest among the
agents and actors of international politics in the political impact of the
popular mobilization across borders. The political interest has been in some
cases transformed into concrete attention that would eventually lead to the
adoption of legal arrangements applicable to the people facing imminent
danger in their home countries or where they seek a refuge to mitigate this
danger. These legal arrangements now play a wide variety of roles, ranging
from identifying the nature of the distress that justify the legal protection to

* Prof. Dr. Department of International Relations, Anadolu University, Turkey (E-mail:
cenap_cakmak@anadolu.edu.tr)
[1] See for instance, Antoine Pecoud and Paul de Guchteneire (eds.), *Migration Without Borders: Essays on the
Free Movement of People* (New York and Oxford: Berghahn Books, 2007).

be extended to the victimized people, to the proper measures to be taken by the hosting state, as well as by the international community.

This paper seeks to first descriptively analyze the legal statuses recognized under international law for the mobilized people and identify these statuses from an international law perspective. Additionally, the paper remains engaged with discussion by offering an analysis of distinction between these statuses including refugees, asylum seekers and (irregular) immigrants. Such a distinction is justified particularly because of the high volume of media reports that almost indiscriminately treat all the mobilized people under the same banner, thus failing to acknowledge the diverse nature that each status may hold. Such a treatment and approach may also potentially lead to misconception of the particular cases and miscalculation of the policy measures to be taken in an attempt to address the problems associated with mobilization of the people. Thus, clarification of the legal statuses will help both policy makers and analysts identify the problem and offer well-grounded solutions.

### Placing the refugee in an international legal context: Who is a refugee and what privileges are attached to their status under international law?

International law is a mere reflection of interstate conducts and of mostly what happens in the international political arena.[2] Because there has, for a number of decades, been no concern commonly upheld by the members of the international society over what should be done in respect to people who left their original countries, international law has not been restructured or reinterpreted in a way to incorporate the concept and issues of the refugees. Only recently was international law extended to include the refugees as group of people whose needs should be attended and whose rights should be taken under protection within an international legal context. The realm of the rights and privileges of the refugees, like many other sections of international law, has been defined in the aftermath of the Second World War, the United Nations (UN) being the pioneer of the relevant political and legal endeavors.

The 1951 Convention Relating to the Status of Refugees,[3] adopted as a final text at the United Nations General Assembly by a resolution, and praised as "the centrepiece of the international refugee protection," is the first comprehensive attempt to address the threats the refugees face and to improve their conditions in a way to raise their status to that of a regular national. As an international legal instrument adopted post-Second World

---

[2] See Martti Koskeinnemi, *Politics of International Law* (Oxford: Hart Publishing, 2011).
[3] The United Nations Conventions Relating to the Status of Refugees, Geneva, 28 July 1951, available at https://www.unhcr.org/5d9ed32b4 (accessed 13 December 2020).

War, the 1951 Convention had a limited mandate only applicable to the people escaping persecution or any other imminent threats and to the escaping occurrences within Europe before 1 January 1951. This limitation was lifted by the 1967 Protocol,[4] thus introducing a universal coverage. Under the Convention, a refugee is a person who "as a result of events occurring before 1 January 1951 and owing to wellfounded fear of being persecuted for reasons of race, religion, nationality, membership of a particular social group or political opinion, is outside the country of his nationality and is unable or, owing to such fear, is unwilling to avail himself of the protection of that country; or who, not having a nationality and being outside the country of his former habitual residence as a result of such events, is unable or, owing to such fear, is unwilling to return to it." (Article 1).

Apart from providing a comprehensive and working definition, the 1951 Convention is of great importance for several reasons. Above all, the deliberations were performed with the involvement of relevant non-state stakeholders (albeit as observers), particularly the international non-governmental organizations (INGOs) with a particular emphasis upon refugees. Secondly, the 1951 Convention reaffirms and consolidates previous legal endeavors relating to the rights and privileges of the refugees at the international level. In contrast to earlier instruments, the 1951 Convention raises a single definition that applies to all featuring the same characteristics that make the person eligible to be considered under the status of refugee.

The Convention not only defines the status of the refugees but also prescribes rights attached to this status. Accordingly, it further introduces fundamental principles that serve as the basis of this status and these rights, including non-discrimination, non-penalization and non-refoulement, which together constitute the backbone of the international refugee law. In practice, these principles and the legal rules they generate are translated into common application of the Convention provisions without discrimination in terms of race, religion or country of origin (Article 3).

The Convention also stresses that refugees may not be subjected to legal prosecution for their illegal entry or stay, suggesting that the act of taking refuge may in some cases require the refugees to violate the immigration rules. The legal actions the Convention prohibits may include being charged with immigration or criminal offences associated with the act of taking refuge or being arbitrarily detained simply on the basis of this act. This is to ensure the general safety of the refugees and to send the message that those who consider taking refuge should not hold worries as to whether they will be incriminated in one of the contracting parties. The relevant provision reads

---

[4] Protocol Relating to the Status of Refugees, New York, 31 January 1967, available at https://www.unhcr.org/5d9ed66a4 (accessed 13 December 2020).

as follows:

> The Contracting States shall not impose penalties, on account of their illegal entry or presence, on refugees who, coming directly from a territory where their life or freedom was threatened in the sense of article 1, enter or are present in their territory without authorization, provided they present themselves without delay to the authorities and show good cause for their illegal entry or presence (Article 31).

The principle of non-refoulement, marking the epicentre of the Convention, is so important that no reservations or derogations (among some other provisions) are allowed to it. According to the principle, the host state may, under no circumstances and in any manner whatsoever, not expel or return a refugee to the jurisdiction of a state where they fear of persecution or other life-threatening conditions. The non-refoulement provision of the Convention reads:

> No Contracting State shall expel or return ("refouler") a refugee in any manner whatsoever to the frontiers of territories where his life or freedom would be threatened on account of his race, religion, nationality, membership of a particular social group or political opinion (Article 33).

Once they are in the host state, the refugees automatically become candidates to become natural parts of the original community. The Convention, in other words, seeks to remove the inherent barriers and differences between the nationals and the refugees. To fulfil this objective, the Convention first stresses that the refugees are required to comply with the rules of the domestic law:

> The personal status of a refugee shall be governed by the law of the country of his domicile or, if he has no domicile, by the law of the country of his residence (Article 12.1).

Additionally, the Convention is careful to protect the previously recognized rights, particularly civil rights, of the refugees:

> Rights previously acquired by a refugee and dependent on personal status, more particularly rights attaching to marriage, shall be respected by a Contracting State, subject to compliance, if this be necessary, with the formalities required by the law of that State, provided that the right in question is one which would have been recognized by the law of that State had he not become a refugee (Article 12.2).

The Convention takes further steps and urges hosting states to take the status of the refugees closer to the nationals:

> The Contracting States shall as far as possible facilitate the assimilation and naturalization of refugees. They shall in particular make every effort to expedite naturalization proceedings and to reduce as far as possible the charges and costs of such proceedings (Article 34).

Even though the states parties to the Convention undertake the obligations pertinent to the protection of the refugees, the United Nations also participates in the process in supporting the parties while implementing the Convention provisions:

> The Contracting States undertake to co-operate with the Office of the United Nations High Commissioner for Refugees, or any other agency of the United Nations which may succeed it, in the exercise of its functions, and shall in particular facilitate its duty of supervising the application of the provisions of this Convention (Article 35.1).

It should be noted that the status of refugee is the one that extends the broadest set of rights for people who experience distress. In other words, the refugee status is the primary one reserved under international law for individuals who, due to immediate threats, have to leave their home countries and seek refuge in another one. As a result, the scope of the Convention offers a broad definition of the term refugee. Although not explicitly stated in the Convention, the following, among others, cases may make the sufferers qualify for this international legal status:

- persecution for reasons of race, religion, nationality, membership of a particular social group or political opinion;

- armed conflict, which may be rooted in and/or conducted along the lines of race, ethnicity, religion, politics, gender or social group divides;

- violence perpetrated by organized gangs, traffickers, and other non-State actors, against which the State is unable or unwilling to protect;

- persecution on the basis of sexual orientation or gender identity;

- disasters (including drought or famine) where they are linked to situations of persecution or armed conflict rooted in racial, ethnic, religious, or political divides, or disproportionately affect particular groups.[5]

---

[5] The refugee concept under international law: Global compact for safe, orderly and regular migration (New York, 12-15 March 2018), United Nations High Commissioner for Refugees (UNHCR), p. 1, available at https://www.unhcr.org/en-my/5aa290937.pdf (accessed 14 December 2020).

While the Convention is clear as to what constitutes the status of a refugee, a decision of granting this status to an individual in practice always appears to be a complicated one as it requires the involvement of different stakeholders:

> The determination of refugee status is a legal or administrative process by which a government or UNHCR, according to its mandate, determines whether a person seeking international protection is considered a refugee under international, regional or national law. Such determinations can be made on an individualized basis or through group-based mechanisms (such as prima facie recognition or the provision of temporary protection).[6]

**Living in purgatory: Seeking asylum is staying in between joy and anxiety**

The status of asylum is not exactly a legal one, particularly when it is treated from an international law perspective. The UN Refugee Agency (UNHCR), on the other hand, provides the following note where it attempts to define the term asylum-seeker:

> A person who leaves his country of origin because of persecution or a well-founded fear of it has a primary and essential need to receive asylum in another country. Asylum implies the possibility of remaining in a country either permanently or at least on a temporary basis pending resettlement elsewhere.[7]

Amnesty International defines an asylum seeker as follows:

> An asylum-seeker is a person who has left their country and is seeking protection from persecution and serious human rights violations in another country, but who hasn't yet been legally recognized as a refugee and is waiting to receive a decision on their asylum claim. Seeking asylum is a human right. This means everyone should be allowed to enter another country to seek asylum.[8]

This quote, placing emphasis upon seeking asylum as a human right, refers to the Universal Declaration of Human Rights, a resolution adopted by the UN General Assembly on 10 December 1948 that serves the nucleus of the contemporary international human rights law. Article 14 of the Declaration

---

[6] Ibid., p. 2.
[7] UN Refugee Agency, "Note on Asylum," EC/SCP/4, 24 August 1977, available at
https://www.unhcr.org/excom/scip/3ae68cbb30/note-asylum.html (Accessed 11 December 2020).
[8] "Refugees, Asylum-Seekers, and Migrants," Amnesty International,
https://www.amnesty.org/en/what-we-do/refugees-asylum-seekers-and-migrants/ (accessed, 10.12.2020).

reads:

> (1) Everyone has the right to seek and to enjoy in other countries asylum from persecution.
>
> (2) This right may not be invoked in the case of prosecutions genuinely arising from non-political crimes or from acts contrary to the purposes and principles of the United Nations.[9]

It should be noted that the Declaration does not identify a legal status for the asylum-seekers, but rather prescribes seeking asylum as a basic right enjoyable by all. Claiming the right to asylum does not, however, necessarily have to translate into automatic recognition of a relevant status associated with this right by the state where asylum is being sought. Since international law does not define such a status that needs to be clarified and incorporated into the national laws, seeking asylum is often associated with the refugee status. In other words, certain conditions have to be met for the claim of the right to asylum to turn into a concrete legal status:

> To be granted asylum, a person must demonstrate that he or she is a "refugee," that he or she is not barred from asylum for any of the reasons listed in our immigration laws, and that the decision-maker should grant asylum as a matter of discretion.[10]

This indicates that every state has some discretion in terms of identifying the status of an asylum-seeker. The 1967 UN Declaration on Territorial Asylum confirms this, noting in article 1 that the State granting asylum is "to evaluate the grounds for the grant of asylum." However, in a sign of attempting to protect the asylum-seekers, the same article further stresses that "asylum granted by a State, in the exercise of its sovereignty, to persons entitled to invoke Article 14 of the Universal Declaration of Human Rights...shall be respected by all other States."[11]

Additional legal documents adopted on a regional level, on the other hand, paid a more specific attention to the question of admission for asylum. For instance, the Organization of African Union's Convention Governing the Specific Aspects of Refugee Problems in Africa (1969) provides:

> Member States of the OAU shall use their best endeavours consistent with their respective legislations to receive refugees and to, secure the settlement of those refugees who for well-founded reasons are unable

---

[9] The Universal Declaration of Human Rights, UN General Assembly, Resolution No. 217A, Paris, 10 December 1948, Article 14.
[10] "Asylum Law and Procedure," Human Rights First, https://www.humanrightsfirst.org/asylum/asylum-law-and-procedure (accessed, 10.12.2020).
[11] UN General Assembly, Declaration on Territorial Asylum, 14 December 1967, A/RES/2312(XXII), available at: https://www.refworld.org/docid/3b00f05a2c.html (accessed 10 December 2020).

or unwilling to return to their country of origin or nationality.[12]

The same Convention further states,

> Where a refugee has received the right to reside in any country of asylum, he may be granted temporary residence in any country of asylum in which he first presents himself as a refugee pending arrangements for his resettlement.[13]

A review of this article particularly reveals that the Convention, the first legal text towards legal recognition of the right to asylum, gives "a measure of normative content to the discretionary competence of states to grant asylum."[14] Similarly, the EU Charter also recognizes a legal form of asylum-seeking, thus prescribing binding provisions for the EU members. Article 18 of the Charter of Fundamental Rights of the European Union states that "the right to asylum shall be guaranteed" by the member states, also bound by article 19 of the same Charter which reads,

> 1. Collective expulsions are prohibited.

> 2. No one may be removed, expelled or extradited to a State where there is a serious risk that he or she would be subjected to the death penalty, torture or other inhuman or degrading treatment or punishment.[15]

Hence, it is safe to argue that international law recognizes the right to asylum, particularly in a regional setting, whereas it does not prescribe a separate legal status for the asylum-seekers. Rather, it appears that a meaningful exercise of the right to asylum is contingent upon affixing a refugee status to those who seek asylum.

### Moving freely across national borders? Not really, particularly if you are a migrant

International migration is now a global phenomenon, attracting a great deal of attention within the community of states and of global civil society elements. The UN notes on this matter as follows:

> The international movement of people is an integral part of a

---

[12] Article II(1), OAU Convention Governing the Specific Aspects of Refugee Problems in Africa, Addis Ababa, Ethiopia, 10 September 1969, available at https://au.int/sites/default/files/treaties/36400-treaty-oau_convention_1963.pdf (accessed 11 December 2020).

[13] Article II(2), Ibid.

[14] Guy S. Goodwin-Gill, "The International Law of Refugee Protection," in Elena Fiddian-Qasmiyeh, Gil Loescher, Katy Long, and Nando Sigona (eds.), *The Oxford Handbook of Refugee and Forced Migration Studies* (Oxford: Oxford University Press, 2014): 42.

[15] Articles 18 and 19, Charter of Fundamental Rights of the European Union, 2012/C 326/02, 26 October 2012, available at https://eur-lex.europa.eu/legal content/EN/TXT/PDF/?uri=CELEX: 12012P/TXT&from=EN (accesed 11 December 2020).

globalizing world; with more than 215 million international migrants currently living outside their country of origin, migration is also a response to growing global inequalities. As the scale, scope and complexity of international migration has grown, states and other stakeholders have become increasingly aware of the need to engage in international dialogue to address migration, and to enhance the international governance of migration.[16]

International legal protection is recognized and offered under international law to the people who experience severe forms of distress including but not limited to persecution, discrimination, fear of life, displacement and political/religious violence. This is partly due to the humanization of international law in a way to address the grave situations caused by instances of domestic turmoil such as ethnic or sectarian clashes. Whether or not this tendency towards humanization extends to include all human beings, however, remains controversial. The hardships and grave situations eligible for recognition of legal protection under international law towards the victims and sufferers seem to be limited in scope and in number, applicable to only a small number of people.

Refugees enjoy particularly strong and comprehensive legal protection whereas the asylum-seekers are considered less important and vulnerable; still, however, the latter has made huge stride towards recognition. Therefore, it appears that it is the rest (those who are not included in the scope of refugees and/or asylum-seekers) which presents troubles in terms of how they should be analyzed from an international law perspective. While the term immigrant, as a broad umbrella concept, encompasses the refugees as well as the asylum-seekers, is often utilized to refer to those who are not precisely protected under international law, namely those who are not either refugees or asylum-seekers.

The problem is mainly about the absence of a working definition of an immigrant that may serve as a basis for a proper engagement of international law. Noting that there is no internationally accepted legal definition, Amnesty International regard migrants as people staying outside their country of origin, who are not asylum-seekers or refugees. Amnesty's approach does not suggest a legal definition of an immigrant that international law may borrow. This is primarily because immigrants are often considered a major concern of national jurisdictions which are recognized as the sole competent entities to address immigration issues.

---

[16] Migration and Human Rights: Improving Human-Rights Based Governance of International Migration, The United Nations Human Rights Office of the High Commissioner, available at https://www.ohchr.org/Documents/Issues/Migration/MigrationHR_improvingHR_Report.pdf (accessed 12 December 2020).

What complicates the matter is the plethora of reasons for people to migrate to another country:

> Some migrants leave their country because they want to work, study or join their family, for example. Others feel they must leave because of poverty, political unrest, gang violence, natural disasters or other serious circumstances that exist there.[17]

These are the major challenges that those who may want to ensure inclusion of immigrants in the discourse and sphere of international law. On the other hand, there is, despite these challenges, still a reason for paying attention to the issue of immigration on the international level:

> Lots of people don't fit the legal definition of a refugee but could nevertheless be in danger if they went home.[18]

Even though international law does not prescribe a specific set of protections for immigrants (other than refugees and asylum-seekers), a review of the international legal texts as well as of the principal customs and practices reveals that international law provides an indirect and implicit coverage:

> It is important to understand that, just because migrants do not flee persecution, they are still entitled to have all their human rights protected and respected, regardless of the status they have in the country they moved to. Governments must protect all migrants from racist and xenophobic violence, exploitation and forced labour. Migrants should never be detained or forced to return to their countries without a legitimate reason.[19]

As a result, immigrants have become entitled to the same human rights protections as all individuals; however, states may limit their rights, particularly with regard to voting and political participation. A number of human rights treaties, on the other hand,

> ...explicitly prohibit discrimination on the basis of national origin and require States to ensure that migrants' human rights are equally protected. Additionally, like other particularly vulnerable groups, migrants have been given special protections under international law, to address situations where their rights are most at risk, such as in the workplace, in detention, or in transit.[20]

---

[17] Refugees, Asylum-Seekers and Migrants, Amnesty International, available at https://www.amnesty.org/en/what-we-do/refugees-asylum-seekers-and-migrants/ (accessed 13 December 2020).
[18] Ibid.
[19] Ibid.
[20] Immigration and Migrants' Rights, International Justice Resource Center, available at https://ijrcenter.org/thematic-research-guides/immigration-migrants-rights/ (accessed 12 December

Additionally, the UN has, in recent decades, assumed roles towards introducing new mechanisms for global governance of the international migration issues. Although it is not clear as to whether these initiatives will eventually translate into legally binding documents, several developments within the UN draw particular attention:

> In 2005 the Global Commission on International Migration (GCIM) was established and recommended that the international community should formulate a more consistent and coherent approach to international migration governance in respect of the legal and normative framework affecting international migrants, and embed it more visibly in the existing international architecture of the UN System.21 The GCIM called for new directions for action on irregular migration, integration, protecting the human rights of migrants and enhancing governance, in addition to action on the economic impact of migration.[21]

In recognition of the need for comprehensive cooperation on a global scale, the Global Migration Group (GMG), involving a number of UN-affiliated bodies and agencies, was launched in 2006. The GMG has identified its priority as follows:

> Working to ensure the full respect for the human rights and labour rights of international migrants so as to pro- mote human security and development and, in par- ticular, provide protection to vulnerable migrants, including asylum-seekers, refugees, stranded migrants and victims of exploitation and trafficking.[22]

The brief discussion above and the accompanying quote confirm a visible tendency, particularly within the UN as a primary institution of global governance, to address the migration issues and to place the migrants into a global context so that they would receive the attention they deserve from other pieces of global governance, national states being the most responsible in legal terms. However, such attempts have so far fallen short to generate a strong and comprehensive international legal regime with a particular emphasis upon migration and the migrants.

---

2020).
[21] Migration and Human Rights: Improving Human-Rights Based Governance of International Migration, p. 24.
[22] Global Migration Group, Terms of Reference, available at: http://www.globalmigrationgroup.org (accessed 12 December 2020).

## Drawing lines between refugees, asylum seekers and migrants: Comparing and contrasting people on the move

It is possible, based on the definitions and clarifications provided above, to draw working conclusions on the similarities and differences between refugees, asylum seekers and migrants from an international law perspective. Such an endeavor is especially useful because it helps readers and bystanders better analyze the legal context applicable to the people who move around the globe and understand why or why not they receive recognition and legal protection accordingly. This analysis further contributes to our understanding of how international law responds to the dynamism and change (or continuity) in international politics and interstate interactions.

### Similarities

A review of the three types of people on the move reveals one primary similarity, particularly if looked at from an international law perspective: that it appears that international law takes the issues affecting all these three groups from the lens of international human rights law. In other words, all major legal and political discussions have been made in reference to the protection of the human rights of these three categories and incorporation of these rights into international and national legal documents and mechanisms. Despite legal conundrums and inherent hardships embedded in the nature of the subject matter, all major international human rights documents have been interpreted in favor of the people on the move, regardless of whether they have a legal standing and status under international law. As a result, not only the refugees who have a separate legal status and specific rights accorded to them, but also asylum seekers and migrants who do not qualify as either refugees or asylum seekers enjoy the protections and privileges recognized under the international human rights mechanisms including supervision bodies and international courts. Even in cases where they have not entered the territories of the hosting states legally, these mechanisms extend their protection to them without making any distinction between nationals, legal residents and the illegal and undocumented migrants. Therefore, a person who illegally crossed the national border of a country that is party to certain human rights protection conventions and mechanisms may still enjoy protection in terms of fundamental rights.

Secondly, in all three major categories, it is possible to identify certain elements of distress; in other words, had they were leading a normal life in their home countries, the people on the move would not have felt the need of leaving their homes to build an uncertain future in another country. This is most obvious in the case of refugees and perhaps of the asylum seekers; but migrants would also be appealed by better life conditions beyond their national borders; they may be appealed by greater freedom, better job or education opportunities, or anything that would make them live a more comfortable life. This, in fact, provides a normative basis for the international legal protection since it tells that there is a valid reason for these people to change their lives radically; in recognition of this, the international community adjusts itself to accommodate the needs and concerns of these people.

### Differences

Similarities between refugees, asylum seekers and migrants may be detected; but differences between these terms are far more visible and analytically significant. The primary difference is observable in the legal status accorded to these three categories under international law. Roughly, it is possible to argue that a refugee, under international law (particularly international refugee law), in addition to enjoying rights (mostly similar to fundamental human rights), is able to exercise privileges attached to a specific legal status. A refugee status gives its holder the ability to claim certain rights vis-à-vis not only the hosting state but also the others that are part of the international refugee regime. Well-defined (and strong) exceptions are also recognized to the refugees for the sake of their protection against what they may encounter in their home countries. Owing to these exceptions (non-refoulement, non-discrimination and non-penalization), the refugees are allowed to stay safe in the receiving state. Such clarified privileges are not defined for the asylum-seekers; however, they are considered future refugees; therefore, once they go through the relevant legal process, asylum seekers, in most cases, are expected to acquire a privileged status as refugees. This, on the other hand, is not the case with the migrants. Even though there is tendency within the international legal community to attend their issues, migrants are concretely protected by national laws only; in such instances, the coverage does not extend to other countries. In other words, migrants holding certain rights in one country may not raise a claim of exercising these rights in another country.

Secondly, the refugee status is relatively clarified; therefore, it is almost safe to argue that there will be no serious disagreement as to who is entitled to be recognized as a refugee. This is mostly due to the historical attention paid to the refugee issues. On the contrary, the status of a migrant is not clear-cut, and in most cases, depends on the national jurisdictions' preferences and tendencies. The emerging attention paid to the migration issues still remains a political one, holding the promise of being transformed into a normative aspiration. Until it happens, however, the migration status is destined to stay vague, complicated and unclarified in legal terms.

# Conclusion

International law adjusts itself to what actually takes place in the international political space; this is what makes it pretty dynamic and flexible. The broad issue of people who have to move is no exception. It appears that international law has been attentive to the issue of refugees since early twentieth century when multilateral arrangements in different fields also started to emerge. However, the most concrete regulations applicable to the refugee issues have been introduced as late as post-World War II era that could be characterized as the inception of a working global governance. Certain areas have come to life as autonomous (but interlinked) realms in international politics; separate particular attentions have been paid to global economic issues, human rights violations and multilateral use of force. The refugees have been considered an exclusive type of victims mostly affected by human rights breaches.

Owing to the strong emphasis upon the problems refugees were facing (mostly associated with the gravity of violations and notorious practices during the Second World War), the UN has committed itself to adopting strong mechanisms towards their protection under international law, thus leading to the emergence of a two-fold protection regime. On the one hand, the refugees were made part of the broad protection of international human rights law. A separate body of law, on the other, has been developed to address peculiar needs of the refugees. This tendency generated strong principles agreed upon and shared by the members of the international community that raisable not only in the hosting states but also in all others that are part of this exclusive regime. As a result, the refugees have acquired a clear-cut legal status as well as broad set of rights that aim at ensuring their safety.

This is not, however, necessarily the case with the asylum seekers and migrants. In other words, they do not have a strongly defined and well-established status under international law, although they are able to enjoy rights and privileges specified within international human rights law, in addition to what has been prescribed to them in separate arrangements. Asylum-seekers are often portrayed as people who wait for (and legitimately expect) legal recognition which will identify them as refugees. However, because certain requirements are prescribed for such recognition and because not all states implement the international refugee law in favor of the victims, asylum seeking may not all the time be translated into a full-fledged refugee status. Thus, it is necessary to address the possible status of asylum seeking in a separate legal setting.

Defining the status and prescribing the rights of migrants under international law is far more challenging. First, migrants may constitute a fairly large community, characterized by extreme diversity in terms of motives, needs and priorities. It is, thus, very hard to address all these motives and to prescribe international legal obligations for the hosting states which would be able to raise legitimate objections. Despite these challenges, however, the issues of the migrants are now being discussed from a global governance perspective.

# CHAPTER 7

# CONCEPTUAL FRAMEWORK ABOUT MIGRATION

Mehlika Özlem Ultan[*]

## Introduction

People who migrated in the early ages due to natural disasters or not being able to meet basic living needs such as nutritional needs; later, with the industrialization, continued to migrate, mostly for economic and political reasons. This is how the migration spread to the world geographically. In this context, it can be said that migration has existed since the beginning of human history and is an integral part of societies. Migrations one of the effective factors in the demographic structure, culture, economy and politics of societies in every period of history; because of this versatility, it has become a phenomenon which studied by different scientific disciplines. International human movements are changing the economic, social, political and cultural structure of sending and receiving countries. Migrations, which have affected and still affect all societies, have emerged in different ways depending on various reasons, such as forced migration, voluntary migration, seasonal migration, internal migration, international migration or illegal migration.[1] This study aims to describe the conceptual framework of migration related literature. As a part of the 'Refugee Crisis in International Policy', it is needed to explain the main and mostly accepted definitions of migration literature. Thus, the book project can be more comprehensive with a conceptual framework.

## Terminology of Migration

In order not to be confused during reading and analyzing the migration studies, the definitions of all the migration related terminology should be understood. For this reason, the origin of the terms and their legal background should be explained.

Drawing on dictionary definitions of migration, it can be determined as "a seasonal movement of populations between regions where conditions are alternately favourable or unfavourable".[2] Despite the diversity of definitions regarding the phenomenon of migration, the element of displacement stands

---

[*] Assoc. Prof., Kocaeli University, International RelationsDepartment, ozlemultan@gmail.com.
[1] Mehlika Özlem Ultan, Avrupa Birliği'nde Yasa Dışı Göçün Önlenmesi ve Ülke Uygulamaları, Ankara, Nobel Yayıncılık, p. 1.
[2] Hugh Dingle and V. AlistairDrake, "What Is Migration?", **Bioscience**, Vol. 57, No. 2, 2007, p. 114.

out as the common point of all definitions. Displacement within the definition of migration covers very short distances as well as expressing inter-city or international changes. In short, migration is the movement from the main place to the place desired to be reached. Migration can also be defined as permanent or semi-permanent displacement.[3] In this context, migration is comprehensively expressed as a displacement movement that includes short, medium or long-term settlement goals from one place to another for political, economic, cultural or individual reasons.[4]

From this point of view, generally, migration is defined as the movement of a person or a group of people from one country to another or anywhere within a country's borders. Migration is a population movement that includes all kinds of displacement of people, including refugees, economic migrants or those who are displaced for other purposes, regardless of distance or reason.[5]

The types of migration can be categorized as internal and international migration. Internal migration is described as the movement of people within a state involving the establishment of a new temporary or permanent residence.[6] It can include both nationals and non-nationals who move away from their place of habitual residence and who decide to move to another place, like in the case of rural-urban migration.[7] Whereas international migration is the movement of people away from their place of usual residence and to go to another country of which they are not nationals. People who move internationally due to recreation, business, visits to friends and relatives, holiday, medical treatment or religious pilgrimages reasons are excluded from this definition.[8]

Apart from the migration term, the definitions of immigration and emigration can also be confusing. While immigration can be described as "from the perspective of the country of arrival, the act of moving into a country other than one's country of nationality or usual residence, so that the country of destination effectively becomes his or her new country of usual residence"; emigration is defined as "from the perspective of the country of departure, the act of moving from one's country of nationality or usual residence to another country, so that the country of destination effectively

---

[3] Everett S. Lee, "A Theory of Migration", **Theories of Migration**, RobinCohen, (Ed.) Cheltenham, Edward Elgard Publishing, 1996, p. 16.

[4] Cemal Yalçın, **Göç Sosyolojisi**, İstanbul, İmge Yayınları, 2004, p. 13.

[5] "Key Migration Terms", InternationalOrganizationfor Migration, https://www.iom.int/key-migration-terms, (Access: 19.11.2020).

[6] International Organizationfor Migration, World Migration Report 2015, p.12.

[7] International Organizationfor Migration, op.cit.

[8] Ibid.

becomes his or her new country of usual residence".[9]

Although many works have been written about migration, the first known scientific study is the article "The Laws of Migration" published by Ravenstein in 1885. In this article, Ravenstein stated that large industrial and commercial centres are preferred by long-distance migrants.[10] This situation shows that migration policies are generally economically based.[11]

It is seen in the literature that it is possible to classify migration from many aspects. But these classifications are not clearly separated from each other. It can be seen that an immigrant is in more than one category at the same time.[12] There have been changes in the migration structure over time. Accordingly, the primitive migration period was associated with natural disasters, and the idea that people migrated due to their desperation in the face of this situation was kept in the foreground. Then, the driving force of migration was tried to be explained with the social structure. In 19th century Europe, immigration was seen as the decision of individuals and expressed as a free immigration wave. With the increase of participation in this migration process carried out by a small number of people of their own will, mass migrations started to occur.[13]

### Regular and Irregular Migration

After explaining migration as a term, another classification can be observed: regular and irregular migration. According to the International Organization for Migration, regular migration occurs in compliance with the laws of the country of origin, transit and destination.[14]

It is the human activity that people carry out for any purpose to go out of their own countries and continue their lives in other countries.[15] Irregular and illegal migration can also be confused. On the subject of illegal immigration, it is possible to say that there is no clear definition that is universally determined. Generally speaking, "Leaving the country where a person is legally located and entering another country illegally; It refers to living and/or working in that country for a long time without having a legal permit, by not

[9] Ibid.
[10] E. G. Ravenstein, "The Laws of Migration", **Journal of theRoyal Statistical Society**, Vol. 52, No. 2, 1885, pp. 198-199.
[11] Uğur Tekin, "Avrupa'ya Göç ve Türkiye", **İstanbul Üniversitesi Siyasal Bilgiler Fakültesi Dergisi**, No. 37, 2007, p. 44.
[12] Fuat Güllüpınar, "Göç Olgusunun Ekonomi-Politiği ve Uluslararası Göç Kuramları Üzerine Bir Değerlendirme", **Yalova Sosyal Bilimler Dergisi**, No. 4, 2012, p. 57.
[13] Serdar Sağlam, "Türkiye'de İç Göç Olgusu ve Kentleşme", **Hacettepe Üniversitesi Türkiyat Araştırmaları Enstitüsü Yayını**, No. 5, 2006, p. 35.
[14] International Organization for Migration, op.cit.
[15] Asar Aydoğan, Türk Yabancılar Mevzuatında Yabancı ve Hakları, Ankara, Emek Ofset, 2004, p. 242.

leaving the country in due time after entering through legal means".[16] Although a generally accepted irregular migration definition does not exist, it is usually used to identify persons moving except regular migration channels. Thus, irregular migration is "the movement of persons that takes place outside the laws, regulations, or international agreements governing the entry into or exit from the state of origin, transit or destination."[17]

If the rights of the irregular migrants are evaluated, it can be seen that migrating irregularly does not relieve states from the obligation to protect their rights. Refugees, asylum seekers, unaccompanied migrant children or victims of trafficking can use some of the irregular migration channels.[18] At this point, the terms of migrant, refugee, asylum seeker, and stateless person should be defined.

## Migrant

Although migrant is not defined under international law, the generally accepted definition of migrant was developed by the International Organization for Migration. According to IOM, migrant reflects people who move away from their place of usual residence, whether within a country or across an international border, temporarily or permanently, and for a variety of reasons. It can be categorized related to the reason for migration; thus, it includes migrant workers, smuggled migrants, or international students.[19] The United Nations Department of Economic and Social Affairs also define the immigrant as "A person who moves to a country other than that of his or her usual residence for a period of at least a year (12 months), so that the country of destination effectively becomes his or her new country of usual residence. From the perspective of the country of departure, the person will be a long-term emigrant and from that of the country of arrival, the person will be a long-term immigrant".[20] It can be evaluated from the perspective of the country of arrival, and the country of destination effectively becomes their new country of usual residence. Some migrants can move to another country for less than 12 months and they are described as short-term emigrants. A person who stays away from the country for a period of less than twelve months is considered a short-term emigrant, while a person who stays away from the country for a period of more than twelve months is considered a long-term emigrant. The definition of short-term or long-term emigrant depends on the duration of stay within the border in the country of

---

[16] "International Migration LawGlossary on Migration", International Organization for Migration (IOM), Geneva, 2004, p. 34, http://publications.iom.int/bookstore/free/IML_1_EN.pdf, (Access: 20.11.2020).

[17] International Organizationfor Migration, op.cit.

[18] Ibid.

[19] Ibid.

[20] "Recommendations on Statistics of International Migration", **UN DESA**, Revision 1, 1998, p. 10.

destination.[21]

## Refugee

Even though there is no accepted definition of refugee, after the 1951 Convention Relating to the Status of Refugees has been accepted, a general definition of the term can be made. According to the Convention, the term refugee should be applied to any person who "owing to a well-founded fear of being persecuted for reasons of race, religion, nationality, membership of a particular social group or political opinion, is outside the country of his nationality and is unable or, owing to such fear, is unwilling to avail himself of the protection of that country; or who, not having a nationality and being outside the country of his former habitual residence, is unable or, owing to such fear, is unwilling to return to it".[22]

According to some sources, refugees can be defined as 'unprotected persons', because they are not accepted as a part of national protection.[23] However, the protection of refugees can be evaluated by many aspects, such as safety from being returned to danger, access to fair and efficient asylum procedures, or measures to ensure that their basic human rights are respected.[24]

The definition of the refugee term and their protection rules are determined in international law. The 1951 refugee Convention is a vital document at this point. According to the Convention, refugee is "someone who is unable or unwilling to return to their country of origin owing to a well-founded fear of being persecuted for reasons of race, religion, nationality, membership of a particular social group, or political opinion."[25] Thus, they are protected under international law for not being penalized for unauthorized entry or stay if they have travelled from a place where they could be at risk.[26]

According to the United Nations provided by the High Commissioner for Refugees (UNHCR), by the end of 2017, there were 25.4 million refugee people who are registered across the world.[27] International Organization of Migration accepts that under international refugee law, recognizing the refugees is declaratory and not constitutive. Thus, if a person fulfils the criteria related to the definition of the 1951 Convention is seen as a refugee

---

[21] InternationalOrganizationfor Migration, op.cit.
[22] Conventionrelating to the Status of Refugees (adopted 28 July 1951, enteredin to force 22 April 1954), (189 UNTS 137) Art. 1A(2).
[23] Antonio Fortin, "The Meaning of "Protection" in the Refugee Definition", **International Journal of Refugee Law**, Vol. 12, No.4, 2000, p. 548.
[24] "Refugees", UNHCR, https://www.unhcr.org/refugees.html, (Access: 28.11.2020).
[25] "What is Refugee?", UNHCR, https://www.unhcr.org/what-is-a-refugee.html, (Access: 28.11.2020).
[26] International Organization for Migration, op.cit.
[27] UNHCR, op.cit.

and had all the rights. "This would necessarily occur prior to the time at which his refugee status is formally determined. Recognition of his refugee status does not therefore make him a refugee but declares him to be one. He does not become a refugee because of recognition, but is recognized because he is a refugee."[28]

### Asylum Seeker

According to the International Organization of Migration, asylum seeker is "someone whose claim has not yet been finally decided on by the country in which he or she has submitted it. Not every asylum seeker will ultimately be recognized as a refugee, but every recognized refugee is initially an asylum seeker".[29] In some of the countries with official procedures, it is accepted as an individual who is seeking international protection within the territory of the country that he or she has submitted.

United Nations High Commission for Refugees also made a definition of the asylum seeker. According to UNHCR, an asylum seeker is "a person who has left their country of origin, has applied for recognition as a refugee in another country, and is awaiting a decision on their application". Thus, an asylum seeker is someone who has asked the related government for refugee status and is still waiting to learn the result of their application.[30]

### Stateless Person

According to United Nations High Commissioner for Refugees, the criteria of being accepted as a stateless person "is limited to the states with which a person enjoys a relevant link, in particular by birth on the territory, descent, marriage, adoption or habitual residence".[31] Thus, the definition is accepted as underlying a person who is not considered as a national by any state under the operation of its law.How a state applies its laws of nationality in the case of individuals as well as of any decisions that may have had an impact on the status of the individuals need another kind of analysis. The 1.1 article of the UNHCR which is related to stateless persons can be applied in both migration and non-migration aspects. Being stateless can be correlated with either a cause or a consequence of the migration flows. In some cases, it can be seen that a stateless person has even never crossed an international border. And also, a stateless person can become a refugee if he/she is

---

[28] United Nations High Commissioner for Refugees, Hand book and Guidelines on Procedures and Criteria for Determining Refugee Status, 2011, HCR/1P/4/enG/Rev. 3.

[29] International Organization for Migration, op.cit.

[30] Simon Goodman and Susan A. Speer, "Category Use in the Construction of Asylum Seekers", **Critical Discourse Studies**, Vol. 4, No. 2, 2007, p. 166.

[31] UNHCR, "Handbook on Protection of Stateless Persons under the 1954 Convention Relating to the Status of Stateless Persons", 2014, p. 12.

unwilling or unable to return to his/her place of residence because of fear of persecution on one of the parts of the refugee definition.[32]

## Conclusion

Migration is on the agenda of both many countries and international organizations. It is accepted as a multi-faceted phenomenon which can be evaluated within many aspects for political organization and society. From this point of view, it is a vital issue which is related to the cause of the many problems within the borders of countries. The issue of migration emerges as an important phenomenon that the whole world is facing. In other parts of the study, many issues related to migration will be discussed. Before these issues are elaborated, it is thought that all concepts related to migration should be analyzed and tried to present the conceptual framework.

[32] International Organization for Migration, op.cit.

101

# CHAPTER 8

## HISTORY OF REFUGEE MOVEMENTS: A BRIEF OVERVIEW

### Akın Kiren[*]

### Introduction

Throughout history, large numbers of people around the world have suffered dislocation as a result of persecution, conflict, violence, human rights violations or any event disrupting the general public order. Some of these people have been internally displaced,[1] and some have been forced to cross borders. In most instances, while some very small numbers eventually have been able to reach an industrialized Western state, the overwhelming majority have resettled in neighbouring countries. Besides, substantial numbers of displaced people have been housed in refugee camps.

According to the latest data from the United Nations High Commissioner for Refugees (UNHCR), by the end of 2019, there are more than **79.5 million** people around the world who have been forcibly displaced from their lands, and only some **26 million of them are in the position of statutory refugee.**[2] **This means 1% of the world's total population has escaped from their homes, and refugees constitute more than one-third of this ratio. An** estimated 30 to 34 million (38-43%) of these 79.5 million are children under the age of 18. **In addition to them, millions of people are defined as stateless, which** means they are not considered as nationals by any state and they lack access to basic rights such as education,

---

[*] Ph.D., akinkiren@gmail.com
[1] Internally Displaced Persons (IDPs) are in a separate but related category with refugees. Much like refugees, IDPs are forced to flee their homes and their livelihoods and to move to another place in order to secure safety. However, they donot cross their states' borders. This is the only thing that differentiates them from refugees. As of 31 December 2019, there were 45.7 million people living in internal displacement in 61 countries and territories because of conflict and violence, and this is the highest number ever recorded. *See* Mark Gibney, **Global Refugee Crisis: A Reference Handbook**, Second Edition, Santa Barbara, California, ABC-CLIO, 2010, p. 2; https://www.internal-displacement.org/global
-report/grid2020/ (Access 2 December 2020).
[2] The word refugee is defined in the Article I of the 1951 Convention Relating to the Status of Refugees. According to this, a refugee is someone who *"is outside his or her country of nationality or habitual residence; has a well-founded fear of persecution because of his/her race, religion, nationality, membership in a particular social group or political opinion; and is unable or unwilling to avail himself/herself of the protection of that country, or to return there, for fear of persecution."* See *"Convention and Protocol Relating to the Status of Refugees"*, p. 14.
https://www.unhcr.org/ 3b66c2aa10 (Access 12 November 2020); *"The 1951 Convention Relating to the Status of Refugees and its 1967 Protocol"*, p. 2. https://www.unhcr.org/3bbdb0954.pdf (Access 12 November 2020).

health care, employment and freedom of movement.[3]

Table 1 below presents data on the first five countries that produced the largest number of refugees and asylum seekers by the end of 2019. As it is seen,more than two-thirds (68%) of all refugees under UNHCR's mandate and the Venezuelans displaced abroad come from these five countries.

**Table 1.** Top Five Refugee Producing States, 2019[4]

| | Country of Origin | Refugees under UNHCR's mandate | Asylum-seekers |
|---|---|---|---|
| 1 | Syrian Arab Rep. (SYR) | 6,616,983 | 118,435 |
| 2 | Venezuela (Bolivarian Republic of) (VEN) | 93,280 + 3,582,202 (Venezuelans displaced abroad) | 794,496 |
| 3 | Afghanistan (AFG) | 2,728,853 | 251,024 |
| 4 | South Sudan (SSD) | 2,234,814 | 5,622 |
| 5 | Myanmar (MMR) | 1,078,268 | 37,452 |

On the other hand, Table 2 shows states which housed the largest number of refugees by the end of the same year, 2019. Among the major refugee hosting countries, developing countries host 85% of the total refugees (and Venezuelans displaced abroad), and the least developed countries provide asylum to 27% of the total. Clearly, Turkey, as a developing country, hosts the largest number of refugees with 3.6 million. After Turkey, Colombia hosts 1.8 million people, most of whom are Venezuelans displaced abroad.

**Table 2.** Major Refugee Hosting Countries, 2019[5]

| | Hosting Country | Refugees under UNHCR's mandate |
|---|---|---|
| 1 | Turkey | 3.6 million |
| 2 | Colombia | 1.8 million |
| 3 | Pakistan | 1.4 million |
| 4 | Uganda | 1.4 million |
| 5 | Germany | 1.1 million |

In the meantime, although one of the great fictions about externally displaced persons is that the bulk of them are housed in the industrialized countries of the West, only Germany from the developed countries is near the top of the list according to the statistics.

The purpose of this study is to briefly look at the history of refugees and

---

[3] "Data on some 4.2 million stateless people residing in 76 countries was reported at the end of 2019. The true global figure is estimated to be significantly higher." Seehttps://www.unhcr.org/figures-at-a-glance.html (Access 12 November 2020).
[4] https://www.unhcr.org/refugee-statistics/download/?url=3JLm (Access 13 November 2020).
[5] https://www.unhcr.org/refugee-statistics/ (Access 13 November 2020).

to examine what reasons have become more important in different eras. However, in order to realize how serious a problem it is still today as it has been in the past; first, some current data is presented above.

The next part of the study examines the refugees of the periods before an international refugee regime was established in the 20th century. Refugees who had to leave their homeland during the years of religious conflicts and border changes, following nationalist movements, are examined under the heading of classic refugees. The third subtitle of the study is about the international refugee regime. After the World War I, the first High Commissioner for refugees was appointed in 1921 by the League of Nations. Since then, various international measures have been taken either under the responsibility of the League of Nations and United Nations (UN) or by the countries experiencing the problem. Despite these measures, during the 20th century, a large number of refugee movements took place, and the total number of refugees reached record levels. For this reason, an evaluation regarding the responsibility of states is presented in the conclusion part.

Meanwhile, it is impossible to explain all the details of such a broad topic in a short study. Therefore, only some of the noticeable examples cited in the sources are included here.

## Classic refugees

It is widely recognized that especially two World Wars of the 20th century caused huge numbers of people to leave their homes. However, as a result of similar reasons, people sought refuge in other places even long before 1900. As mentioned at the beginning of this study, the history of immigration and asylum goes back to old times.[6] In history, there are too many examples of displacement of individuals and large populations because of their religious beliefs and/or political opinions.

Gatrell gives a few examples without going too far back into old ages, and first makes a mention of the time of *Reconquista*;[7] ending the Moorish rule that lasted hundreds of years in Spain and forcing 200,000 Muslims and Jews out of the country in 1492, is a very well-known incident at the end of the Middle Ages. As a second example, he refers to the German Protestants who left their lands at the end of the seventeenth century. After being expelled from the Palatinate (Middle Rhine), the German Protestantsresettled first in England and then in North America. At around the same period, one million

---

[6] Elemer Balogh, Political Refugees In Ancient Greece: From The Period Of The Tyrants To Alexander The Great, Roma, L'erma Di Bretschneider, 1972.

[7] Peter Gatrell, **The Making of the Modern Refugee**, Oxford, Oxford University Press, 2013, p. 2; for more examples, *see* Philipp Ther, **The Outsiders: Refugees in Europe since 1492**, Translated by Jeremiah Riemer, Princeton, Princeton University Press, 2019.

Calvinists left France due to the persecution of the French Catholic government, and created Huguenot settlements all over Europe, America and South Africa.

These were the years when the word *refugee* was first used in English.[8]After being introduced in French more than a hundred years previously, it was derived from and used to define the same Huguenots, who fled to England before and after the revocation of the Edict of Nantes by Louis XIV, in October 1685.[9]

Gatrell'slast example regarding the period preceding the 20th century is on the Revolution in Haiti in 1791. During this revolution, a slave revolt erupted on the French colony, and the colonial white population had to flee from the island.[10]

On the other hand, Zolberg, Suhrke and Aguayostart their work with a more detailed analytic review of the Western historical record. First of all, considering the criteria used in international law today, they also support the idea of accepting the victims of *Reconquista*as *refugees*, who had to flee from Spain after the fall of Granada. They claim that it would be appropriate to call it a classic case of *unrecognized refugees*. Moreover, they make this case more concrete with numbers. According to them, the wave of migration after the fall of Granada reached its peak in the five years after1609; 275,000 people migrated to other shores of the Mediterranean Sea in these years.[11]

Secondly, they use the definition of *classic refugees*, while explaining the years before an international refugee regime emerged. Under this category, they draw attention to increased numbers of *religious refugees* of the sixteenth and seventeenth centuries.

The years between the Protestant Reformation and the Peace of Augsburg (1555), and between 1618 and 1648, when the Thirty Years' War took place, are amongst the most destructive and turbulent years of European history. In addition to other casualties, thousands of German Catholics and Lutherans had to move from their lands in these years, because of the serious conflicts and wars.[12]

Another example of religious refugees are the Irish Catholics who were

---

[8] "Originating in France in the late seventeenth century, the word refugee is recorded as having been used in 1573 in the context of granting asylum and assistance to foreigners escaping persecution." **Le Petit Robert**, Paris, Societe du Nouveau Littre, 1978, p. 1641, as cited in Aristide R. Zolberg, AstriSuhrke and Sergio Aguayo, **Escape from Violence: Conflict and the Refugee Crisis in the Developing World**, New York and Oxford, Oxford University Press, 1989, p. 5.

[9] **Oxford English Dictionary**, Oxford, Oxford University Press, 1971, p. 2468.

[10] Gatrell, The Making of the Modern Refugee, p. 2.

[11] Zolberg, Suhrke and Aguayo,**op.cit.**, p. 7.

[12] Stephen J. Lee, **Aspects of European History, 1494-1789**, Second Edition, London and New York, Routledge, 1984, p. 82.

forced to flee from their homes during the late sixteenth and especially in the mid-seventeenth century. According to Terpstra, *"In the seventeenth century, England began using refugees and migrants in order to secure and develop new and troubled areas in Ireland and Americas."* To illustrate, *"about 125,000 settlers were shipped over to Ireland in the space of a few decades, with 80,000 sent to Ulster alone."*[13] Not surprisingly, in a short while, problems arose between natives and Protestant settlers, and, following a limited but exaggerated conflict, Oliver Cromwell found an opportunity to reshape Ireland. Only in between 1649 and 1653, 50,000 people were deported from Ireland. But yet, considering the fact that nearly 600,000 people out of a population of 1,400,000 died due to famine, the Black Death and war in these years, somewhat ironically, the deported ones could even be considered to have been fortunate.

On the other hand, Catholics were not the only religious victims of English governments. Particularly in the seventeenth century, some Protestant groups known as *dissenters* rejected the privileged powers of the Church of England and became another target. Eventually, in the 1680s, they were encouraged -or forced- to move to America, in order to form new settlements in this wild New World.[14]

Zolberg and his colleagues' second focus under the title of *classic refugees* is on *political refugees* of the last decades of the eighteenth century and the nineteenth century. Results of longstanding conflicts between revolutionaries and counter revolutionaries, or between fighters of national independence movements and imperial rulers created new migration flows in the West during these years. And sometimes, as in post-Restoration France, it gave way to the return of former exiles. Thus, two-way movements of political refugees became very commonplace.

The French Revolution is one of the well-known periods of the political refugee movements. Palmer states that 129,000 people left France during the Revolution. Since the population of France was about 25 million in those years, it can be said that five out of every thousand people fled abroad. However, only fifteen years ago, the rate was five times higher in America. During the American Revolution, approximately 100,000 people left their lands to go to Canada or England. This means the ratio of the loyalist colonists, who were supporting the British cause, to America's population of 2.5 million in 1776 was about twenty-four per thousand.[15]

One of the notable population flows of the nineteenth century originated

[13] Nicholas Terpstra, Religious Refugees in the Early Modern World: An Alternative History of the Reformation, New York, Cambridge University Press, 2015, p. 123-124.
[14] Terpstra, Religious Refugees in the Early Modern World, p. 124-126.
[15] Robert R. Palmer, **The Age of the Democratic Revolution: A Political History of Europe and America**, 1760–1800, Princeton and Oxford, Princeton University Press, 2014, p. 141.

inthe Russian Empire. About 7,000 Polish rebels, that failed at the November Uprising of 1830-31, were forced to leave Russian-held Polish land, and 5,000 of them reached and settled in France.[16] Less than a quarter of a century later, a second wave occurred in 1863-64after a similar revolt. And this time, most of the exiles divided into two main groups and went to London and Paris. As it is seen, the numbers in this example are not as high as other refugee groups mentioned in this study. However, some of these Polish refugees and the organizations they formed *"were perhaps the most active and effective groups of their kind in the nineteenth century."*[17] For instance, who arrived in Turkey brought with themselves valuable technological and political skills and enterprise, and provided the local government *"with a viable and valuable resource as foreign advisors, technicians, and political allies."*[18]

The Crimean War was another period of huge population movements in the nineteenth century. Besides the mass migration of Orthodox Christian Bulgarian peasants in 1854, more than 300,000 Muslim Tatars left their homes to relocate in the territories of the Ottoman Empire.[19]Later on, Circassians and other Muslim groups were expelled from the Caucasus during the 1860s, again by the Russians.[20]

Meanwhile, as a result of the mid-nineteenth century crisis, tens of thousands of people, mainly from France, Germany, Italy, and Austria-Hungary sought refuge in countries like Belgium, Switzerland, the United States, and Britain. In addition to these, relatively smaller groups from Italy, Spain, and Russia fled to new places during the other difficult periods. The number of these groups also reaches an important level in total.[21]

One last point to be mentioned about the 19th century is that, crises started in the last decades of the century continued until the mid-20thcentury.[22] Confirming this, Gatrell draws attention to the Jewish refugees. According to

---

[16] Jolanta T. Pekacz, *"Deconstructing a 'National Composer': Chopin and Polish Exiles in Paris, 1831-49"*, **19th-Century Music**, Vol. 24, No. 2, Special Issue: Nineteenth-Century Pianism, Autumn, 2000, p. 164.
[17] Barbara Jelavich, *"The Polish Emigration, 1831-1871: The Challenge to Russia"*, **L'émigration Politiqueen Europe**,Year: 1991, No. 146, p. 235.
[18] After the 1830s, some of the Polish refugees arrived in Turkey in 1848 and 1863. *See* Andrew A. Ubranik and Joseph O. Baylen, *"Polish Exiles and the Turkish Empire, 1830-1876"*, **The Polish Review**, Vol. 26, No. 3, 1981, p. 43.
[19] Justin McCarthy, **Death and Exile: The Ethnic Cleansing of Ottoman Muslims, 1821–1922**, Princeton, N.J., Darwin Press, 1995, p. 17, 29, 47-8.
[20] Stalin mostly ended the Tatar presence in Crimea. Rest of the Tatars had stayed in their homes after the Crimean War of 1853-1856 were deported by his order, in 1944. Gatrell, **The Making of the Modern Refugee**, p. 21.
[21] Zolberg, Suhrke and Aguayo, **op.cit.**, p. 11; Although it has been stated that there is no detailed study, it should also be emphasized that there are some studies pointing to singular events. For example, Marrus mentions 45,000 refugees who had to flee from France during the 1871 Civil War. *See* Michael R. Marrus, **The Unwanted: European Refugees in the Twentieth Century**, New York, Oxford University Press, 1985, p. 24.
[22] Zolberg, Suhrke and Aguayo, **op.cit.**, p. 11.

him, when the word refugee was used at the turn of the century, people would have mostly understood it to have been about the Jews who went to North America and Western Europe due to the poverty and persecution in Eastern Europe.[23] Between 1881 and 1914, because of the institutionalized discrimination, more than 1.9 million Jews left Russia, Austro-Hungary and Romania in order to reach the United States of America. Nearly three quarters ofthree-quartersdeparted from the western provinces of Russia, known as the *Pale of Settlement*.[24]

### Refugees in the era of international refugee regime

Studies focusing on the 20th century show that developments of this century were more brutal and bloodier than those of past centuries. Therefore, the number of refugees has been seen to have relatively increased as well. Marrus describes the increase that started in the 1880s as "*astronomic*."[25] However, his description is not sufficient to explain the severity of the new situation in its entirety. The number of refugees, which was expressed mostly in tens of thousands in the 19th century, started to be expressed not even in hundreds of thousands but in millions. In general terms, refugees became a prominent element of international politics and started to affect inter-state relations in the 20th century.[26]

One of the most important features of the 20th century is the fall of the last remaining multi-national empires. In this process, modern nation states, similar to those established in Europe in the 19th century, replaced empires all around the world. However, such a major transformation did not happen without blood and war, the First World War became one of the most important turning points.

The emergence of the Great War increased all existing tensions. Before, during and after the War, groups whose loyalty was considered suspicious faced deportation and relocation.Besides, people who seized power in the newly established states, or in the states under establishment, aimed to make their societies nationally homogenous. Their efforts in this context resulted in seeing minorities as the main sources of all problems. Finally, they choose to eliminate "*people without the correct ethnic credentials from their territories*."[27]

Nevertheless, the consequences of the War were particularly dramatic for

---

[23] Gatrell, The Making of the Modern Refugee, p. 21.
[24] Andrew Godley, Jewish Immigrant Entrepreneurship in New York and London, 1880-1914:
Enterprise and Culture, New York, Palgrave, 2001, p. 78.
[25] Marrus, The Unwanted.
[26] Marrus, **The Unwanted**, p. 24; *see also* EwaMorawska, "Intended and Unintended Consequences of Forced Migrations: A Neglected Aspect of East Europe's Twentieth Century History", **The International Migration Review**, Vol. 34, No. 4, Winter, 2000, pp. 1049-1087.
[27] Panikos Panayi and Pippa Virdee (Eds.), Refugees and the End of Empire: Imperial Collapse and Forced Migration in the Twentieth Century, New York, Palgrave Macmillan, 2011, p. viii.

the subjects of the last three empires. The Ottoman, Austro-Hungarian, and Russian empires were multi-national empires, and they had already been experiencing the pains of transition from traditional social and political orders to modern ones.[28] At the end of the War, the first two collapsed and disintegrated, and, a civil war and revolution followed the fall of the Tsarist regime in Russia. Consequently, mass flights of people from all these empires occurred.

The total number of displaced people during and after the Great War was over 3 million.[29] In addition to this number, after the Bolshevik Revolution, another 3 million people escaped from Russia to the west, especially to France and Germany.[30] Hence, as Gatrellpoints out, the word "refugeedom" started to be used in these years in connection with the refugee crisis in Russia.[31]

When it comes to the Ottoman Empire, it is necessary to mention two major population movements that took place during and after the War. First, *"the Ottoman Government ordered, in 1915, the Armenian population residing in or near the war zone to be relocated to the southern Ottoman provinces away from the supply routes and army transport lines on the way of the advancing Russian army."*[32]As a result of this, large numbers of Armenians were subjected to forced migration. And secondly, the Treaty of Lausanne, which is the final treaty of World War I and signed between Turkey and Greece in 1923, introduced a new concept of compulsory population exchange. In the first phase, at least 1.5 million people were directly affected by this exchange.[33] On the other hand, compared to the Russian and Ottoman empires, relatively fewer subjects of

[28] Zolberg, Suhrke and Aguayo, **op.cit.**, p. 12.

[29] Peter Gatrell, **A Whole Empire Walking: Refugees in Russia During World War One,** Bloomington, IN, Indiana University Press, 1999; *see also* Peter Gatrell, "Introduction: World Wars and Population Displacement in Europe in the Twentieth Century", **Contemporary European History**, Vol. 16, No. 4, Theme Issue: World Wars and Population Displacement in the Twentieth Century, Nov., 2007, pp. 415-426; Peter Gatrell and LiubovZhvanko, **Europe on the Move: Refugees in the era of the Great War,** Manchester, Manchester University Press, 2017.

[30] Norman Stone and Michael Glenny, **The Other Russia: The Experience of Exile,** London, Faber and Faber, 1990, p. xv.

[31] Gatrell, The Making of the Modern Refugee, p. 284.

[32] *"The Events of 1915 and The Turkish-Armenian Controversy over History: An Overview"*, http://www.mfa. gov.tr/the-events-of-1915-and-the-turkish-armenian-controversy-over-history_-an-overview.en.mfa (Access 19 November 2020).

[33] Evangelia Balta, **The Exchange of Populations**, İstanbul İstos, 2014; Mehmet Ali Gökaçtı, **Nüfus Mübadelesi: Kayıp Kuşak Hikayesi**, İstanbul, İletişim, 2003; Renée Hirschon, 'Consequences of the Lausanne Convention: An Overview', in **Crossing the Aegean: An Appraisal of the 1923 Compulsory Population Exchange Between Greece and Turkey**, Renée Hirschon (Ed.), New York and Oxford, Berghahn Books 2003; The concept mentioned above was later considered to be applied as a legitimate method in solving other minority problems, especially after the Second World War. *See* Matthew Frank, **Expelling the Germans: British Opinion and Post- 1945 Population Transfer in Context**, Oxford, Oxford University Press, 2007, pp. 13–38.

the Austro- Hungarian Empire had to move during its disintegration.[34]

The interwar period between the two World Wars became a period when fascism was on the rise, and hundreds of thousands of people escaped from Nazi persecution.[35] Nevertheless, a decrease of refugee mobility was observed in these years. The main feature of this period is that the issue of refugees was recognized in the international arena, and urgent need of an institutional structure was clearly understood. So, the League of Nations appointed Fridtjof Nansen as the first High Commissioner for Russian refugees in 1921.[36] This appointment was the first effort of the international community to formally address the refugee problem.

Being experienced for the first time in history, it was clear that such a regime would require substantial support. However, although some efforts were made and at least nine international bodies were created to deal with the crisis, it was not enough to strengthen it.[37]As a result of the inability to provide both political and financial backup of the member states of the League, in a very short time, the weakness of the High Commissioner regime was revealed. Especially after the time of the Holocaust, there was no doubt about its ineffectiveness.[38]

The time of the Second World War is probably the period when refugee movements occurred the most in history. In these years, the world certainly witnessed many more displacement events compared to the First World War. At the beginning of the War, changes began with the Germans' turning their aspirations to the East. Due to their policies in Poland, not only Poles and Jews, but also many Germans had to move and resettle in new places. Likewise, because of the Stalinist practices in the Soviet Union, large numbers of people were forced to move, and many were exiled to Siberia. In Russia, once again, Crimean Tatars were among the groups who suffered the most. In 1944, 190,000 people out of the population that stayed in these lands after the pressures of the 1800s were forcibly sent to the Urals, Siberia, Kazakhstan and Uzbekistan.

[34] Panikos Panayi, "Imperial Collapse and the Creation of Refugees in Twentieth- Century Europe", **Refugees and the End of Empire: Imperial Collapse and Forced Migration in the Twentieth Century**, Panikos Panayi and Pippa Virdee (Eds.), New York, Palgrave Macmillan, 2011, p. 4.
[35] When the victims of Nazi persecution are mentioned, naturally, those who lost their lives in the genocide come to mind first. However, although they survived, lots of additional people had to leave their homes. *See* Panayi, Refugees and the End of Empire, p. viii-x.
[36] https://www.unhcr.org/uk/3eeee0464.pdf (Access 20 November 2020).
[37] Gibney, Global Refugee Crisis, p. 7.
[38] In fact, Nansen's initiative was not expected to be very inclusive at the beginning. He was responsible for only dealing with the problems of the Russian refugees. Gil Loescher, **Beyond Charity: International Cooperation and the Global Refugee Crisis**, New York and Oxford, Oxford University Press, 1993, p. 36, 37; for the situation of Jewish refugees fleeing Nazi persecution, *see* Tony Kushner and Katherine Knox, **Refugees in an Age of Genocide: Global, National and Local Perspectives during the Twentieth Century**, London and Portland, Frank Cass, 1999, pp. 126–71.

Moreover, 1945 did not put an end to the refugee mobility. From the last months of the War to the early 1950s, migration flows took place in all directions across Europe. The peak of these flows was in between 1945 and 1947, and the total number of refugees in these two years reached 25 million. Of course the majority of this number consisted of people fleeing from or to Germany. From the fall of Nazi Germany until 1947, approximately 13 million Germans moved west to resettle in the remaining parts of the country. Besides, the nation-states liberated from the Nazi yoke also expelled the Germans who had been living on their lands since the time of the Austro-Hungarian Empire. Most of these people from countries like Czechoslovakia, Hungary and Romania had to take refuge in Germany. Thus, Germany became the new home of millions of refugees. By 1950, the population of the newly founded Federal Republic of Germany was about 50.8 million, and 7.9 million of them were refugees and expellees. In the 1950s, an additional 1.6 million people left the German Democratic Republic and emigrated to Federal Germany.

In fact, although Germany was at the centre of the displacement during this period, due to the border and regime changes, similar developments emerged all over Europe. Nearly 145,000 Poles stayed in Britain instead of returning to the Soviet-controlled Polish state. With the redefinition of the Italian-Yugoslavian border, 900,000 ethnic Italians remained in Yugoslavia, and 300,000 of them decided to cross to the other side. In the same way, Italians from Tunisia, Egypt, Libya and other parts of Africa migrated to Italy. Lastly, concerning Italy, as many as 100,000 anti-Communist Yugoslavs took refuge in this country, besides Austria. After all, considering all these numbers, an estimated total of more than 30 million people became refugees during and after the Second World War.[39]

Meanwhile, it should be emphasized that the late 1940s also witnessed the beginning of one of the most long-lasting refugee crises in the world. For the establishment of a territorial Israeli state, besides the systematic ethnic cleansing efforts, Israeli governments forced some 750,000Palestinian Arabs to leave their homes only at this phase.[40]

The most important result of the intense refugee movements of the Second World War is the realization of more effective and competent regulations and institutionalization. Firstly, the United Nations High Commissioner for Refugees (UNHCR) was established in 1950. As an agency of the United Nations (UN), the UNHCR has become the principal

---

[39] Panayi, Refugees and the End of Empire, p. viii-x.
[40] Ilan Pappé, "*The 1948 Ethnic Cleansing of Palestine*", **Journal of Palestine Studies,** Vol. 36, No. 1, Autumn 2006, pp. 6-20; Benny Morris, **The Birth of the Palestinian Refugee Problem Revisited**, Second Edition, Cambridge, Cambridge University Press, 2004; for the most recent data on the situation of Palestinian refugees, *see* https://www.unrwa.org/palestine-refugees (Access 22 November 2020).

mechanism of the international community to help and protect refugees for almost seventy years now.[41]

Secondly, the first international legal regulation on refugees, *the Geneva Convention Relating to the Status of Refugees*, was adopted in 1951. In the beginning, there were some geographic and temporal limits in this Convention. In order to revise and remove these limits, a Protocol was accepted in 1967. As being the only amendment, the Protocol gave the Convention its final shape, and the 1951 Convention is still the most important document of international refugee protection today.[42]

From the end of the 1940s, the intensity of refugee movements of the Second World War period decreased gradually in Europe. However, with the increase of Communist influence in Eastern Europe, a few examples emerged in the region. To illustrate, about 100,000 Greeks fled from the Civil War of 1944-1949, and sought refuge in the East.[43] The Bulgarian government implementing a policy of so-called "re-educating" the Turkish minority forced approximately 180,000 people to leave the country between 1949 and 1951. After the 1956 Hungarian Revolution was crushed by the Soviets, more than 200,000 people migrated primarily to Austria and Yugoslavia, and some of them later moved to countries such as Britain, France, Switzerland and Germany.

After the 1960s, there were few movements in Europe until the 1980s, and these came mostly as a result of Soviet pressure. Seeking political freedom and better living standards of people or events like the 1968 Prague Spring were the main reasons of these movements. And when it comes to the end of the 1980s, particularly under the influence of the intolerant and repressive policies of the weakening Soviet Bloc regimes, new examples such as Polish migration to West Germany, flight of ethnic Germans and Hungarians from the Ceausescu regime, and the escape of the Turkish

---

[41] According to Gibney, the statute of the UNHCR, which was adopted by the General Assembly on 14 December 1950 as Annex to Resolution 428 (V), *"assigns responsibility to the agency of providing international protection for refugees and seeking permanent solutions for the problems of refugees."* Gibney, **Global Refugee Crisis**, p. 7; *see also "Statute of the United Nations High Commissioner for Refugees"*, https://www.unhcr.org/ 4d944e 589.pdf (Access 22 November 2020).

[42] The Convention Was Prepared On The Basis Of Article 14 Of The Universal Declaration Of Human Rights. As It Is Known, The Declaration Is A Milestone Document In The History Of "Human Rights" And It Was Declared In 1948 By The Un General Assembly As A Common Standard Of Achievements For All Peoples And All Nations. The Article Mentioned Recognizes The Right Of Persons To Seek Asylum From Persecution In Other Countries. According To Gatrell, *"The United Nations Adopted A Definition That Centered Upon The Individual Victim Of Persecution"* With The Convention. *See*gatrell, The Making Of The Modern Refugee, 2013, P. 284. Besides, The Scope Of The Convention Was Initially Limited To The People That Fled Before 1 January 1 1951 And The Events Occurred Within Europe. *See "Convention And Protocol Relating To The Status Of Refugees"*, P. 2. Https://Www.Unhcr.Org/3b66c2aa 10 (Access 25 November 2020).

[43] Edgar O'Ballance, **The Greek Civil War, 1944-1949**, New York, Frederick A. Praeger, 1966.

minority from ethnic cleansing in Bulgaria took place.[44]

In the meantime, concerning the post-Second World War era, a social progress that is at least as important as the examples mentioned above is the decolonization of Asia and Africa. Between 1945 and 1960, nearly three dozen new states obtained their independence or autonomy from European colonial rulers. As a result of this, huge population movements -or forced displacements- occurred in these parts of the world. For instance, following the end of the British Empire, India faced disintegration, and, an estimated 15 million people were displaced during the establishment of Pakistan as a new state.[45] Besides, from the 1960s onwards, new refugee crises emerged especially in the developing world.[46] Also, with the failure of American policies in Vietnam, many people had to leave this country in the ensuing years.[47]

The third and the last wave of mass refugee crises in 20th century Europe reached its peak in the 1990s. In fact, the number of displaced people after the Cold War was not as large as the previous two major eras, and refugees within Europe were mostly from the former Eastern Bloc countries and the newly collapsed Yugoslavia. However, unlike in the previous examples, the people who pursued a new life by taking a European path came mostly from outside of the continent.

On the other hand, a total of some 25 million ethnic Russians remained outside of the Russian Federation, on the borders of the former republics. Until 1995, mostly from Tajikistan, Georgia and Azerbaijan, approximately 2 million people immigrated to Russia. But of course this was not the only movement from the Russian periphery. A few movements which occurred in the Caucasus in the mid-90s are as follows: First, during the war between Azerbaijan and Armenia over the Azerbaijani territory Nagorno-Karabakh, approximately 1.6 million people, most of whom were Azerbaijani Turks, fled from the region until 1995.[48] Secondly, as a result of the struggle for independence that broke out in the South Ossetia region of Georgia, 120,000 refugees crossed to the Russian side of the border. And thirdly, due to

[44] Panayi, Refugees and the End of Empire, p. ix.
[45] Addressing these issues in detail goes beyond the limits of this study. *See* Gatrell, **The Making of the Modern Refugee**, pp. 223-252; for Decolonization, *seealso* Dane Kennedy, **Decolonization: A Very Short Introduction**, New York, Oxford University Press, 2016; Martin Shipway, **Decolonization and its Impact: A Comparative Approach to the end of the Colonial Empires**, First Edition, Oxford, Blackwell Publishing, 2008.
[46] Loescher, **op.cit.**, pp. 75–92.
[47] Gatrell, The Making of the Modern Refugee, pp. 203-223; *seealso* William Courtland Robinson, Terms of Refuge: The Indochinese Exodus and the International Response, London, Zed Books, 1998; Barry Wain, The Refused: The Agony of the Indochina Refugees, New York, Simon and Schuster, 1981.
[48] While these lines are being written, the second phase of the Nagorno-Karabakh War has finalized. Having won this phase, Azerbaijan started to relocate some of the refugees to their homes.

another separatist conflict in Georgia, 80,000 people left Abkhazia.[49]

The war in the former Yugoslavia resulted in one of the greatest displacement crises since the Second World War. During the war between 1990 and 1992, large numbers of people fled to other former Yugoslav republics. According to Panayi, Yugoslavia *"resembled a vast refugee camp"* in these years,[50] and almost one fifth of the total population of the former Yugoslavia, which was about 22.4 million in 1981, had to leave their homes. However, a great majority of these refugees were from Bosnia-Herzegovina, which was ethnically the most diverse republic.[51] Later on, after the conflicts in Kosovo, further displacements took place in the same region.[52]

What happened in Yugoslavia showed that the centre of Europe could not be exempt from the refugee crises even at the end of the 20th century. However, in the same years, crises and refugee movements continued in many different parts of the world. For instance, one of the biggest and most dramatic displacements of the immediate aftermath of the Cold War was happening in Iraq. After Saddam Hussein persecuted and killed thousands of Kurds and Shi'ites, nearly 2 to 3 million people flocked into the mountainous regions near the borders with Turkey and Iran.[53] Besides, due to inter-clan civil war and food shortages, millions of Somalis were forcibly displaced during the 1990s. Only in 1992, about 800,000 people fled to Kenya and Ethiopia from Somalia.[54] Regarding these years, it is possible to add more displacement examples from other African countries like Mozambique, Rwanda and Somalia, or from Caribbean countries like Haiti and Cuba, or from Venezuela.

## Conclusion

In the current century, a new time period that can be called "era" in terms of refugee movements has begun after the September 11 attacks. Invasion of Afghanistan and then Iraq made millions of people feel obliged to leave their homes. These two crises were followed by the so-called Arab Spring, that began in early 2010, and the Syrian crisis, in which almost all the population

---

[49] For the population displacement after the dissolution of the Soviet Union, *see* Gatrell, **The Making of the Modern Refugee**, pp. 259-261.
[50] Panayi, Refugees and the End of Empire, p. 8.
[51] The term *ethnic cleansing* began to be used for the first time in the spring of 1992, in order to describe the Serbian attacks on Bosnian Muslims. *See* Norman M. Naimark, **Fires of Hatred: Ethnic Cleansing in Twentieth- Century Europe**, Cambridge, Harvard University Press, 2002.
[52] Panayi, "Imperial Collapse and the Creation of Refugees in Twentieth-Century Europe", p. 4-9; for the dissolution of Yugoslavia and the population displacement after the dissolution of the Soviet Union, *see also* Gatrell, **The Making of the Modern Refugee**, pp. 259-267.
[53] Loescher, **op.cit.**, p. 3, 4.
[54] Laura Hammond, "Somali refugee displacements in the near region: Analysis and Recommendations Paper for the UNHCR Global Initiative on Somali Refugees", https://www.unhcr.org/55152c699.pdf (Access 27 November 2020).

of this medium sized country was affected. When only crises of Pakistan, Libya, Yemen, Somalia and the Philippines are added to the abovementioned three countries', with a conservative estimate, more than 37 million people fled their homes and became the new migrants, asylum seekers and/or refugees of the first two decades of the 21st century.[55] This figure only stems from these eight wars after 2001. And the common characteristics of these wars is that they are the wars in which the United States sent troops or was directly involved.

On the other hand, by December 31, 1999, the UNHCR'stotal population of concern was about 22.3 million.[56] Remembering the latest data which gives the same number by the end of 2019 as 79.5 million, it is quite clear that the figure has increased almost four times in the last two decades.

Since the Second World War, probably, refugees may have never occupied world politics as much as they did after the Syrian crisis. For this reason, the importance of the international refugee regime and its necessity for both refugees and states have been re-understood. The 1951 Convention, which forms the basis of the international refugee regime, is aimed to address both humanitarian and political aspects of the problem. While the first purpose in the preparation of this Convention was to provide international protection to refugees, the second was to prevent a possible tension between states by not putting burdens on only certain states. However, due to the reluctance of some states to provide international protection and to share responsibility, the point the international refugee regime has reached today shows that both goals could not be achieved. In other words, despite the existence of the UN regime and a binding agreement with wide participation, the states parties still shape their policies individually and according to their own interests. Even in some cases, governments manipulate refugees on the grounds of their national security while undermining the security of other states.

The difficult journeys of refugees, confrontation with death, and problems they face in the countries they reach frequently attract media

---

[55] The first report on this subject, prepared by David Vine and his students, includes the following statements: "Using the best available international data, … conservatively … at least 37 million people have fled their homes in the eight most violent wars the U.S. military has launched or participated in since 2001." However, they also say that the number could be closer to 48-59 million. See David Vine, Cala Coffman, KatalinaKhoury, Madison Lovasz, Helen Bush, Rachael Leduc, and Jennifer Walkup, "Creating Refugees: Displacement Caused by the United States' Post-9/11 Wars", 21 September 2020. https://watson.brown.edu/costsofwar/files/cow/imce/papers/2020/Displacement_Vine%20et%20al_ Costs%20of%20War%202020%2009%2008.pdf(Access 28 November 2020); see also Dawn Chatty, "Dispossession and Forced Migration in the 21st-century Middle East and North Africa", **Bulletin for the Council for British Research in the Levant**, 5/1, 2010, pp. 39-42.
[56] "The State Of The World's Refugees 2000: Fifty Years Of Humanitarian Action",P. 10. https://Www.Unhcr.Org/Publications/Sowr/4a4c754a9/State-Worlds-Refugees-2000-Fifty-Years-Humanitarian-Action.Html#:~:Text=The%20state%20of%20the%20world's%20refugees%202000 %20provides%20a%20detailed,Of%20the%20last%2050%20years (Access 28 November 2020).

attention and are discussed publicly. Besides, political leaders emphasize their responsibilities and the importance of international cooperation. Though, there is no indication of new refugee movements will not occur in the future. Considering the examples mentioned in this study, roughly four different factors seem to be effective in the emergence of refugee movements. Clearly, the most common factor is the war between states. Another important factor is ethnic, religious or sectarian conflicts within or between states. Thirdly, civil wars and/or revolutions that result from class or ideological differences constitute another factor. And the fourth factor is the practices of oppressive, authoritarian or fascist regimes. In addition to these, sometimes natural disasters and environmental problems may force people to flee abroad. Since all these problems are almost certain to emerge in the future, unfortunately, it can be said that refugee movements will continue to exist as well.

# CHAPTER 9

# DEVELOPMENT ASSISTANCE AND REFUGEE CRISIS

## Hakan Sezgin Erkan*

## Introduction

The concept of post-Cold War globalization has been one of the rare concepts with a worldwide direct effect. Security concerns have been replaced by concerns over economic development, welfare of societies and removal of borders with the effect of the decreasing levels of threats perceived by states from each other.

After the Cold War, emerging former Soviet countries tried to integrate into the free market economy and in doing so, had difficulty as a result of being ruled by long-term communist administrations. In addition, even if these states wanted to integrate into the free market economy, they have neither adequate infrastructure nor sufficient manpower.

One of the most emphasized concepts to integrate these countries into the system in the period following the Cold War was the provision of development assistance. Although development assistance and being an assistance provider country began in the 1960s, it gained importance in the post-Cold War era.

In the wake of the 9/11 attacks, the importance of development assistance has increased further with the restructuring of security understanding and perception of threats not directly from other states but from terrorist organizations that can easily recruit people. Although development assistance was initially seemed to only aim at integrating former Soviet countries into the system, it has been systematized over time and all countries have started to be supported in becoming donor countries with the impact of realizing that it could have consequences such as narrowing the fields of terrorist organizations, preventing migration and decreasing regional conflicts.

Although being a donor of development assistance was not initially a concept that was attributed enough importance by countries, with soft power gaining importance in international relations, countries have begun to use development assistance to achieve the above-mentioned results and to increase their soft power in international relations.

* Dr., ORCID ID: 0000-0002-6204-8689, E-mail: hakansezginerkan@gmail.com

As a result, development assistance is of great importance in the 21ˢᵗ century to ensure the economic development of underdeveloped and developing countries all over the world, that people living in these countries are not subject to forced migration, and reduce conflicts in regions and therefore refugee crises.

This study will seek an answer to the question of whether development assistance can prevent refugee crises. At the same time, the study will investigate development assistance, as well as refugee crises in detail.

The first section of the study will discuss development assistance, its emergence and contributions to countries. The second section of the study will explain migration and the causes of refugee crises based on migration theories. Finally, the third section of the study will dwell upon the relations between migration, refugee crisis and development assistance, followed by the conclusion.

### Development assistance

The Organization for Economic Cooperation and Development (OECD), by its own definition, is an international organization that builds better policies to create better lives. The concept of development assistance is defined by the OECD as aid provided by developed countries with relatively better economies to improve the economies of developing and underdeveloped countries with the purpose of improving the economic conditions of the receiving country.

According to its narrower-scope definition, development assistance is aid to countries or regions on the Official Development Assistance Committee's (DAC) Official Development Assistance (ODA) Recipients List within the OECD, where there are multilateral institutions. The DAC has determined which aid will be development assistance and its exceptions. Accordingly, there are two rules for aid to be considered as official development assistance. These are:

- Development assistance shall be provided by official agencies, including states and local governments, or by their executive agencies; and

- Development assistance must have the main characteristic of being privileged[1] donation or low interest loan) and supporting the economic development and wealth of the receiving country.

Two exceptional circumstances have been determined not to consider

---

[1] It is concessional in character and conveys a grant element of at least 25 per cent (calculated at a rate of 10 per cent discount).

aids as official development assistance. These circumstances are as follows:

- Military assistance and aid supporting the donor country's interests in its security[2]

- Mutual transactions, whose primary purpose is commercial, are not considered official development assistance.[3]

**Table 1.** Declarations, Year, Conference Name & Goals of Development Assistance

| DECLARATION | YEAR | CONFERENCE NAME/ATTENDEES | GOAL |
|---|---|---|---|
| Official Development Assistance (ODA) Concept | 1969 | DAC | 0.7% of GNP Target |
| Shaping the 21st Century: The Contributionof Development Cooperation | 1996 | The DAC High Level Meeting, OECD Ministerial and the G7 Summit | Economic Well-being, Social Development, Environmental Sustainability, |
| The Millennium Development Goals | 2000 | The UN Millennium Summit | A Better World for All: Progress Towards the International Development Goals |
| Monterrey and OECD Action for a Shared Development Agenda | 2002 | OECD Ministerial Council | OECD Action for a Shared Development Agenda |
| Rome High Level Forum on Harmonization | 2003 | Members of DAC | DAC's Six Good Practice Papers |
| Paris High Level Forum | 2005 | DAC High Level Meeting | To increase efforts in harmonization, alignment and managing assistance |

The principles of official development assistance were first defined by the DAC in 1970. Member states of the DAC[4]set the first target for official

---

[2] Official Development Assistance (ODA), OECD, Paris, 2020, p. 1.

[3] http://www.oecd.org/development/financing-sustainable-development/development-finance-standards/officialdevelopmentassistancedefinitionandcoverage.htm (Access 24.11.2020)

[4] Development Assistance Committee was established on June 23, 1961 as part of the OECD as a result of the Ministerial Resolution. For details, see Helmut Führer, **A History of the Development Assistance Committee and the Development Cooperation Directorate in Dates, Names and Figures**, Paris, OECD, 1994, pp. 11-15. DAC is an organization that brings together the world's largest development assistance donors with a total of 30 members including 29 countries and an international organization (European Union). The World Bank, IMF and United Nations Development Programme attend DAC meetings as observers and development assistance providers. http://www.oecd.org/dac/development-assistance-committee/ (Access 24.11.2020)

development assistance this year. DAC member states have committed to give 0.7% of their gross national product as official development assistance. After this first meeting, DAC members have updated their objectives with various declarations in regular meetings.

Development assistance is classified under 8 different headings[5]. These are:

**Budget support:** Budget support means direct budget support from donor countries to receiving countries.

**Pool programs and funds:** It is the kind of assistance that donor countries or countries provide through NGOs, the private sector or international organizations. Pool programs are usually carried out with the contribution of multiple donors rather than a single donor.

**Project-type interventions:** These are projects managed and executed within the boundaries of receiving countries. Humanitarian and other assistance sent through NGOs can also be accepted within this category.

**Expertise and other technical assistance:**Donor countries can assign consultants, teachers, researchers, academics and volunteers to countries receiving assistance for sustaining or improving economic development. This also includes training and research conducted in countries receiving assistance. Conferences, seminars, workshops, exchange visits and publications are also considered to be in this type of help.

**Scholarships:** This includes financial aid and tuition fees provided for students in countries receiving assistance to study abroad.

**Debt relief:** This type of assistance includes actions related to the debt of the receiving country like exemption, conversions, swaps, buy-backs, rescheduling, and refinancing.

**Administrative costs:** This type of assistance includes covering expenses and salaries arising from administrative work.

**Other expenditures:** This type of assistance includes various activities to increase public support of donor country. In addition, the costs of housing refugees in the donor country are also accepted in this type of assistance.

While one of the actors of development assistance is the state, NGOs, international institutions and international organizations are also among the actors of such assistance. Since NGOs can easily go to many countries, states can encourage NGOs to take roles and responsibilities in development assistance. On the other hand, international institutions and organizations

---

[5] Better Aid Managing Aid Practices of DAC Member Countries, OECD, Paris, 2009, pp. 63-64.

(i.e. OECD, UN) can develop various projects for the countries on the DAC List and send invitations to countries to participate in these projects. Countries can provide development assistance themselves or by being involved in the project of an international organization, yet the underlying motivation for donor countries to support development assistance can be classified into 5 different categories:

**Political motivation:** Although development assistance is based on improving the economic and social conditions of the country receiving the assistance, donor countries also attach importance to their political relations with the country receiving the assistance. A country tends to provide more assistance to the country with which it previously had historical relations. For example, many of the countries that were colonial powers in the past allocate large portions of development assistance to their former colonies[6].

**Table 2.** Bilateral assistance to former colonies, 1970 to 1994[7]

| Bilateral assistance to former colonies, from 1970 to 1994 | |
|---|---|
| Donor | Colony Share Percent |
| Australia | 55.5 |
| Belgium | 53.7 |
| France | 57.0 |
| Germany | 2.6 |
| Italy | 9.0 |
| Japan | 6.3 |
| Netherlands | 17.1 |
| New Zealand | 22.5 |
| Portugal | 99.6 |
| Spain | 4.8 |
| United Kingdom | 78.0 |
| United States | 2.9 |

As can be understood from the table, many of the countries that used to be colonial powers in the past send a significant portion of their development assistance to their former colonies. However, it would be wrong to say that development assistance is provided only on the basis of colonial ties. Countries that do not have a colonial background and do not provide assistance according to such colonial ties consider their own interests when choosing the countries where they will provide development assistance, as well as their influence in the region where the receiving country is located. If the donor country has been able to have a say in the geography where a foreign country is located, as well as its foreign policy or its relations with other countries, it has achieved the purpose of using development assistance.

---

[6] Alberto Alesina & David Dollar, "Who Gives Foreign Aid to Whom and Why?" **Journal of Economic Growth**, Vol. 5, No. 1, 2000, p.37.
[7] ibid. p. 37

**Security motivation:** The period of decolonization ended with many problems such as conflicts, civil wars, ethnic conflicts, soldiers seeking to seize power by arms and economic problems burdened on colonial countries. At the same time, famine and starvation have emerged as one of the main problems in ex-colony countries due to the reasons mentioned above. Many problems in this region have turned into two basic security problems for developed countries. The first of these problems is that people living in difficult living conditions here become members of radical terrorist organizations and turn into human resources for terrorist attacks. Another reason is that people here have become refugees due to problems in their countries and want to emigrate to developed countries illegally due to starvation and famine. In order to prevent these two situations, developed countries provide development assistance to countries that are experiencing or have the potential to experience the aforementioned problems. To support this, the DAC has launched a program called Security System Reform and is trying to eliminate threats in this area. The main value of this system is described as *"people-centreed and locally-owned democratic norms and internationally-accepted human rights principles as well as the rule of law"*[8].

**Humanitarian development motivation:** One of the main objectives of the UN in the post-Cold War process has been to achieve humanitarian development. For this purpose, the UN encourages various international organizations, states and even NGOs to provide development assistance for humanitarian purposes. The Human Development Index[9] is used to measure human development levels. The Human Development Index measures with three basic social dimensions. These are long and healthy life, knowledge and a decent standard of living. Donor countries need to influence these three areas when they provide assistance with the human development motivation so that their assistance is considered development assistance.

**Democratization motivation:** The development of democracy in a country also increases the stability of that country in the international area and its contribution to world trade. Development assistance contributes to the development of democracy in these countries along with the social and economic development it provides.[10] Scholarships, expert assistance and guidance as well as technical support provided by donor countries are important to empower the country's state institutions against any conflict in

---

[8] Dylan Hendrickson, Nicole Ball, Lisa Williams, Francesca Cook, Maria Consolati, Paul Isenman, **Security System Reform and Governance,** Paris, OECD Publications, 2005, p. 22.

[9] It consists of health, education and standard of living. Health is evaluated by life expectancy. Education is quantified by means of years of schooling and expected years of schooling. Standard of living is quantified by gross national income per capita. http://hdr.undp.org/en/content/human-development-index-hdi (Access 25.11.2020)

[10] A. Maurits van der Veen, **Ideas, Interests and Foreign Aid,** Cambridge, Cambridge University Press, 2011, p. 56.

society. Especially the generations raised with the scholarships provided in the field of education have a great value in terms of strengthening democracy in that country.

**Underground resource motivation:** When evaluated by simple logic, if a country has rich underground resources, the level of development assistance should decrease. However, not every country has the technology, manpower or expertise to extract or process these resources. In such cases, it is important to use the necessary technological equipment with the help of experts. Donor countries assign their own experts in the assistance-receiving country to ensure that they strengthen their economic development by extracting underground resources.

Evaluatingthe underlying reasons for donor countries to provide development assistance, it can be observed that they are all assistance intended to improve the economic and social conditions of the receiving country. Thanks to such assistance, the living standards of people living in developing and underdeveloped countries are rising. In order to raise these standards, world leaders at the UN Millennium Summit in 2000 determined The Millennium Development Goals[11]. All donor countries have reached consensus to achieve the goals.

**Figure 1.** The Millennium Development Goals

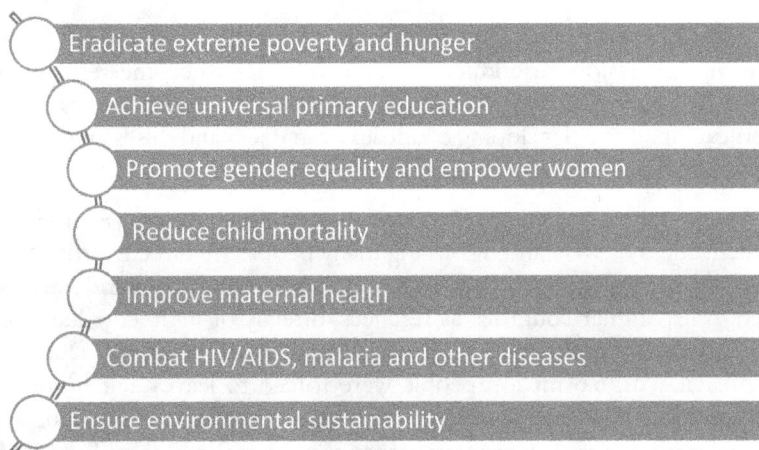

Eradicate extreme poverty and hunger

Achieve universal primary education

Promote gender equality and empower women

Reduce child mortality

Improve maternal health

Combat HIV/AIDS, malaria and other diseases

Ensure environmental sustainability

**Refugee crisis**

According to figures for June 18, 2020, 79.5 million people around the world have been forcibly displaced, and about 26 million of them are

---

[11] Reaching Our Development Goals: Why Does Aid Effectiveness Matter?, OECD, Paris, 2015, p. 3.

refugees[12]. This figure is quite high given how difficult states grant the refugee status.

Pinpointing the origin of refugee problems is important for solving refugee crises. Therefore, it is essential to analyze the reasons of refugee crises rather than the problems emerging in refugee crises.

Looking at the causes of refugee crises by several reports of UNHCR and many other international NGOs, it is revealed that there are four main causes of refugee crises. When these four reasons are basically viewed, the common cause is that they are seen in economically and socially underdeveloped societies.

The first and most common cause of refugee crises is persecution. It can appear in many forms such as religious, national, social, racial, or political, and this is the first reason that displaces most people as refugees. This discrimination can be applied to religious, racial, social, national or political minorities within the states themselves, as well as to others by groups that hold political power despite being in the minority in the country.

Although countries and their decision makers have reached a consensus on the existence of natural human rights in accordance with the convention on human rights, this discrimination and oppression continue in many countries of the world for many reasons.

Revisiting persecution of individuals, persons or a group through collective oppression, discrimination and causing to become refuges on a country-by-country basis, it is seen thatthis situation generally takes place in underdeveloped and developing countries even if less and this is an important fact for building relations with development assistance.

The second most common cause of refugee crises is wars. Although the destructiveness of wars and displacing many people are directly proportional to their length, a significant number of refugees around the world have been forced to leave their countries as refugees, directly or indirectly due to civil war, conflict of ethnic groups or direct wars between countries. Due to the Syrian Civil War, 6.6 million people were forced to leave their homes and change places within their country. According to official UNHCR figures, the number of people with temporary protection status[13]who sought refuge in Turkey due to the Syrian Civil War is 3.6 million [14]. The total number of

---

[12] https://www.unhcr.org/refugee-statistics/ (Access 26.11.2020)
[13] Turkey attached the annotation of "geographical limitation" to the 1967 Protocol. Accordingly, Turkey only accepts refugees coming from European countries and does not grant refugee status to those coming from other countries. Since it is on the transit migration route and the first destination of Eastern country citizens who want to migrate to Western countries, Turkey has brought this limitation and has been continuing to implement it.
[14] https://www.unhcr.org/tr/unhcr-turkiye-istatistikleri (Access 26.11.2020)

people fleeing the country due to the war is over 5 million.

Looking at the conditions of the 21ˢᵗ century, it can be observed that wars often occur in countries with low economic and social development. Countries, whose economic system cannot meet the welfare and needs of people, cannot adequately produce and who are left behind as education levels have to deal with problems such as civil war, ethnic and religious conflict. In this regard, the relationship between development assistance and wars –the second cause of refugee crises –is important as well.

Another cause of refugee crises is gender/sexual orientation. UNHCR issued a new guideline in 2012 on the refugee status of people discriminated by their sexual orientation and thus their lives threatened. According to UNHCR regulations,*"[w]here an individual seeks asylum in a country where same-sex relations are criminalized, these laws can impede his or her access to asylum procedures or deter the person from mentioning his or her sexual orientation or gender identity"*[15].

This guideline stated that criminal laws in some countries directly prohibit same-sex relationships, threaten individuals with oppression and torture, or that this situation is used to blackmail them, and that people have to hide their own sexual identities. With the UNHCR new regulation, it is stated that it may be involved, including determining refugee status under its authority[16].

Even though gender debate arises in every country in the world, there are various laws, pressures and interventions to prevent gender equality in economically and socially underdeveloped countries while laws or society look at sexual orientation as one's choice. Thus, it is important to provide various development assistance to underdeveloped countries.

The fourth cause of refugee crises is famine. According to the latest UNHCR figures, a total of 20 million people from Somalia, Nigeria, South Sudan and Yemen have become refugees due to drought and famine and have been forced to leave their homes to emigrate to places with better food sources. Looking at the African continent, about 17 million people have left their homes to emigrate to Europe, where there is no food problem. Only a small number of them reached the European continent, while most of these people remain in various refugee camps.

Famine, as in four other causes, is mostly seen in economically and socially backward countries. With various equipment, training and expert support to be provided with development assistance, people here can find solutions to the problem of famine.

In total, all four major causes of refugee crises are seen in economically,

---

[15] https://www.unhcr.org/lgbti-persons.html (Access 20.11.2020)
[16] https://www.refworld.org/docid/50348afc2.html (Access 23.11.2020)

socially and culturally backward countries. Since people living in these regions lack democracy, economy, education, expertise and equipment to deal with wars, persecution and discrimination against sexual orientation, they are forced to abandon their geography and become refugees in other regions where there are no such problems.

## The impact of development assistance on preventing refugee crises

Development assistance is a type of aid provided by countries with better economic conditions to economically underdeveloped or developing countries so that they solve a large part of their problems, and this type of assistance can make a big difference in the short term. This part of the article will discuss whether the various types of development assistance can produce solutions to the causes that reveal refugee crises.

**Figure 2.** Relations Between Types of DA, Millennium Development Goals and Causes of Refugee Crises

| Types of Development Assitance | Millenium Development Goals | Causes of Refugee Crises |
|---|---|---|
| • Budget Support<br>• Pool Programs and Funds<br>• Project-Type Interventions<br>• Expertise and Other Technical Assistance<br>• Scholarships<br>• Debt Relief<br>• Administrative Costs<br>• Other Expenditures | • Eradicate extreme poverty and famine<br>• Achieve universal primary education<br>• Promote gender equality and empower women<br>• Reduce child mortality<br>• Improve maternal health<br>• Combat HIV/AIDS, malaria and other diseases<br>• Ensure environmental sustainability<br>• Develop a Global Partnership for Development | • Persecution<br>• War<br>• Gender-Oriented Discrimination<br>• Famine |

Before looking at the relationship between development assistance and the causes of refugee crises, it is important to remember that most refugee crises are observed in underdeveloped countries because the country's economic, social, and cultural levels are not sufficiently developed. In this context, the fundamental aim of providing development assistance to underdeveloped countries is to foster development in all areas, which is an element that will prevent the emergence of refugee crises due to the forced displacement of people.

As one of the support provided as development assistance, budget support is of great importance for countries with limited resources to be spent for society. With budget support provided directly by governments, underdeveloped countries are able to meet their water needs in many regions, provide food to the public against famine and meet some needs of schools. As a result, famine, which is one of the causes of refugee crises, can decrease with direct budget support and can be an obstacle to people's forced displacement.

Many international institutions, international organizations and NGOs organize various projects to ensure the development of underdeveloped countries and to improve the living standards of people living in these geographies. These projects aim to partially or completely solve the specific problems of the targeted country as a result of the pool and funding created with the joint participation of many countries. Projects are organized in many areas such as food, agriculture, education, culture, and prevention of famine and discrimination and invitations are sent to countries to participate in projects. Thanks to the large sums that arise with the participation of many countries, permanent solutions can be brought in many areas. Therefore, pool programs directly affect all the causes of refugee crises.

Donor countries can offer development assistance by producing a project at the request of a country or as a result of the gap seen in a specific area. Countries can directly provide support to such projects managed and carried out within the borders of the country receiving assistance or they can offer assistance through NGOs. Project-based assistance can often be created to combat famine, as can also be provided to schools and hospitals. In this context, project-based assistance can also prevent three of the causes of refugee crises, as the decrease in persecution and gender-based discrimination is directly proportional to the increase in education level, while hunger will decrease in the relevant region along with the food aid sent.

Expertise and technical assistance are probably needed the most in underdeveloped countries followed by budget support and donor countries can send consultants, teachers, academics, experts, researchers and volunteers to recipient countries to provide education, take part in economic development projects and train experts. Thus, the countries receiving assistance can benefit from the know-how and experience of the donor country to achieve development in the country, create employment projects, develop agriculture and livestock, and have the chance to raise expert personnel who can provide trainings. As a result of the trainings supported and provided by experts, agriculture and livestock projects will help solve the famine problem that causes refugee crises. Furthermore, with the employment created in various fields and the training provided by teachers and academics from donor countries, it is made difficult for armed organizations to reach human resources and persecution and gender-oriented discrimination are prevented.

Donor countries organize special scholarship programs for countries receiving assistance. Such programs contribute to the development of the given country by educating people in developed countries to ensure they educate people in their own country or producing projects in areas that will foster development. At the same time, higher education students do not participate in armed organizations and human resources are cut off for organizations that lead to civil war in the country. Another important aspect of scholarships is avoiding persecution and gender-oriented discrimination. With the increase in educational level, awareness of gender equality increases while oppression and persecution due to discrimination against religion, language and race decrease.

One of the biggest problems of underdeveloped countries is the payment of debts received. Especially in the payment of loans and debts received due to investments for development, donor countries can provide development assistance by methods such as exemption, conversions, swaps, buy-backs, rescheduling, and refinancing. Thanks to such kind of assistance, the countries receiving assistance can solve the famine problem and create jobs thanks to the investments they make.

Donor countries can also cover expenses and salaries arising from the administrative work of the country receiving assistance. In general, this development assistance with experts and technical staff contributes to the development of the country receiving that assistance.

As stated before, all development assistance prevents one or more of the reasons for the emergence of refugee crises in the short, medium and long term. Development assistance supports the given country in various ways such as through projects, training and financial aid to eliminate the causes of migration and refugee crises in underdeveloped countries. Given that refugee crises took place in underdeveloped geographies in the 21st century, the role of development assistance in curbing forced migration is revealed.

The steps to be taken to prevent refugee crises overlap with the Millennium Development Goals. Eradicating extreme poverty and hunger, which is the first of millennium development goals, directly targets hunger that is one of the causes of refugee crises. Achieving sustainable development specified in Goal 7 is related to wars and conflicts in a region. Global primary education given in Goal 2 lays the groundwork for the elimination of religious, national, social, racial, or political persecution, which are among the reasons of refugee crises. In other words, the intended result of development assistance and millennium development goals are directly aimed at solving the problems that lead to refugee crises.

## Conclusion

Although development assistance has been a concept within international relations since the 1960s, it gained importance in the post-Cold War period. In this new period that states no more perceive threats from each other,importance has started to be given to the development of societies. Especially with the changing security paradigm after the 9/11 attacks, the development of underdeveloped regions has become more important as threats move from the level of states to the level of terrorist organizations.

As a result of the instant news from all regions of the world with globalization, refugee crises that arise due to wars, hunger, persecution and gender-oriented discrimination have started to attract more attention from societies. The reluctance of developed states to take in refugees and their desire to solve this problem on the spot has been another factor that increases the importance of development assistance. Therefore, developed countries have tended to provide more development assistance due to both their reluctance to accept refugees, pressure from societies and security concerns.

Development assistance has visibly changed the lives of many people in many regions of the world and ensured the development of societies along with the integration of countries into the international system. Although the first aim of such assistance is not to prevent refugee crises or forced migration, they bring solution to this problem in the short term and will continue to do so in the long term. Many of the results that millennium development goals are trying to achieve are actually the same as solving refugee crises. Therefore, development assistance is not directly related to refugee crises, but with the effect it has, it can eliminate refugee crises.

# CHAPTER 10

## REFUGEE WELL-BEING AT WORK

Merve Mamacı[*]

### Introduction

According to United Nations Refugee Agency, the definition of a refugee is "someone who is unable or unwilling to return to their country of origin owing to a well-founded fear of being persecuted for reasons of race, religion, nationality, membership of a particular social group, or political opinion."[1]

Statistical data shows that; there are 4,000,000 refugees and asylum-seekers in Turkey. As registered refugees and asylum seekers, Syrian nationals and other nationalities are distributed as 3,600,000 and approximately 330,000.[2]

Although hosting refugees may be evaluated as *"unwanted resource sharing"* with foreigners by natives, accepting refugees may also have a positive effect for the country in terms of social and human capital, labour force, economic development and productivity. By integrating them into the workforce, protecting and educating refugees, providing a healthy environment for them to work efficiently, a country may have a chance to increase its human resources potential. Refugees may have different KSAO'S (knowledge, skills, abilities and other characteristics) then natives, that's why it can be considered as prosperity. So it is crucial to assess and develop well-being at work for refugees.

One aspect of work life is well-being. When literature is reviewed, it can be seen that the physical and mental health of workers are highly related with workplace productivity.[3,4,5] On the other hand, WHO[6] states that; well-being is *"a state of complete physical, mental and social wellbeing and not merely the absence of*

[*] Assst. Prof İstanbul Kent University, Psychology Department
[1] https://www.unhcr.org/what-is-arefugee.html (Accsess 1.12.2020).
[2] https://www.unhcr.org/tr/wp-content/uploads/sites/14/2020/11/UNHCR-Turkey-Operational-Update-October-2020.pdf(Accsess 1.12.2020).
[3] Dame Carol Black, David Frost (2011). "Health at work – an independent review of sickness absence",http://moodle.nottingham.ac.uk/pluginfile.php/4281894/mod_resourc e/content/1/Black Frost - Absence Review 2011.pdf (Accsess 1.12.2020).
[4] https://www.ons.gov.uk/employmentandlabourmarket/peopleinwork/e mploymentandemployeetypes /datasets/sicknessabsenceinthelabourm arket (Accsess 1.12.2020).
[5] Parick Collinson, "Sick Days Taken By UK Workers Fall To Lowest Rate On Record" https://www.theguardian.com/money/2018/jul/30/sick-days-taken-ukworkers-fall-lowest-rate-on-record(Accsess 1.12.2020).
[6] https://www.hsl.gov.uk/media/202146/5_kim_who.pdf (Accsess 1.12.2020).

*disease or infirmity.* That's why companies and governments should better to approach this topic in much more detailed and carefully. It will also bring out great advantages for companies to improve refugee employees' well-being levels by assessing organizational factors and by psychological interventions.

In this chapter, several theories on psychological well-being will be presented. Also, fundamental factors which have a relationship with well-being will be shared. These factors are listed as; xenophobia, prejudice, discrimination, organizational justice, leadership and importance of cultural tendencies. A short guide for companies to develop better refugee well-being will be shared.

## Well-being

Are you happy? Are you satisfied with your life? Do you think you have a fulfilled life? Which features may help to build a meaningful life? Is it enough to build a good life with just positive emotions? Or do we need something more? Although these questions stay the same from the beginning of history, the answers vary according to different philosophers and psychologists. It can be said that all these questions aim to seek answers for a good life and to explain well-being. It should be noted that; well-being is defined as *"the optimal psychological experience and functioning."*[7]

When the literature is examined, it can be seen that there are two distinct well-being approaches in Philosophy and Positive Psychology. Although these approaches have distinct ideas and have their own ideas about a good life, they both have a contribution to building a definition for well-being. These approaches are named as hedonic and eudaimonic well-being [8,9].

The concept hedonia has derived from ancient Greek and itis composed of several constructs. In the field of Psychology, hedonia is described as subjective well-being (SWB) and it has three dimensions; (a) presence of positive emotions-positive effect, (b) the absence of negative emotions – low levels of negative affect and (c) high levels of life satisfaction- which is a cognitive evaluation for one's own life. Subjective well-being is generally used interchangeably with happiness. This idea basically puts stress on maximizing positive feelings and minimizing negative feelings.

According to Waterman,[10] one can maximize positive feelings and

---

[7] Edward Deci, Richard Ryan, "Hedonia, Eudaimonia, and Well-Being: An Introduction", **Journal of Happiness Studies**, Vol.9, No. 1, 2008, pp. 1-11

[8] Richard Ryan,Edward Deci,"On Happiness and Human Potentials: A review of Research on Hedonic and Eudaimonic Well-Being", **Annual Review of Psychology**, Vol. 52, 2001, pp. 141–166.

[9] Veronika Huta, Alan Waterman, "Eudaimonia and Its Distinction From Hedonia: Developing a Classifcation and Terminology for Understanding Conceptual and Operational Defnitions", **Journal of Happiness Studies**, Vol.15, No.6, 2014,pp. 1425–1456.

[10] Alan Waterman, "Two Conceptions of Happiness: Contrasts of Personal Expressiveness

minimize negative ones but at the same time still can be lack of psychological health and well-being. From this point, another approach emerges: eudaimonia. The second approach *"eudaimonia"* is defined as living well with one's authentic nature and achieving one's own virtuous potentials. Unlike hedonic perspective, eudaimonic well-being approach gives importance to the process but not the outcome. It can be said that eudaimonic approach does not oppose to feel positive feelings, but opposing to run after positive feelings. If one lives in accordingly to his nature, naturally he will obtain a good life.

In summary, throughout the history of Psychology, researches on well-being fall on to two categories: hedonic and eudaimonic wellbeing. Although there are different types of well-being models, the PERMA[11] model (a multidimensional model) draws attention to the explanation of psychological well-being by combining eudaimonic and hedonistic features of a good life.

## Theoretical foundations of well-being

*Subjective well-being theory*

The term subjective well-being (SWB) was first coined by Diener[12] to understand evaluations of individuals of their lives. SWB can be defined as; one's perception and the evaluation of experiencing emotions such as negative and positive ones, also general life satisfaction about one's own life. According to Diener, Lucas and Oishi[13] subjective well-being is *"a person's cognitive and affective evaluations of his or her life."* Therefore; SWB can be considered as both an emotional and cognitive evaluation.[14]

Three components of SWB is categorized under three dimensions: Life Satisfaction (LS); Positive Affect (PA) and Negative Affect (NA).[15]

*Six-factor model of psychological well-being*

Another multidimensional psychological well-being theory was put forward by Ryff and Singer[16] named as *Six-Factor Model of Psychological Well-being.* According to this theory, well-being basically consists six dimensions.

(eudaemonia) and Hedonic Enjoyment"**Journal of Personality and Social Psychology,** Vol. 64, 1993, pp. 678–691.
[11] https://positivepsychology.com/perma-model/ (Accsess 1.12.2020).
[12] Ed Diener, "Subjective Well-Being",**Psychological Bulletin**, Vol 95, 1984, pp. 542–575.
[13] Ed Diener, Richard, E. Lucas, Shigehiro Oishi, "Subjective Well-being: The Science of Happiness and Life Satisfaction"**Handbook of Positive Psychology**, Charles R. Snyder, Shane J. Lopez (Ed.), Newyork, Oxford University Press, 2002, pp. 63–73.
[14] Ed Diener, E., Eunnkook M. Suh, Shigehiro Oishi, "Recent Findings on Subjective Well-Being",**Indian Journal of Clinical Psychology**, Vol 24, 1997, pp. 25–41.
[15] Ed Diener, Eunkook M. Suh, Richard E. Lucas, and Heidi L. Smith, "Subjective Well-Being: Three Decades of Progress", **Psychological Bulletin**, 1999, Vol. 125, No. 2, pp. 276-302
[16] Carol D. Ryff, Burton Singer, "The Contours of PositiveHuman Health",**Psychological Inquiry**, Vol. 9, 1998, pp.1–28.

These dimesions are stated as; (a) self-acceptance, (b) positive relations with others, (c) autonomy, (d) environmental mastery, (e) purpose in life and (f) personal growth.

*(a) Self-Acceptance:* Authors put stress on the importance of having knowledge about ones own strengths and weak features, understanding one's own motivations, behaviours and also emotions. Such kind of understanding points the level of knowledge of one's self. After all by such kind of an understanding, one can accept himself as the way he is. This high level of being one's own self and accepting oneself is defined as *positive self-regard.*

(b) *Positive Relations with Others:* Ryff[17] defined positive relations as "strong emotions of empathy and love established with others in a clear and reliable way".

*(c) Autonomy:* Autonomy dimension has an emphasis on one's ability for self-determining ability and independence. It is also related to evaluating personal standards, resisting social pressures and a certain way of thinking which is forced by society. So it can be said that the autonomy dimension is related to several qualities such as self-determination, independence, and the regulation of behaviour from within.

*(d) Environmental Mastery:* Authors has seen environmental mastery as an ability to choose or change the environment using one's physical or mental capabilities as well as having the capability to control events.

*(e) Purpose in Life:* This dimension of well-being lies on Frankl's *"search for meaning"*. Finding meaning in suffering, and creating a meaning out of that suffering and directing life in accordance with that meaning is so important and precious.

*(c) Personal Growth:* According to authors, personal growth is, positive functioning mostly related with self-realization of one's self. It has also seen as a dynamic process in which an individual continues developing his potential day by day. This term can be seen as becoming rather than reaching a point.

In general, all these factors contribute to one's well-being.

*Social well-being theory*

Another theory for describing well-being has introduced by Keyes[18] into the field of Positive Psychology. *"Social well-being"* has defined as an evaluation

---

[17] Carol D. Ryff, "Happiness is Everything, or Is It? Explorations on The Meaning of Psychological Well-Being"*Journal of Personality and Social Psychology,* Vol. 57 No. 6, 1989, pp. 1069- 1081.
[18] Corey L. M. Keyes, "Social Well-Being", **Social Psychology Quarterly**, Vol. 61, No. 2,1998, pp. 121–140.

of an individuals' conditions and functioning in the community. According to this theory, social well-being can be evaluated through several dimensions such as;

*(a) Social Integration*: quality of the relationship an individual develops with the society

*(b) Social Acceptance*: trust other people, an ideation that other people are able to be kind kindness, accepting one's self in a society

*(c) Social Contribution*: positive evaluation of individuals social value

*(d) Social Actualization*: the evaluation of the community potential

*(e) Social Coherence*: the perception and evaluation of the social world

Keyes[19]has also provided an comprehensive approach for conceptualizing and studying *"flourishing."*According to Keyes people who have flourishing tendency have higher levels of emotional, social and psychological wellbeing.

## PERMA well-being model

PERMA[20] model is derived from Authentic Happiness Theory[21]and developed by Martin Seligman. The model combines both hedonic and eudaimonic well-being features.

PERMA has five essential dimensions; (a) *positive emotions, (b) engagement,(c) relationships, (d) meaning,* and*(e) achievement/ accomplishment*. Each dimension can be measured and all dimensions contribute to well-being.

Dimensions of PERMA model has defined as;

(P): *Positive emotions* (not just feeling of happiness and joy but also different types emotions which can be evaluated as positive emotions such as; hope, compassion, contentment, empathy, gratitude and love)

(E): *Engagement* refers to concerns whether an individual is deeply engaged with specific activities such as; work, personal interest, or hobby. Csíkszentmihályi[22] put forward the term *"flow"* which means being fully absorbed in a specific activity. Flow is also attached to the PERMA model.

(R): *Positive Relationships* are seen as important sources for positive

[19] Corey L. M. Keyes, "The Mental Health Continuum: From Languishing to Flourishing in Life"**Journal of Health and Social Research**, Vol. 43, 2002, pp. 207–222.
[20] Martin Seligman, Flourish: A Visionary New Understanding of Happiness and Wellbeing, New York, NY Free Press, 2011.
[21] Martin Seligman, Authentic Happiness: Using the New Positive Psychology to Realize Your Potential for Lasting Fufillment, New York, NY: Free Press, 2002.
[22] Mihaly Csíkszentmihályi,**Flow: The Psychology of Optimal Experience**, New York, Harper Collins, 1990.

emotions. The main point for positive relationships are developing and forming positive relationships with other people. These relationships can arise from several social contexts such as; work, school, family, romantic or platonic relationships.

(M): *Meaning is* also labelled as purpose. It refers to building a purposeful life in order to build a meaningful existence for oneself. A meaningful life can be acquired by using strengths, not for just one's self but also for others. A way of a meaningful life is also obtained by dedicating oneself for something greater.

(A): *Achievement / Accomplishment* is also fundamental for a good life. It can be defined as sensing a feeling of productivity and accomplishment. Achievement / accomplishment pathway is seen as for its own sake, even if it doesn't result in positive feelings.

### Organizational threats for immigrants

Migration is a difficult and also traumatic experience for refugees and also a beneficial way of increasing welfare and well-being of themselves. But it can not be denied that refugees may be the target of negative attitudes such as xenophobic reactions, prejudice, discrimination in their social lives and work lives. In work life, organizational factors may also inhibit refugees' general psychological well-being. As a result, in this section, several factors are presented as a threat to refugees' well being.

### Xenophobia, prejudice and discrimination

The phenomenon *"xenophobia"* has investigated by law professionals and also social scientists. As stated above, refugees, unfortunately, may be exposed to xenophobia in both everyday life and work life. As being a part of social science, business psychology is also trying to understand xenophobia in workplaces,

The word *"xenophobia"* comes from a Greek word and it has two components: the first component is *"xenos"* which means foreigner, The second component is *"phovos"*, and it means "fear."[23] So, *"xenophobia"* can be referred to as fear of the foreigner. It can be seen that this term has emotional content.

According to Hjerm[24] xenophobia can be defined as "high levels of fear, dislike, and hostility towards to foreign including anything and anybody from

---

[23] Dionisis Philippas, *"Xenophobia"*, **Encyclopedia of Quality of Life and Well-Being Research**, *Alex C. Michalos (Ed.)*, Dordrecht,Springer, 2014, pp. 7275–7278.
[24] Mikael Hjerm, "Anti-immigrant Attitudes and Crossmunicipal Variation in the Proportion of Immigrants", **Acta Sociologica**, Vol. 52, No. 1, 2009, pp. 47–62.

outside one's own social group, nation, or country". With this definition, the term "xenophobia" gains attitudinal and behavioural dimension.

According to tripartite perspective, [25]attitudes have three types of components: (a) affect (b) behaviour and (c) cognition. Affect points to one's feelings towards an attitude object. Cognition refers to beliefs which one holds about the attitude object. Lastly, the behaviour is described as responses and actions towards attitude object. In accordance with this explanation; refugees may be exposed to negative emotions by others such as fear, anger, disgust and rage. Such kind of attitudes may trigger native workers to behave in such a way that leads to prejudice and discrimination.

As a social psychology model for understanding attitudes, A-B-C model can also be transferred to workplaces and work life of refugees. Stereotyping can be defined as a cognition/belief (positive or negative) about a social group and its characteristics. "Immigrant people are useless and incompetent" can be an example for stereotyping. Native people may also generate unjustifiable negative attitudes about refugees, which can emerge as prejudice. It can be said that by our cognitions/beliefs, we create behaviours, so stereotyping and prejudice may also bring discrimination towards refugees, eventually end up with decreased levels of refugee well-being.

## Organizational justice

"Justice" is important and precious for all people. Likewise, it seems that immigrants' perception of the organization in which they work may have an effect on their work life, social life and also on their work outcomes. The perception of justice is a precursor of organizational and individual outcomes in working life. That's why it is an issue worth exploring.

Historical development of organizational justice theory is based on the Equity Theory proposed by Adams[26]. According to this theory, employees compare their job inputs (effort, training, quality of performance, etc.) with their work outcomes (economic gain, recognition and other awards). At the same time, employees compare themselves with other coworkers. If they detect an imbalance or inequality between inputs and outputs, or if they perceive a difference between themselves and other employees, the process ends up trying to restore equality. Employees use several strategies to balance equality. These strategies vary such as; reducing productivity, decreasing the quality of the output or showing absenteeism.[27] So it can be hypothesized

---

[25] Morris Rosenberg, Carl Hovland, "Cognitive, affective, and behavioral components of attitudes", Morris Rosenberg, Carl Hovland , William McGuire , Robert Abelson , Jack Brehm (Ed.), **Attitude, Organization and Change,**New Haven, CT: Yale University Press, 1960, pp. 1-14.
[26] Stacy Adams, "Toward an Understanding of Inequity"**Journal of Abnormal and Social Psychology,** Vol. 67, 1963, pp. 422-436.
[27] Jerald Greenberg, **Managing Behavior in Organizations**, New Jersey, Prentice Hall, 1999.

that refugees may also show typical balancing strategies. On the other hand, natives may evaluate these strategies by prejudiced thoughts.

Organizational justice has been studied with different definitions by different authors. According to Moorman[28] organizational justice is perceptions of how fair employees are treated in the workplace. Colquitt[29] defined organizational justice as employees' perceptions of what is fair and what is not fair in their institution. According to Greenberg[30] organizational justice includes the perceptions of employees on the basis of the fairness of the decisions taken by the institutions, the processes (procedures) they use in situations involving decision-making processes in the business process, and the interpersonal interaction that the employees face.

Also, different authors have studied organizational justice with different dimensions. For example, according to Masterson, Lewis, Goldman and Taylor[31] organizational justice is consisted of three dimensions: distributive justice, procedural justice, and interactional justice. Colquitt et al.[32]examined organizational justice in four dimensions.

These dimensions are; *distributive justice* (perception of justice regarding the distribution of resources), *operational / procedural justice*(perception of the fairness of the procedures applied in the distribution of resources, *interactional justice* (quality of interpersonal relationship shown to the employee when procedures are applied) and *knowledge-based justice* (the level of competence, honesty and compliance of the information conveyed about why the procedures used for resource allocation are used in a certain way or how the results are determined. So, it can be hypothesized that perceived organizational justice of refugees' will have a relationship with their well-being because justice is a basic need for living beings.

## Leadership in the workplace and cultural differences

According to Hofstede[33], culture is "the collective programming of the

[28] Robert H. Moorman, "Relationship Between Organizational Justice and Organizational Citizenship Behaviors: Do Fairness Perceptions Influence Employee Citizenship?" **Journal of Applied Psychology**,Vol. 76 No. 6, 1991,pp. 845-855.
[29] Jason A. Colquitt, "On the Dimensionality of Organizational Justice: A Construct Validation of a Measure", **The Journal of Applied Psychology**, Vol. 86, 2001,pp. 386-400.
[30] Jerald Greenberg,"Organizational Justice: Yesterday, Today, and Tomorrow", **Journal of Management**,Vol. 16,1990, pp. 399-432.
[31] Suzanne Masterson, Kyle Lewis, Barry Goldman, Susan Taylor, "Integrating Justice and Social Exchange: The Differing Effects of Fair Procedures and Treatment on Work Relationships", **Academy of Management Journal**, Vol. 43, 2000, pp. 738–748.
[32] Jason A. Colquitt, Brent A. Scott, Jessica B. Rodell, Dvid M. Long, Cindy P. Zapata, Donald E. Conlon, Michael Wesson,"Justice At The Millennium, a Decade Later: A Meta-Analytic Test of Social Exchange and Affect-Based Perspectives", **The Journal of Applied Psychology**, Vol. 98,2013, pp. 199-236.
[33] Geert Hofstede, **Culture's Consequences: Comparing Values**, Thousand Oaks, CA: SAGE, 2001.

mind that distinguishes the members of one group or category of people from another."He states five dimensions for different countries and cultures.

These dimensions are defined as follows:

(a) Power Distance: "the extent to which the less powerful members of institutions and organizations accept that power is distributed unequally".

(b) Uncertainty Avoidance: "the extent to which people feel threatened by ambiguous situations, and have created beliefs and institutions that try to avoid in such situations."

(c) Individualism: "a situation in which people are supposed to look after themselves and their immediate family only."

Collectivism: "a situation in which people belong to in-group or collectivities, which are supposed to look after them, in exchange for loyalty."

(d) Masculinity: "a situation in which the dominant values of society are success, money, and things."

Femininity: "a situation in which the dominant values of a society are caring for others and quality of life."

(e) Longterm orientation: "long term orientation stands for the fostering of virtues oriented towards future rewards, in particular perseverance and thrift."

Short term orientation: "short term orientation, stands for the fostering of virtues related to the past and present, in particular, respect for tradition, preservation of 'face' and fulfilling social obligations."

Congruence of national culture-organizational culture and employees' values are determinants of well-being and work life. Work systems, processes and behaviours which are held in the workplace are affected by cultural norms and values. Also, leadership is effected by cultural tendencies. Each country may have its own values and also have its own preferred leadership styles. Incongruency between cultural values held in a country and expectations of refugees' as followers may differ and this may result in conflict between followers and leaders in the workplace.

## Conclusion

In conclusion, factors that are related to organizations and nations may have a relationship with refugee well-being. In this chapter, concepts of xenophobia, prejudice, discrimination, perceived organizational justice, leadership in organizations and cultural differences between refugees' and the actual country are summarised.

In terms of well-being, there are dominant theories each with its own strengths and weaknesses. In addition to that, the PERMA model has a comprehensive understanding of psychological well-being in terms of taking into account both hedonistic and eudaimonic approach. It can be hypothesized that all these presented threatening factors and PERMA levels of refugees' have a negative relationship. So, further research may investigate this topic.

It is really important to take care of refugee employees as well as native employees' well-being in organizations. One way to build strength in organizations by developing well-being is to recruit clinical psychologists who are specialized in PTSD (post-traumatic stress disorder) and psychological assessment. Clinical psychologists may also offer clinical therapy sessions, help the organization at the micro level. Another helpful way is to recruit business psychologists who are specialised in HR functions and management functions to make the systems work better. Business psychologists may have a chance to support employee well-being at the macro level.

Also, organizations may present well-being programs for immigrants. Such kind programs may conduct immigrant employees surveys and questionnaires to understand the needs and interests of immigrants. It may help to assess the organisational climate and perception of the employees. The second step may be to get organizational support from higher positions, such as managers and other workers in the workplace. Also raising awareness on coworkers may help to build a new climate and to prevent negative attitudes to immigrants and also fear of change. Training sessions, individual clinical sessions may also help immigrants to develop their self-efficacy and well-being their professional lives. These programs may go hand in hand with occupational health specialists. Lastly, building trust with refugees may help to get them involved in these steps.

# CHAPTER 11

# INTEGRATION OF REFUGEES INTO THE SOCIETY

Saadat Demirci[*]

## Introduction

In 2015, more than 1 million refugees were destined to the European borders, considering the mortal journey. The migration and refugee movement triggered by international and civil wars covers ever-expanding geographies. The Syrian war and persistent terrorist movements and political disorder in the Middle East regions have increased forced migration rate. Immigrants and refugees have created serious economic, security and demographic problems for countries that open their borders to them. Determining the refugee status through internal regulations in every state has caused serious status problems. The refugee crisis in Europe has determined that a single definition of status should be made under international law and the conditions required for status should be connected to a single level system and become valid for all states.

The refugee and migration crisis showed that there are serious crisis management deficiencies in the international legal system. The diversity of refugee identification is one of the first problems to cause confusion. The multitude of definitions such as immigrants, refugees, asylum seekers and displaced persons and the importance of a single international definition of "refugee" status has become apparent. The regulation of this system should be established in a way that takes into account the present-day developments and events that trigger forced migration. The determination system of refugee status has been established according to the order developed by the internal institutions of the states. The status conditions determined by the constitutional system determine the precedent legal order which is the source of international law. The system of granting asylum to foreigners by states is being developed in each state's constitutional order. According to the 1951 Geneva Convention Relating to the Status of Refugees and its 1967 Protocol, it has been documented that it is required that the states should protect having legal rights at the international level and the rights and responsibilities of the refugees who are outside the country of their citizenship and cannot benefit from the protection of that country because they fear persecution for good reasons because of their race, religion, nationality, membership of a certain social group or political opinions or who do not want to take

---

[*] Assoc. Prof. Dr., Çankırı Karatekin University

advantage or have no nationality because of aforementioned reasons and who are outside their country of residence as a result of such events and cannot return there or do not want to return because of the fear in question.

The protection and recognition of States of these rights is an indication of the level of protection of international community values. In this study, the development phase of the documentation regulations shown for the legal protection of refugees is examined, and the historical process is interpreted.

The integration policy of refugees covers every part of the migration process, regardless of the purposes and routes migrants come through. A successful integration process conveys positive developments for both immigrant and governmental societies. On the other hand, the integration process's failure causes the feelings of grudge and hatred to take root in the society where the refugees trigger the conflict with the local people and causes security problems related to these. This reinforces both sides' distrust of the state administration. Studies conducted with the integration process are included in the second part of the study. The migration crisis has now turned into the post-crisis problem of integrating the refugees into society. This section reflects the integration process approaches and policies of states.

The studies on multiculturalism developments determined as an integration policy solution are the third part of the study. Multiculturalism has become popular as a result of the policies implemented by the states established thanks to the immigrant societies such as America and Canada, and it has been tried as a part of the integration policy in European countries struggling with immigration and its failure has been accepted. There are determinations that multiculturalism, which is determined to cause social problems in Europe, will be an important source that will provide a way out for Europe's demographic problem in the near future.

This study aims to interpret the refugee problem in the light of current developments and to take a direction to view the problem in terms of a sociological problem outside of the usual legal, economic and political aspects.

## Historical development process of the legal status of refugees

A refugee is a person who seeks the protection of a foreign state by leaving the country of his / her nationality or residence due to various pressures or discriminatory legal proceedings, entering the country of a foreign state, diplomatic representation or consulate buildings, warships or state aircraft[1]. According to the applied international law, the only authorized actor for foreigners to enter and stay in the country is the state. In accordance with

[1] Hüseyin Pazarcı, **Uluslararası Hukuk**, Ankara 2003, pp.210

this main principle, whether a state grants asylum to foreigners in its country or not is an issue to be evaluated within the framework of the international obligations and national legislation of that state[2].

The first regulations on the protection of refugees were made in 1921 during the League of Nations period. In the chain of events that triggered the forced migration (World War, the collapse of the Ottoman Empire, the Bolshevik dictatorship in Russia), refugees had to be protected within a legal framework. In 1921, the League of Nations held its first congress on the refugee problem. By the decision of the Congress, F. Nansen has been appointed as High Commissioner for Refugee Issues. The duty of the Office of the High Commissioner for Russian Refugees, which was initially established for Russian Refugees, was to carry out activities related to the protection of refugees, such as determining the status of refugees who had to leave their country due to the Russian revolution, determining the states that could grant refugees asylum, and organizing aid organizations[3]. Decisions were taken to grant support and asylum rights to refugees between 1921 and 1928 at first with the identity and travel documents of Armenian and Russian, and later on, other refugees. In 1933, the extradition and non-refoulement principle of refugees was confirmed[4]. In the same year, a decision was taken to give some refugees the right to education and work. The lack of definition given to refugees in the conventions was tried to be overcome in 1938 by the International Law Institute and the Interstate Committee. Previously the definition of a refugee was made as "a citizen or an individual who left the region voluntarily or compulsorily as a result of sudden political events in the state of residence" in the decisions taken in 1936. 1938 Interstate Committee added racial and religious discrimination as reasons for forced migration. Although these decisions did not have legal status, they contributed greatly to the definition and protection of refugee rights under international law[5].

The International Refugee Office, one of the most important works on the protection of refugees' rights, was established in 1931 after Nansen's death. The chairman of the Board of Directors was elected by the League of Nations. The office was obliged to provide all kinds of legal support to refugees and operated until 1938[6]. The Office work ended. With the

---

[2] Pazarcı, 211

[3] Yury Sarashevsky, "Rol Ligi Natsiy v Formirovaniyi Prava Bejentsev", **Belorussky Jurnal Mejdunarodnogo Prava i Mejdunarodnıh Otnosheniy**, No1, 2000, pp.33

[4] Natalya İvanova, " K Voprosu o Statuse Bejentsa v Mejdunarodnom Prave", **İzdatelstvo Gramota**, No3 (4), 2009, pp. 74

[5] Lyudmila Pavlova ve Yuriy Sarashevskiy, " K Voprosu o Ponyatiyi Bejenets v Mejdunarodnom Prave", pp.15

[6] Sarashevskiy, pp.34

appointment of the High Commissioner for Refugees in 1938[7]. The High Commissioner for Refugees coming from Germany was established in 1933 for German refugees escaping Nazi Germany.

After World War II, the issue of refugees became the most occupying issue on the international agenda. In 1946, the UN underlined the need for a serious international platform to solve this problem, and affirmed the principle that refugees or displaced persons who have valid reasons not to return to their country of residence or to their countries of residence will not be returned[8]. The International Refugee Organization was established in 1947. As stated in the organisation's founding decision, the organization was in temporary status and its activity ceased in 1952[9]. The organization has designed to deal with every aspect of refugees' lives. Considering the agreements made by the organization with states, the organization was supranational[10]. At that time, the protection of victims prosecuted by the Nazi German regime, deported refugees and people without citizenship was a priority. In line with the decisions of the International Refugee Organization, those who were followed because of their race, religion or political views and who could not or did not want to accept the aid of their country of origin were granted the status of "refugee"[11]. The International Refugee Organization was the first UN organization to deal with post-World War II refugee issues. A series of problems related to the living conditions of refugees, protection of their legal rights and granting refugee status were under the responsibility of the organization. The organization's bylaw prohibited those on trial for treason and the Military Penal Code, as well as aid to ethnic Germans escaping from the Soviet army and alliance forces.[12].

The UN's attempts for refugee rights have been stated on two factors: i. Objective - To bring the refugee problem to the international platform at the UN and to seek solutions jointly with the member states for the problems of sheltering and protecting refugees, which increased in number after World War II; ii. In the founding treaty of the UN, the organization's duty definition was determined as the regulation and development of inter-state cooperation as well as the promotion and protection of all states "respect for human rights

---

[7] Elif Uzun, " Uluslararası Hukuk Çerçevesinde BMMYK'nın Yapısı, Görevleri ve Uluslararası Mülteci Hukukunun Gelişimindeki Yeri, **Göç Araştırmaları Dergisi**, Volume 2, No 2,July-December 2016, pp.63

[8] BM 12 Şubat 1946 8(I) Kararı, Gay S. Goodwin-Gill, "Convention relating to the Status of Refugees Geneva, 28 July 1951, **Audiovisual Library of international Law**, https://legal.un.org/avl/ha/prsr/prsr.html, 21.10.200

[9] Gay S. Goodwin-Gill, **Status Bejensa v Mejdunarodnom Prave**, Çev. A.İvanchenkova , Ed.Levina, , Budapeşte COLPİ 1997, pp.437

[10] Uzun, pp. 66

[11] Goodwin-Gill, pp.443

[12] A. İbragimov, **Rejim Bejensev v Mejdunarodnom Prave**, yayınlanmamış doktora tezi, Kazan 1999, pp.11

without discrimination of race, religion, language, gender"[13]. In short, the UN Charter has made it possible to deal with the concept of human rights at the international level[14]. On December 10, 1948, the Universal Declaration of Human Rights was declared by the UN General Assembly Resolution 217 A (III). The purpose and the article 1 of the declaration was stated as to undertake the duty of ideal measurement guide in order to respect the human rights and freedoms of the member states and to ensure that these rights are effective worldwide[15]. Article 2 of the declaration stated that all humanity has equal rights, regardless of race, colour, sex, language, religion, political or other opinion, national or social origin, property, birth or any other discrimination[16]. In addition to fundamental rights, the Declaration made certain regulations on refugee law and refugee rights. The right of every person to leave the state of his / her birth and citizenship has been stated in Article 13/2 of the declaration and the refugee right has been confirmed. Article 14/2 has determined the right of people to seek asylum. In order to determine the difference between immigration and being a refugee, it has been underlined that 1) the individual has the right to ask, not to claim asylum and 2) this right has a right granted only to individuals who are persecuted and oppressed in other states, it has been important that the repression only carries a political motive, it has been explained that this right is not given to persons who are wanted for non-political criminals or crimes contrary to UN fundamental principles[17]. The 1948 Declaration of Human Rights served as a foundation for the 1951 Refugee Convention and its Fundamental principles. In those days, the awareness of the necessity of protecting human and human rights as an individual at states was newly established. Based on this, the 1948 Declaration primarily undertook the guidance of states regarding the protection order to be created for individuals who were persecuted[18]. Thus, the Universal Declaration of Human Rights explained the important principles of the granting of asylum and determined the most important decision-making centre of the state in this matter[19]. On this basis, the 1951 convention determined the principles of states' treatment of refugees and the international protection system. At the beginning of the convention, there was no regulation regarding the protection system of individuals within the borders of the state while crossing the state borders. As a result of long-term negotiations, the UN Security Council decided to establish 428 (V) High Commissioner for Refugees dated 14 December 1950

---

[13] Charter of UN 3rd paragraph of Article 1

[14] Bozkurt Enver, İnsan Haklarının Korunmasında Uluslararası Hukukun Rolü, Ankara 2003, pp. 55.

[15] Universal Declaration of Human Rights, Article 1, https://www.danistay.gov.tr/upload/insanhaklari evrenselbeyannamesi.pdf, 25.10.2020

[16] Universal Declaration of Human Rights Article 2.

[17] Universal Declaration of Human Rights Articles 13/1/2, 14/1/2

[18] Gay.S. Goodwin-Gill,pp.1-2

[19] Pavlova, Sarashesky, pp. 17

instead of the International Refugee Organization at the 3rd Committee. The definition of the refugees under the status of High Commissioner for Refugees who will fall under the auspices of this organization has been made[20]. Initially, the High Commissioner for Refugees was supposed to operate for 3 years, but as the refugee problem became a permanent problem, the working period of the Commissioner was continuously extended for 5 years, and in December 2003, the decision of the Commissioner's Office was annulled [21].

The duty of the High Commissioner was determined as the resolution of the refugee problem by overseeing the provision of "international protection" to refugees and ensuring that the states comply with the decisions taken in this regard, in the 1st clause of the 428 (V) Resolution[22]. The 1951 Convention only dealt with asylum seekers outside the country of nationality due to pre-1951 events as a time limit. In other words, it was aimed at European refugees after World War II, and protection was subject to both time and geography limits. The time limitation was deregulated by signing the 33rd Agreement together with the additional protocol in 1967, but the right to geographical limitation was preserved in the 1967 protocol[23]. In addition, this protocol stated that the initiative of granting the right to asylum belongs entirely to the states and that the right to housing will be granted only in accordance with the decision of the states [24]. It was considered that the decisions would be taken in a way that both the protection of refugee rights and the non-violation of the state sovereignty and the decision-making centralist system would protect the refugee rights under the UN roof[25]. However, the 1951 Convention was determined to be European- centreed in terms of both scope and purpose, and therefore it was criticized by developing countries. Although the 1967 additional protocol derestricted the time limit in response to these criticisms, it was criticized for a narrow approach to the refugee concept and lack of attempts to solve the refugee movement that caused forced migration such as natural disasters, internal conflicts and famine.[26] In the "Protection Agenda" published by the United Nations High Commission in 2013, it has been called for inviting the states who put the geographical reservation to lift the reservation, paying special

---

[20] Cenevre'de 1951 tarihinde imzalanmış olan Mültecilerin Hukuki Durumuna dair Sözleşmenin tasdiki hakkında kanun tasarısı ve Dışişleri Komisyonu raporu (1/125), https://www.tbmm.gov.tr/tutanaklar/TUTANAK/KM__/d00/c002/km__00002024ss0053.pdf, 25.10.2020
[21] BM Güvenlik Konseyi 22 Aralık 2003, 58/153 tarihli Kararın 9.bendi
[22] Mültecilerin Hukuki Statüsüne ilişkin Sözleşme, http://www.multeci.org.tr/wp-content/uploads/2016/12/1951-Cenevre-Sozlesmesi-1.pdf, 25.20.2020
[23] Arzu Güler, "Mülteci Sorunu ve 1951 Mültecilerin Hukuki Durumuna İlişkin Sözleşme: Siyasi Gerçeklik ve Normatif Düzen İkilemi", **Uluslararası İlişkiler**, Volume 13, No 51, 2016, pp. 46-47
[24] 19967 Ek Protokol Madde 1/3
[25] Pavlova, Sarashesky, pp. 18
[26] Ersan Barkın, **"1951 Tarihli Mülteciliğin Önlenmesi Sözleşmesi"**, pp..338, http://www.ankarabarosu.org.tr/siteler/ankarabarosu/tekmakale/2014-1/12.pdf, 25.10.2020

attention to individuals who are in the vulnerable group such as children and elderly in order to strengthen refugee rights and make protection more effective and making it an international standard by including it in the national legislation to protect refugee rights [27].

As the post-World War II period continued to be shaken by civil wars, the chain of mass migration to Europe and other countries was getting longer. Refugees escaping from the wars of liberation that started in Asian and African countries were not included in the "refugee" status determined by the High Commissioner. The UN Security Council, with its resolution 1167 of 26 November 1957, instructed the High Commissioner to assist those who are not "refugee" but who are victims of war and other situations whose situation raises concerns among nations. [28]. Those who had to leave their country due to civil war or international conflicts were not in refugee status under the 1951 and 1967 Conventions. For their protection, the 1949 Geneva Convention and the International Protocol on the Protection of Victims in Armed Conflicts No I and the Protocols on the Protection of Victims in Non-International Armed Conflicts No II annex to the convention were signed.[29]

The concept of refugee was discussed in a wider scope in the decisions of the UN Security Council and the UN Economic and Social Council in the early 1970s. Except for people who escaped from their state and took refuge in another state, there were individuals who were displaced within the state during the civil war.[30]

The 1951 and 1967 conventions included the general status of refugees, an explanation of the concept and the principles that states will set for the protection of refugee rights. Despite this, the problems of individuals who were refugees due to regional and national problems remained outside these concepts. In order to meet these problems, the 1969 Organization of African Union agreement was signed on September 10, 1969, which deals with the special dimension of the refugee problem in Africa[31]. In paragraph 2 of Article 1 of this convention, which entered into force in 1974, it has been included all those who are forced to leave their permanent place of residence to seek asylum elsewhere outside of their country of origin or the country of

---

[27] https://www.unhcr.org/tr/wp-content/uploads/sites/14/2017/02/koruma_gundemi.pdf, 25.20.2020
[28] BM Güvenlik Konseyi 1167 (XII) Kararı, 26 Kasım 1957, Gay.S. Goodwin-Gill,pp.18
[29] Handbook and Guidelines on Procedures and Criteria for Determining Refugee Status under the 1951 Convention and the 1967 Protocol Relating to the Status of Refugees, December 2011, HCR/1P/4/ENG/ REV. 3, http://www.refworld.org/docid/4f33c8d92.html, 27.10.2020
[30] N.N. Zinchenko " Mejdunarodnoye Migratsionnoye Pravo: Osnovı Teorii i Praktiki", **Nauchnaya Kniga 2011**, pp. 179
[31] Koruma Gündemi 3. Baskı, Ekim 2003, pp.2, https://www.unhcr.org/tr/wp-content/uploads/sites/14/2017/02/koruma_gundemi.pdf, 26.11.2020

their citizenship because of foreign attack, occupation, foreign sovereignty or events that seriously disrupt public order in their country of origin or some or all of the country of their citizenship, within the definition of a refugee.[32]. Another convention structured on the special status of refugees was the 1984 Cartagena Declaration. The Declaration recommended expanding the concept of refugee and including those who escape their countries on the grounds that their lives, security or freedoms are threatened due to widespread violence, external assault, internal conflicts, widespread violations of human rights or other serious disruption to public order[33]. The Declaration focused on issues such as facilitating the implementation of the Convention and Protocol among countries in the region to address the problems of refugees at the regional level, encouraging the adoption of necessary national laws and regulations and, if necessary, establishing internal processes and mechanisms to ensure the protection of refugees[34].

The Declaration foresaw a different approach and perspective to the refugee problem. Unlike the previous documents, it emphasized that the concept of refugee should be expanded and be created a conceptual framework reflecting the problems of the day. Decisions prohibiting refugees from crossing the border were identified as the building blocks of the refugee problem with non-refoulement. It emphasized that these principles should be accepted by all states and applied as a *jus cogens* norm. The 1984 Cartagena Declaration has been an international document that is frequently cited by the Organization of African Unity and has reflected the views of Latin American countries.[35]

The Council of Europe and European Union organizations based their refugee policy on the 1951 Convention and the 1967 additional protocol. Despite the many codification decisions and declarations taken by the Council of Europe on the protection of human rights, it has not made a separate concept study for the protection of refugee rights other than these conventions. This issue has limited to the instructions given by the Council of Europe to the Committee of Ministers on granting asylum to refugees in European countries. Accordingly, there has been a recommendation of the Committee of Ministers dated October 5, 1981 that refugees should be allowed to stay in the country until they are granted asylum. The 1984 recommendation of the Committee of Ministers has covered the protection

---

[32] **Afrika Birliği Örgütü Afrika'daki mültecilerin özel sorunlarına dair 1969 Sözleşmesi**, : http://www.refworld.org.ru/docid/528634864.html, 28.10.2020

[33] Özcan, M.,**Avrupa Birliği Sığınma Hukuku**, Ankara, Uluslararası Stratejik Araştırmalar Kurumu 2005, pp. 21

[34] 1984 Cartagena Mülteciler Bildirisi, http://sorular.rightsagenda.org/Uploads/MULTECI%20MEV/ 1984%20CARTAGENA%20M%C3%9CLTEC%C4%B0LER%20B%C4%B0LD%C4%B0R%C4%B0 S%C4%B0.pdf, 28.10.2020

[35] Gay.S. Goodwin-Gill, **Status Bejentsev v Mejdunarodnom Prave**, Budapeşte 1997, s.147-148

of asylum seekers who do not have refugee status and has stipulated that the principle of "non-refoulement" applies to this group of asylum seekers. The recommendation has foreseen that this principle applies without discrimination between those with refugee status and those who have entered the country illegally or are living.[36].

In 1990, the European Union built its refugee policy on organizational unity and common policy. European countries have linked their decisions on refugees from individuality to a single European Union policy. Decisions on this matter were included in the 1990 Dublin Convention. The 1990 Dublin convention stated which European Union member country would consider applications for refugee status. The Convention has guaranteed that refugees whose asylum claims are not met will not be returned from country to country. The fingerprints of refugees who have applied for asylum since 2000 have been collected in a single database. This prevents the application to two or more countries and the re-entry of those whose applications are rejected into the EU country[37]. The strategic aspects of the EU countries' refugee policy were determined at the 1999 EU meeting held in Tampere, Finland. The rights and obligations of third-country nationals were determined through an international agreement between the EU country and the country concerned. It created the first regulations on the refugees' right to free movement, security and fair justice. The next development in this regard took place at the Brussels meeting held by the European Council on November 5, 2004, with the preparation of the 2005-2010 Hague program. The 2005-2010 Hague program was about organizing a joint refugee program of European countries within the specified dates. Based on this program, it has been foreseen that a special EU body related to the common European refugee policy will be put into action. These initiatives continued with the 2009-2014 Stockholm program. In 2012, preparations for the CEAS program, which includes a single European system for asylum, were carried out. As a result of the CEAS program, the European Office EASO (European Asylum Support Office) was established with regard to asylum problems. Within the scope of the program, "Asylum, Migration and Integrated Finance Foundation" was established for the years 2014-2020. The Dublin III or Dublin Convention on refugee policy has entered into force by year 2013. The purpose of this convention is to create a common European refugee policy and to carry out the evaluation of asylum applications on the same system in all European states. The assessment of asylum status is carried out by the country of application and the status is valid only within the territory of the given state. According to the new articles of the convention,

[36] H. Lambert, " Comparative Law and practice in Selected European Countries, London 1995, s. 127-128
[37] İ.Aleshkovski, Z. Botcharova, "Bejentsı Stanovleniye i Evolutsiya Statusa i Razvitiye Sistemı Zashitı", **Rossiya XXI**, No2, 2017, s.21

151

homosexual and women under the threat of circumcision who had to escape their country will be able to apply for asylum. One of the most important developments in this regard has been the restriction of the asylum application assessment process. While the evaluation process of states was extended up to 1 year before, with this convention, the period must be completed within 6 months. The task of the European Office is to provide technical and urgent support to the European states suffering from the refugee flow, to cooperate about refugees with the Council of Europe and the UN High Commissioner for Refugees[38]. With the definition of refugees in the 1951 UN Refugee Convention and 1964 Additional Convention, refugees are classified into different categories. While refugees have a status and legal protection protected by international agreements, those who have not yet achieved this status and seek international protection are protected by the UN High Commissioner for Refugees with asylum seeker status. The UN Relief and Works Agency for Palestine Refugees (UNRWA) has been organized to give Palestinian refugees a separate status and to protect their rights. UNRWA provides assistance to more than 5 million refugees in the West Bank, Gaza, Jerusalem, Jordan, Lebanon and Syria[39]. Those who try to escape from the civil war in Syria by sea are considered in a different group. 6.6 million refugees from Syria constitute about a third of the global refugee population, followed by Afghanistan and South Sudan with 2.7 million and 2.2 million, respectively. Among those seeking protection, the largest group of asylum seekers in 2019 was Venezuelan citizens. Turkey is one of the neighbours of Syria and sheltering the most Syrian refugees with more than 3.77 million people. This corresponds to 65.5 per cent of Syrian refugees in the countries of the region[40]. According to the Clause 1 of (B) Paragraph of Article 1 of Geneva Conventions, Turkey describes those who are coming from Europe as refugee by making a geographical reservation. Those who come from outside European countries and seek asylum are in the status of "conditional refugees" according to Article 62 of the Law on Foreigners and International Protection[41]. Syrians do not meet the definition of either a migrant or a refugee. Due to the gap in the legislation, the "Law on Foreigners and International Protection" was enacted regarding the status of Syrians and the status of Syrians was specified as "temporary protection"[42].

Even though it is not covered much in international and domestic law,

---

[38] **Eurostat. EU statistics agency**, http://ec.europa.eu/eurostat/statistics-explained/index.php/sylum_ tatistics, 09.11.2020
[39] https://tr.sputniknews.com/tags/organization_Birlesmis_Milletler_Filistinli_Multecilere_Yardim_Ajansi_UNRWA/, 10.11.2020
[40] M. Hamsici, " **Komşu Ülkelerdeki 6 mln Suriyeli Ülkelerine Döner mi?**", https://www.bbc.com/turkce/haberler-dunya-50502393, 10.11.2020
[41] Ş. Çakran, V.Eren, " Mülteci Politikası: Avrupa Birliği ve Türkiye Karşılaştırması", **Mustafa Kemal Üniversitesi Sosyal Bilimler Enstitüsü Dergisi**, Volume: 14, Issue: 39, pp. 6
[42] Çakran, Eren, pp.7

people who have been displaced due to forced migration are in another category. Internally displaced persons (IDPs) differ from refugees in that they do not leave their country and remain within the borders of the country. This group is the people who had to leave the region they live in because of the civil war, irregular conflicts and systematic human rights in their country. States have obligations to displaced persons under international human rights law. Although it is not legally binding, the most important document on this subject is the Guiding Principles on Internal Displacement prepared by Françoise Deng, the Special Representative of the UN Secretary General. Many of the principles reflect the obligations that states already have. UNHCR carries out its assistance activities regarding IDPs through cooperation with other UN aid agencies.[43]

The definition of a refugee has undergone great changes since the first time it entered international law. Irregular migration movements due to conflicts have triggered these changes. Today's refugee is stateless, displaced, forcibly displaced and a third-world citizen or stateless person who has fled various threats and pressures from his/her country. What makes them different from foreigners who change countries is that there is no protection initiative on the country's government. Refugee status is stated in international documents on the basis of conditions and acceptance of each state. In 1997, the Executive Committee of the UN High Commissioner for Refugees (EXCOM) called for states to comply with the UN general requirements on refugee status[44]. Temporary offices on refugee issues were left in permanent status, as the refugee problem could not be solved in a short time and there was no cessation in the refugee flows in the light of the agenda events.

### Countrywide distribution of refugees and integration processes

European countries have been the focal point of refugees forced to escape their countries and seek refuge in other countries due to conflict, civil war, repression and other human rights violations. The process of integrating the refugees into the countries was carried out within the framework of the domestic policies of the states according to the refugee policy specified in international documents. Refugee mobility, which started in the light of recent conflicts, has exposed European countries to an unexpected migration wave.

As the European Asylum Support Office (EASO) stated in its 2019 asylum report, UNHCR stated that there are total 79.4 million people including 3.9 million stateless persons under the auspices of UNHCR, 20.2

---

[43] Uzun, pp.74
[44] Aleshkovski, Botcharova, s. 25

million refugees, 3.7. million asylum seekers, 531,000 repatriate refugees and 43.9 million internally displaced persons (IDPs) in June 2019. 6.6 million refugees from Syria constitute about a third of the global refugee population, followed by Afghanistan and South Sudan with 2.7 million and 2.2 million, respectively. Among those seeking protection, the largest group of asylum seekers in 2019 were Venezuelan citizens. After 9 years of internal conflict in Syria, 6.6 million Syrian refugees constitute 1/3 of the global refugee population. Turkey is the country that hosts the highest number of Syrian refugee community by hosting 3.6 million. Pakistan is home to around 1.4 million refugees, most of them Afghanistan-origin[45]. Around 80% of the refugees were accepted by Germany, France, England and Sweden between 2015-2017. Except for England, the number of refugees accepted by these three countries is much higher than the average population rate. For every 1 million citizens of Germany, there are 2402 refugees. This figure is 220 in Sweden and 1359 in France. Germany is the region where refugee groups are most heavily settled. In 2017, Germany accepted 31% of refugees at 198.300, Italy accepted 19.5% at 126.550, France accepted 14% at 91.070, Greece accepted 8.8% at 57.020, England accepted 5.1% at 33.310, Spain accepted 4.7% at 30.445, Sweden accepted 3.4% at 22.190, Austria accepted 3.4% at 22.160, Belgium accepted 2.2% at 14.035 and Netherlands accepted 2.5% at 16.090[46]. The asylum request of refugees in 2017 was mostly positive by European countries. Considering the acceptance statistics of application requests, Denmark is 63%, Norway 55%, Sweden 46%, Germany 40%, Finland 40% and Greece 10%[47]. Among the asylum seekers, the most applications were from Syria, Afghanistan and Iraq, where conflicts are intense, 33% of the applications belong to these countries[48]. The application requests of the group of refugees in question are likely to be accepted. Because the citizens of these countries are in the ranks of the victim group who have the most suitable conditions for refugee status and should be taken under international protection, in this context, considering the positive results of the 2018 applications, 86% positive applications for Syria, 43% for

[45] EASO Sığınma Raporu 2020, Avrupa Birliğinde Sığınma Durumuna İlişkin Yıllık Rapor, https://easo.europa.eu/sites/default/files/EASO-Asylum-Report-2020-Executive-Summary-TR.pdf, 11.11.2020
[46] Countries of Destination: Germany, Italy and France the Main. Eurostat. Asylum Statistics. 16 March 2018 and 18 April 2018 (part of final decisions). Available at: https://ec.europa.eu/eurostat/statistics-explained/index.php/Asylum_statistics#Countries_of_destination:_Germany.2C_Italy_and_France_the_main, 11.11.2020
[47] Asylum Decisions in the EU-EU Member States Granted Protection to More Than Half a Million Asylum Seekers in 2017. Almost One-third of the Beneficiaries Were Syrians. Eurostat Newsrelease. 67/2018. 19 April 2018, http://www.reddit.com/r/europe/comments/8ddbo5/asylum_decisions_in_the_eueu_member_states, 11.11.2020
[48] 650 000 First-time Asylum Seekers Registered in 2017. Eurostat Newsrelease. 47/2018. 20 March 2018. http://ec.europa.eu/eurostat/documents/2995521/8754388/3–20032018-AP-EN.pdf/50c2b5a5-3e6a-4732-82d0-1caf244549e3 , 11.11.2020

Afghanistan and 35% for Iraq were evaluated.[49].

For European countries that are exposed to such a refugee flow, the integration policy of refugees is an important issue in terms of state order, economy and demographic regulations. In many ways, the integration process of refugees is about keeping up with the order of the country they live in. The execution of his/her life is one of the important conditions for the transition to this order, not only to the state, but also to his /her earnings and business life. Another important aspect is that he/she reduces the burden on the state, as a working individual, the need for social assistance will disappear. This is one of the most positive aspects that an immigrant can give to the state where he or she takes refuge. The integration of refugees into the labour market is also at the stage of the development that benefits the receiving countries the most in terms of the national economy. In the "Agenda Report" published by the UN on September 25, 2015, it was emphasized that non-integration of refugees would cause more costs and burdens on states. Especially in states with a high elderly population, the presence of young immigrants in open areas will make a significant contribution to these countries. This pragmatic idea is theoretically considered in the content of national integration programs of all states that accept refugees. However, it is too early to say that the practise has progressed as brightly as the statistics set in theory. The frameworks of the common refugee program of European countries were confirmed by the EU Justice and Home Affairs Council in 2004[50]. In 2015, Jean-Claude Junker, Chairman of the European Union (EU) Commission, in his speech at the European Parliament, stated that EU member states should change their asylum programs and that they should be shared among member countries. European countries, worried about being exposed to a large number of asylum flows and being unable to resist, rejected the Commission's proposal to distribute refugees fairly to EU member states. The Juncker plan envisaged a fine of 6,000 euros for each refugee candidate from countries who did not receive or received little refugees, and that the same amount be paid to countries that exceed their quota[51]. This project, which was prepared for each state to accept a certain number of refugees, was suspended as a result of the states' insufficient interest in this issue. The Asylum, Migration and Integration Fund (AMIF), which organizes a more active work plan to remedy this situation, was established for the period 2014-2020 with 3.137 billion Euros for seven years. It was established with the aim of efficient

---

[49] Decisions on Asylum Applications. Eurostat Statistics Explained. Asylum Quarterly Report. 15 June 2018. https://ec.europa.eu/eurostat/statisticsexplained/index.php/Asylum_quarterly_report# Decisions_on_asylum_application , 11.11.2020

[50] Vedeneeva, T. "İntegratsia Bejentsev v Evrope: Prioritet-Trudoustroistvo", **Mirovaya Ekononmika i Mejdunarodnıye Otnosheniya**, no 63, No 1, pp. 104

[51] Riegert, B., **Juncer Devrimi,** https://www.dw.com/tr/juncker-devrimi/a-18705311, 11.11.2020

management of migration flows and structuring a common asylum policy towards European countries. It has been envisaged for AMIF to make arrangements in four subjects:

Refugees - To organize a single European Asylum System by ensuring that states participate in an equal ground and act on a common system.

Legal Migration and Integration - To ensure that the refugee movement in Europe operates according to a legal system and to direct the migration movement in line with the workforce needs in European countries.

Return - Prepare a safe return order for refugees who want to return to their homeland.

Solidarity - To reduce the burden of migration by transferring excessive refugees to different countries from EU states that are exposed to excessive migration movements that exceed their capacities of interest.

The Fund is also an important source of data that supports the European Migration Network to ensure its work effectively.[52].

The European Migration Network (EMN) was established to create a data network on refugees and to provide up-to-date, reliable and comparable information on asylum.[53].

In 2016, the European Commission prepared several programs on the integration of refugee. One of the projects was presented on 7 June 2016 and the "Action Plan on the Integration of Third-Country Nationals" is responsible for preparing asylum, immigration and integration program for refugees[54]. The documents placed special emphasis on work and workforce, and the issue of providing refugees with immediate job opportunities. Another initiative of European countries on this issue has been guided by the 5 July 2016 Integrated Resolution on Asylum, Political Integration and Labour Market[55]. The resolution includes recommendations for European states to meet the basic social needs of asylum-seekers such as home and accommodation, education and health services. Another project (Skills

---

[52] Bkz: https://ec.europa.eu/home-affairs/financing/fundings/migration-asylum-borders/asylum-migration-integration-fund_en, 15.11.2020

[53] Bkz: https://ec.europa.eu/home-affairs/financing/fundings/migration-asylum-borders/asylum-migration-integration-fund/european-migration-network, 15.11.2020

[54] Communication from the Commission to the European Parliament, the Council, the European Economic and Social Committee and the Committee of the Regions. Action Plan on the Integration of Third Country Nationals. COM(2016) 377 final. Brussels. 07.06.2016, https://ec.europa.eu/home-affairs/sites/homeaffairs/files/what-we-do/policies/europeanagenda-migration/proposal-implementation-package/docs/20160607/communication_action_plan_integration_thirdcountry_nationals_en.pdf, 5.11.2020, Aktaran : Vedeneeva, pp.104

[55] European Parliament Resolution of 5 July 2016 on Refugees: Social Inclusion and Integration into the Labour Market (2015/2321(INI)). Available at: http://www.europarl.europa.eu/sides/getDoc.do?pubRef=-//EP//TEXT+TA+P8- TA-2016-0297+0+DOC+XML+V0//EN, 15.11.2020

Agenda for Europe 2016) prepared to increase the chances of refugees to find employment in European countries is to enable refugees to apply for specialized courses and receive training, as well as to direct them according to their workforce needs, to open agencies and to carry out effective studies on this issue[56]. European countries agree on providing refugees with job opportunities. Each country has determined and taken action to implement various training projects for language learning, vocational training and specialization in line with its own means. This issue creates an important resource that will benefit both the economic and demographic policies of the European countries that provide refuge, beyond the one-sided solidarity project, and meet their labour needs.

In order to increase the working potential of refugees in European countries, language preparation training programs have been organized for candidates who have applied for asylum and are in the waiting period. (Language Training, Skills Assessments). Belgium establishes "integrated centres" and directs the candidates who are likely to meet their asylum requests to various workplaces according to their professional competencies by receiving 50 hours of language training. Belgium stipulated the condition of "social integration certificate" for refugees, requiring applicants to pass a language proficiency test first by year 2016[57]. Germany's decision regarding the asylum conditions of refugees in 2016 has brought both a language requirement and the allowances of candidates who do not attend language courses will be cut[58]. The method of strictly enforcing integration policy encourages refugees to apply for such programs. According to the "Employment and Social Developments in Europe (ESDE) studies supported by the European Commission, while 59% of refugees, who have applied for asylum and have a command of the state language, have found job opportunities, only 29% of those who do not speak the language of the country they live in have the opportunity to work.[59]

## Migration Crisis

While Europe was trying to regulate the influx of refugees, several bomb

---

[56] Communication from the Commission to the European Parliament, the Council, the European Economic and Social Committee and the Committee of the Regions. A New Skills Agenda for Europe. Working Together to Strengthen Human Capital, Employability and Competitiveness. COM(2016) 0381 final. Brussels. 10.06.2016. Available at: https://eur-lex.europa.eu/legal-content/en/ TXT/?uri= CELEX%3A52016DC0381, Aktaran, Vedeneeva, pp.104

[57] Bkz: http://dx.doi.org/10.1787/migr_outlook-2017-fr, 15.11.2020

[58] Gesetzentwurf der Bundesregierung. Integrationsgesetz.doc. BMAS. 24.05.2016. Available at: https://www.bmas.de/SharedDocs/Downloads/DE/PDF-Meldungen/2016/entwurf-integration sgesetz.pdf?__blob=publicationFile&v=4, Aktaran, Vedeneeva, pp. 105

[59] Peschner J. Labour Market Performance of Refugees in the EU. Analytical Support to the Employment and Social Developments in Europe 2016. Working paper 1/2017. Review. ESDE, 2016, pp. 5. Available at: http://ec.europa.eu/social/main.jsp?catId= 738&dangId=fr&pubId=7992&further Pubs=yes, 16.11.2020

and gun attacks took place simultaneously in Paris, the capital of France on 13.11.2015. 140 people died in the attack. After the attack, France closed its borders and declared an extraordinary situation. As a phenomenon that parallels the security threat to the country, refugee migration has put European countries in fear. Despite the heavy effects of the horror of the attack, there has been a rapid increase in the irregular migration movement that has forced Europe on refugee immigration. Towards the end of 2015, the coastal borders of Italy and Greece were exposed to an influx of about one million refugees seeking shelter. Nearly three thousand immigrants died by drowning in the waters during the dangerous passing. Combat against human trafficking and illegal immigration organizations has been initiated in order to stop the influx of refugees and control irregular migration. The "Sophia" military operation in the Mediterranean Sea started by the European Union Foreign Affairs Council within the framework of the European Common Defense and Security Policy. However, the operation that was actually started was cancelled due to the dispute between the EU member states[60]. After four rounds of negotiations which ultimately seeking a solution in other European countries in this regard by December 16, 2013, Turkey signed the Readmission Agreement. The Agreement was approved by Law No. 6547 of 5/6/2014 dated and entered into force as of October 1, 2014[61]. After the Turkey-EU summit on March 18, 2016, "18 March Immigrant Reconciliation" was signed. It has been envisaged to support Turkey, who accept the refugees, in line with the reconciliation in order to prevent the influx of refugees who are in the irregular migration movement to EU and escape from the civil war in Syria. In accordance with the reconciliation, refugees who are passing from Turkey to Greek islands would be returned, and duly asylum applications would be examined by UNCHR[62]. According to Turkey's EU Action Plan, 3 billion euros would be allocated in the first stage on Turkey to prevent the movement of irregular migration and to receive asylum seekers. European Union countries had some demands from Turkey such as closing its borders to asylum seekers, placing the migration chain within the country, providing jobs, training and other social conditions. However, Turkey had also demanded such as speeding up Turkey's accession process to the EU, providing convenience for visa to Turkey's citizens for EU countries apart from the financial aid in front of Refugee Convention[63]. Although the EU do not demonstrate a clear stance

---

[60] https://www.sozcu.com.tr/2020/dunya/avrupa-birliginde-akdeniz-operasyonu-tartismasi-5632985/, 17.11.2020

[61] T.Yıldırım Mat, Selman Özdan, "AB ile Türkiye arasındaki Geri Kabul Anlaşması'nın İnsan Hakları Açısından Değerlendirilmesi (A Review of the Readmission Agreement between EU and Turkey in regard to Human Rights), **Marmara Üniversitesi Hukuk Fakültesi Hukuk Araştırmaları Dergisi •** Cilt 24, Sayı 1, Haziran 2018,pp. 36

[62] https://www.bbc.com/turkce/haberler-dunya-51724776, 17.11.2020

[63] https://tr.euronews.com/2018/03/26/ab-turkiye-multeci-anlasmasi-ab-fonlari-nereye-ve-nasil-harca-

on this issue, the EU negotiation process with Turkey is coming to a deadlock. Although Turkey is only the backbone country supported by the EU as a temporary solution country for refugee crisis, it has not been determined that which countries will benefit more of the alliance agreement. Although a disruption has not been seen in the warm relations, Turkey's importance and effect to EU foreign policy have become apparent with the refugee crisis.

Chair of the EU Commission Jean-Claude Juncker has reported that the organizations shall create an effective fight against the illegal mobility and in the prevention of asylum seekers migrating illegally to Europe with the Refugee Convention with Turkey and the cooperation with Turkey in this field will continue. However, it cannot be said that the EU is in agreement with other EU countries on this issue. International organizations have seriously warned the EU to shift its responsibilities regarding immigrants to weak countries by making it a bargaining issue.[64] The EU Commission has continued its determination that it will act according to the European common plan on migration. In 2015, it announced that it would impose penalties on countries that do not adjust their domestic legislation to the European asylum system. Greece, Croatia, Italy, Malta and Hungary have also been warned in this regard. The Commission attaches particular importance to the protection of sea and land borders. With an additional 31.5 million Euros for 2017, it has been reported that tighter security measures will be taken for the protection of international lines by making Frontex not only security but a semi-military institution.[65] Regarding the issue of immigrants, it can be said that EU countries are weak in many points in terms of human rights and refugee right, which are highly defended. The fact that asylum-seekers are sent back to their countries of origin or stuck in the transition country before they find any opportunity to apply for asylum in the country they are sent to and their applications are not examined with the necessary care, triggers the crisis to become an increasingly serious problem.

While European countries are faced with the migration crisis problem, it is important to overcome the crisis rather than temporary solutions to reach the roots of the problem and to investigate its causes. Although the Arab Spring and the Syrian civil war are important factors that trigger the migration

---

niyor-, 17.11.2020

[64] Melike, A.Köse, "Geri Kabul Anlaşması ve Vizesiz Avrupa: Türkiye'nin Dış Politika Tercihlerini Anlamak", **Marmara Üniversitesi Siyasal Bilimler Dergisi** • Marmara University Journal of Political Science, Volume 3, No 2,September 2015, pp. 204

[65] Communication from the Commission to the European Parliament and the Council: A European border and coast guard and effective management of Europe's external borders / European Commission. – Strasbourg, 2015 d. – 15.12. – COM (2015) 673 final. – 10 p, http://ec.europa.eu/dgs/home-affairs/what-we-do/policies/securing-eu-borders/legal-documents/docs/communication_-_a_european_border_and_coast_guard_and_effective_management_of_europes_external_borders_en.pdf, 17.11.2020

crisis, it is not the only reason. European countries have always been attractive to third-world citizens struggling with poverty, unemployment and other social problems. This time migration crisis has become complicated by the combination of both economic and political and illegal migration Moreover, migrants escaping from the country's disasters are not just looking for a safe haven as they used to. Most of the outgoing migrants see European countries not as a temporary refuge but as a country of permanent residence to live in better conditions. New asylum seekers are more aware of Europe's social assistance mechanism compared to the old immigrants. This information comes from ethnic associations established in European countries as well as social media.

The Syrian civil war, which has been going on for 9 years, is another development that adds a link to the immigration chain. The irregular conflicts that have been going on since 2011 have exhausted the trust of refugees from Syria to the country's administration. According to the EASO 2020 Asylum Report, 6.6 million refugees from Syria constitute about a third of the global refugee population and this is followed by 2.7 million refugees with Afghanistan and 2.2 million refugees with South Sudan.[66]

Until the Refugee Convention signed between EU and Turkey, Mediterranean and Aegean seas were one of the advantageous ways for refugees allowing them to enter Europe illegally. In the first six months of 2015, 137.000 illegal immigrants entered Europe by crossing the waters with boats through the Mediterranean. According to the 2019 data provided by the EU border and coast guard agency, 150.000 people entered the European borders illegally. This shows a 92% decrease compared to 2015, when the crisis peaked, as the lowest level in the last 5 years.[67] Illegal immigrants mostly cross to Greece. However, since Greece is not able to go out of the 2,000 refugees given its industrial area and labour market, immigrants try to cross the borders of Macedonia and Serbia to Hungary[68]. This situation is another important reason for the refugee flow. The allowances made to countries that will accept migrants are determined as 100 million Euros.

European Regional Development Fund (ERDF) has allocated 300 million Euros as a support fund for cross-border cooperation initiatives of neighbouring regions within the EU. Of these allowances, 42 million Euros were given to Greece and 58 million Euros were given to Italy[69]. Despite

[66] EASO Sığınma Raporu 2020, Avrupa Birliğinde sığınma durumuna ilişkin Rapor, https://www.easo.europa.eu/sites/default/files/EASO-Asylum-Report-2020-Executive-Summary-TR.pdf, 17.11.2020
[67] https://www.bbc.com/turkce/haberler-dunya-46768567, 17.11.2020
[68] Reasons Europe's Refugee Crisis is Happening Now, *The Washington Post*. – 18.09.2015, https://www.washingtonpost.com/news/worldviews/wp/2015/09/18/8-reasons-whyeuropes-refugee-crisis-is-happening-now/, 17.11.2020
[69] The EU's response to the refugee crisis: Taking stock and setting policy priorities / Carrera S., Blockmans S., Gros D., Guild E.; Centre for European policy studies (CEPS). – Brussels, 2015. – 16.12.

these attempts, countries that remain indifferent to the refugee crisis in the face of the allowances criticize the EU's refugee policy. Only one of the 5 centres planned to register immigrants arriving in Greece was operational. Greece has accused other European countries of not taking steps to ease the burden on them, stating that it has suffered more refugee flows than it cannot handle. All registration centres established in Greece at the end of February 2016 became operational when the EU, on the other hand, threatened to remove Greece from Schengen[70]. The threat posed to Greece is not just a topic that frightens this country. The Schengen agreement, which currently provides passport-free travel in 26 European countries, is in danger by the migrant crisis. European countries have declared that they will take tight control of their external borders until the refugee crisis is resolved and will suspend the Schengen agreement until the crisis is resolved. The issue that the collapse of the Schengen project, which provides free movement at the internal borders of Europe, will not only close the countries as a border but will lead to great economic problems is the most important issue of concern of European countries. The abolition of the Schengen Union may cause the Euro, which is the common currency, to be out of circulation in the future, as it is obvious that the existence of a single currency behind the closed borders will not be of great importance for the economic development of the countries. For this reason, resolving the refugee crisis is an important challenge that will balance the economic and social balance of European countries.

The following five issues need to be addressed when assessing the migration crisis: 1) Preventing illegal immigration by registering migrants at checkpoints and applying necessary security measures; 2) Ensuring that refugees seeking asylum are equally distributed to EU countries by evaluating their applications; 3) the political crisis within European countries, which is escalating due to the refugee crisis; 4) being one of the points where the borders of Greece and Italy will be the first to be influenced in case of new refugee movement; 5) Integration of refugees who have reached European borders. Although the 2015 migration crisis seems to have been stopped by a hasty and temporary solution, effective steps have not yet to be taken for more stable and definitive solutions. The initiative of Italy to negotiate with the internationally renowned Libyan and Tunisian government and the armed groups controlling Libya's Mediterranean coast is the only concrete step taken in this regard. Italy is trying to come to an agreement with Libya and Tunisia on both sides to prevent smugglers from sending refugees to

---

– N 20. – 22 p, https://www.ceps.eu/system/files/EU%20Response%20to%20the%202015%20 Refugee%20Crisis_0.pdf , 18.11.2020
[70] https://www.sabah.com.tr/aktuel/2016/01/25/abden-yunanistana-schengen-tehdidi, 18.11.2020

European countries illegally[71]. European states seem to understand that the refugee crisis is not an external problem, because this problem is rooted in Europe's colonial period and is the result of external intervention in every region where there are conflicts. It is clear that the slightest irregularity will create a new refugee and migration crisis, unless an international initiative is provided to stabilize the countries with the highest migration flow.

### From migration crisis to integration crisis

The problem of integration is an important issue that stands before the whole migration movement, regardless of the ways in which it is done. The successful integration process has positive contributions to both immigrants and the countries they live in. Conversely, the failure of integration policy will cause problems such as the division of society and marginalization of migrants. Although the migration crisis is not completely over, the issue of integrating the refugees who reach European countries after the crisis phase into the society they live in is one of the most important problems occupying the agenda. Countries faced with this problem have started to transition from temporary refugee crisis solution to permanent integration initiatives. The integration process after basic social, accommodation, education, job opportunities and status evaluations are an issue that countries should spend long-term time for both newcomers and settled refugees. Refugees have less potential than local people in terms of language, education and expertise they can offer to the labour market as a natural flow. This puts immigrants at a disadvantage in the long term, as well as causing local people to separate and marginalize them. Without delay in reacting to the effect, the "marginalizing" approach causes the immigrants to grudge, moreover, some groups react with radical protests[72]. 80-95% of the refugees do not want to return and see their future in European countries. In this case, immigrants should not only speak their language, but also appreciate their values, adopt the social norms prevailing in the culture and the country, by being fully integrated into their society. The reality is that new and old refugees create a separate "parallel society" and live according to the norms they have determined on their own cultural basis. The result is slow progress in language learning, cultural exclusion, low social opportunities, and unemployment and poverty as a result of education. This results in an increase in the crime rate among young migrants and an increase in the rate of members of radical terrorist organizations. Such a social order causes immigrant to lose contact with the local government. Neighbourhoods outside of police control (No Go Areas) in European countries make locals quite anxious. In 2015, Holger Münch,

---

[71] Demetrios G. Papademetriou and Caitlin Katsiaficas, "Seeking Answers to Evolving Dilemmas", **Per Concordiam**, Volume 8, İssue 4, pp. 19-20
[72] Demetrios G. Papademetriou and Caitlin Katsiaficas, pp..24

the head of the German Federal Police Organization (BKA), declared that the increasing number of asylum seekers in Germany threatened the internal security and stated that "The constantly increasing number of asylum seekers makes the security situation serious". Münch reported that 100 people who entered the country with asylum seekers were suspected of terrorists, but their situation was investigated due to the lack of sufficient evidence[73]. On the other hand, there are attacks of reactionary and racist movements against refugees. In a statement Münch gave to the RBB radio, more than 850 attacks were carried out against refugee hostels in 2016. 61 cases were reported about damaging public properties, attempting to kill and wounding with racist motives[74]. Another issue that adds importance is that immigrants and local people in the European community get used to each other without pain during the integration process. In fact, the integration process has many systematic disruptions and the most important problem is the lack of a systematic mechanism that determines the only admission, resettlement and integration stages for states that are generally in a position to accommodate all refugees. It is possible to evaluate these problems in three stages: First system is refugee - immigrant discrimination. Most states treat immigrants as a temporary group. Since they will return to their countries in the near future, no integration policies are applied at the state level. Germany and Austria are among the countries that adopt this approach. The second system is the system of assimilation of immigrants. As migration is considered as a permanent phenomenon, the migrants are asked to mix with the region and society they live in as soon as possible. The problem here is not that immigrants adapt to the society they live in, but they are asked to fully integrate with this society. For this, it is expected that the conditions set forth by the state in which they take refuge and the determined order are fully complied with. This system is valid for France. Third system is "ethnic minorities" or a model of multicultural society. This system envisages the most effective integration of refugees into society. This system is effective in England, Netherlands, Belgium and Sweden. According to this system, the rights given to immigrants and refugees are recognized on an equal basis with the rights given to their native citizens, and social and political rights are granted to take part in all kinds of political and economic order of the country. However, this system, which has many expectations, was accepted by the leaders of European countries in 2010-2011 as a failure of this system within Europe[75]. As one of the countries experiencing the failure of this system, Germany announced by German Chancellor Angela Merkel at the

[73] https://www.dunya.com/dunya/039siginmacilar-guvenligimizi-tehdit-ediyor039-haberi-296427, 18.11.2020
[74] https://www.dw.com/tr/bka-m%C3%BClteci-yurtlar%C4%B1na-850nin-%C3%BCzerinde-sald%C4%B1r%C4%B1-d%C3%BCzenlendi/a-36412338, 18.11.2020
[75] M.Apanovich, " Voprosı integratsii Migrantov v Evrope", https://cyberleninka.ru/article/n/voprosy-integratsii-migrantov-v-evrope, 26.11.2020

Youth Branch congress of the Christian Democratic Union Party in October 2010 that Germany's project to become a multicultural country collapsed[76].

## Multiculturalism policy as an integration concept in immigration policy

The aim of the Multiculturalism policy is the rapid integration of all minorities into society and the possibility of cultural conflict between locals and newcomers to disappear. The most successful period of multiculturalism policy was experienced in America's 1960 period. Everyone who adopted American language and culture was deemed to have integrated into American society. Known as a country of society where every nation can freely live its culture, language and religion independent of each other, America was far from dwelling on a national and cultural value that refugees and immigrants would adopt. Anyone who accepts the values of language and democracy can be an American. These countries can therefore be called immigrants' states, unlike Europe. While Canada determined its multiculturalism policy as state policy in 1971, Australia declared it in 1973[77]. Unlike these countries, European countries see themselves as a "nation state" with cultural values and national heritage[78]. It does not have an immigrant society like America and Australia. It used immigrants and its multiculturalism policy to fill demographic gaps. It was taught that immigrants do not need to undergo cultural change because they have been seen as brain drain and being cheap labour force point and they will not stay in the country for a long time and will return to their country. In the 1980s, multiculturalism was determined as an explicit policy strategy of states. Germany supported the immigration movement as it has seemed migrants a necessary resource for cheap labour and demographic policy. However, Germany's expectation from immigrants to a society that embraced German culture disappointed it. In the light of the multiculturalism policy, a development schedule was set for immigrants to both protect their cultural values and heritage and adopt the values of the society they live in. However, without being stated in theory, it has been revealed that immigrants do not want to be integrated into the language and society of the countries they live in. As a society, while living their own language and culture in the region they live in, there was a real chart that they rejected the country's social values and did not want to learn the language. For a long time, this approach was perceived as a natural concept of rights granted to immigrants, but the increasing number of immigrants and refugees

---

[76] Merkel'in Hristiyan-Demokrat Gençlik Partisine yaptığı konuşma, http://www.bbc.co.uk/russian/international/2010/10/101016_merk el_multiculturalism_failed.shtml, 25.11.2020

[77] Agita Missani, https://www.integration.lv/ru/chto-takoje-multikulturalizm-i-sljedujet-li-jego-opasatsja, 26.11.2020

[78] M.Apanovich, https://cyberleninka.ru/article/n/voprosy-integratsii-migrantov-v-evrope, 26.11.2020

has shown that it causes major demographic and social problems for countries. Europe has been a job gateway for many refugees and multiculturalism has created a new generation immigration group for immigrants who consider their country of residence only from a livelihood perspective. For this generation that feeds terrorist organizations, Europe is only a comfortable source of life. While multiculturalism underlines the necessity of preserving the cultural values of every nation and abandoning the concept of single national cultural values, its failure in Europe does not reduce the success of multiculturalism. Multiculturalism cannot be successful in any society that evaluates the nation on the basis of its nationality. In addition, this concept, which is determined for nations to protect their cultural values, protect their national heritage and live their culture, not assimilated, does not survive in countries with acceptance initiatives for profit. While immigrants are regarded as a necessary resource to increase their voting potential in Europe, the multiculturalism policy criticism of national nationalist party groups also reinforces the failure of this work. In this case, a new integration strategy and multiculturalism policy strategy should be determined, this time more emphasis should be placed on the sociocultural change of individuals, not on a social change[79].

As it can be seen, we cannot say that any of the integration models has achieved success in European countries. It cannot be said that Spain, where liberal laws were adopted, and Germany, where refugees were divided into groups and the social status of each group was determined, has achieved this job. In America, which is determined as the country of immigrants, the reluctance of immigrants and refugees to adapt to the native language and culture is observed. It would not be wrong to determine that it mostly originates from the integration policy of the accepting country. Most countries' refugee policies are determined on temporary visas and residence permits. A very small percentage of foreign immigrants get the chance to nationalization as a result of a long effort. Thus, most of the immigrants are in the position of "temporary guests". The temporary situation of immigrants cannot create a sense of belonging to the country in which they live. They do not need this and continue to live in the "guest" concept. While the integration gap is filled with the continuation of their own cultures, there is no need to even acquire language learning skills. While it is necessary with the comfortable living standards of the country where they live, efforts are made to break the connections with their homeland. While insisting on their unwillingness to integrate with the country they live in, it is even seen that immigrants bring parts of their own culture to the countries they live in. This problem is on the rejection of the innovations that come with the foreign

---

[79] Fukuyama F. Identity and Migration, Prospect, http://www.prospectmagazine.co.uk/features/ identitymigrationmulticulturalis m-francis-fukuyama, 26.11.2020

culture and the efforts of the local cultures to make a living without being adopted by the immigrants. The coexistence of several cultures in a society is possible with an approach of respect for each other. Current developments make it necessary to review the integration processes of immigrants according to their sociological and ethnic characteristics, to deeply analyze the activities of state programs, and to manage the migration movement correctly. Immigration control should be conducted over quotas. Each country should accept immigration and refugees not exceeding their capacity and without exceeding the quotas set on them. Balancing the immigration wave by distributing the remaining numbers to countries that do not fill the quota will help manage migration and integrated policy more effectively.

## Indicators of Integration Policy

Measure values have been determined to monitor the integration process of new immigrants into society. These values are determined according to measures such as the level of immigrants 'involvement in the social life of the country, the assessment of their sense of belonging to the community, and the follow-up of the locals' acceptance of new immigrants. It constitutes the qualitative measurement of these values. There are also quantitative measures and can be listed as follows: the unemployment rate, the number of beneficiaries, the number of children who are in a successful education process and on the contrary, who are expelled from the school or not able to go on. All these values are important to follow the integration stages of immigrants and to clarify the targets to be set. In addition, these values are also necessary for the effectiveness of the decisions and practices taken, the removal of projects with low success rates, and the prevention of events that may pose a threat in the early follow-up process. In 2010, instruments for measuring the integration ratio of immigrants and refugees were determined by the European Union countries. This application is called "Migrant Integration Policy Index". Measurements are made on seven important values and each of these values contains 10 to 100 sub-measurement values[80]. The values are as follows: - Flexibility of the labour market (proportion of employees, opportunities to open their own businesses, working conditions, keeping conditions at the same capacity as locals, validity of specialized documents, certificates and diplomas obtained outside EU countries), Opportunities for family reunification (facilitating and simplifying bureaucratic procedures ); When immigrants stay in the country for more than one year, countries where the conditions for bringing their spouses are regulated are evaluated with 100 points[81]. Educational opportunities (free

[80] Migrant Integration Policy Index. Available at: www.mipex.eu, 28.11.2020
[81] Reitz J. G. Warmth of the Welcome: The Social Causes of Economic Success for Immigrants in Different Nations and Cities. Boulder, CO, Westview Press, 1998, pp. 298

education and scholarship opportunities), political participation (rights to elect and be elected for long-term resident immigrants and refugees), participation in municipal and party elections, establishment of party and non-governmental organizations, appointment to consultancy positions and granting citizenship rights to refugees (facilitating document acquisition during application processes and certain reductions in registration fees). There are 34 criteria for measuring this value. Measurements are made from the prohibition of racism to the criteria of equal conditions without discrimination on race, gender, language and religion. Up to 100 criteria can be specified for measurements. The most criteria belong to Sweden (80 criteria), Portugal and Finland and the least criteria belong the Republic of Cyprus, Slovakia and Lithuania (30 criteria). The important shortcoming of these measures, which are determined as index, is that it is not possible to measure the true value of the efficiency of the system. As the integration process cannot be realized with the efforts of the only accepting state, the efforts of refugees and immigrants from the opposite side are of great importance. Often times, this process is slowed down by their unwillingness and initiative[82].

## Conclusion

The migration and refugee problem are on the list of the most important problems occupying the world agenda. Recently, it has emerged as a result of armed conflict, civil war, ethnic and religious discrimination, hunger and poverty. States that are exposed to refugee and migration waves have to solve many problems related to settlement, health, education, job and social rights of millions of migrants. Apart from these, states should establish coordination with its neighbouring countries for border security and to stop irregular migration, and organize many diplomatic coordinated relations in order to keep the migration wave under control.

No single state can cope with the migration and refugee problem, and the migration problem is doomed to become one of the critical problems of the world without producing a solution-oriented, coordinated international system. The migration problem is not only an economic and demographic problem, it also brings many security problems with it. Therefore, migration and refugee mobility should be looked at more broadly. This problem has not developed due to a single cause. Conflicts, strategies of political interest of states have made the problems deeper, but they are not the point of origin. The reasons for the slow development of this problem that lies beyond conflicts should be investigated. Underdeveloped, economically weak states

[82] Vladimir Malakhov, " İntegratsiya Migrantov Kak Administrativnaya Problema: Opıt Evrosoyuza (Immıgrants Integration As An Administrative Problem: The Case of the European Union)", **Mirovaya Ekonomika i Mejdunarodnıye Otnosheniya**, 2015, No 1, pp.82-83

are focusing on a very sensitive order and any crisis that may develop is sufficient to disrupt the order. The irregularity that develops in these countries has a direct effect on European countries. Irregularity leads to conflicts, increasing terrorist threat and migration crisis. In the international system, the refugee crisis can be resolved with foreign intervention promoting economic development and good control of political order.

It is important that the solution process of the Syrian crisis is uncertain and a different approach to the refugee problem is developed. As the migration problem continues, the focus should be on integrating internally displaced persons in their countries and developing a system of assistance to the countries that accept refugees with them. According to research on refugees, the majority of immigrants (80-85%) do not want to return to their country and want to establish their future in the European country. In this case, they need to be integrated with the country and society they live in. It is especially important to learn the language of the country in which he/she lives and to accept the social order, rules and values of his/her society However, in reality, it is seen that refugees and migrants live in regions where another order of their own has been established. In the 1960s, Western countries opened the doors for cheap labour and a cheap and socially lacking labour market system was arranged for those coming from third world countries for job opportunities. The issue of integrating immigrants, who were regarded as temporary at first, was not the focus of attention, and the migration problem started to cause serious social and demographic problems with settling the families of the immigrants who were thought to go to the countries. Against the increasing racist approach towards immigrants, it was tried to develop a multiculturalism policy and not to assimilate societies, but to establish a social order in which different cultures respect each other and each culture would live by preserving its unique values. Although this approach is successful in America, Canada and Austria, it cannot be said that it has gained a place in Western society. While these countries were established by the migration movement, Western countries have stereotyped large and historical cultural heritage, so multiculturalism could not be a system that for these countries could easily digest. However, on the other side of the coin, another important problem that has not been reflected in the world public opinion much for now and has been overshadowed by the agenda issues is the rapid shrinkage of European countries in terms of demographics. Immigrants are the biggest resource that will fill Europe's demographic gap, so it is inevitable that Europe will become a refugee and immigration country in the near future. States cannot expect all immigrants to unite and assimilate into local society. For immigrants to be a part of society, they must learn to recognize that they are different and to live with their cultural distinctions. The main problem area is determined in this regard, as neither the political elite nor the civil society in European countries are yet ready to accept it. If we look at the parties that won the election victories in European countries, it is seen that the national-nationalist right parties gained more popularity. While these parties are famous for their refugee and anti-immigration policy, they endeavour to develop a policy on the interests of the national and local people. It is not surprising why the parties gathered more and more votes. The desire to protect the rights of the local people and the security uneasiness cause their votes to be favoured by more national and nationalist parties. The fact that the locals vote for these parties can be considered as an outbreak of protest against the waves of terrorism, immigration and refugee flow due to the developing Islamic movement in their country. The immigration and refugee problem caused Britain to leave the EU organization. It has been one of the leading states in the protection of refugee rights and the development of multiculturalism policy among European countries. It tried to take measures in the legislative order to prevent the development of racism over religion, language and culture discrimination. However, this policy of the country caused the local people to face terrorism and security threats caused by the migration wave.

European countries are applying various measures to reduce these threats and integrate migrants. Organization of informatics programs necessary for communication plays an important role in the successful development of immigration and integration policy. The Netherlands and Sweden are exemplary states in this regard. Considering the important role of the language issue in the integration policy, it has established information systems where immigrants can primarily apply not only to schools and classes for language learning, but also to learn languages in any environment they are in. Learning methods transferred to audio sources are adjusted according to the characteristics of each national language. This method, which increases the language learning skills of immigrants under all conditions, enables them to quickly master foreign languages and to adapt to the local society by improving their communication skills. Civil organizations provide free location services to immigrants and refugees in need through housing search engines such as Airbnb. Another building block of the integration policy is the involvement of refugees in the labour market. This issue is one of the important issues brought to the fore by the integration policies of EU countries. In this way, different vocational training courses are opened in many directions, and free education opportunities are provided to refugees. However, many of these efforts are disappointed by the low education level of most refugees and their unwillingness to improve their language skills. Although the countries that accept migration and refugees have different integration policies, their general approaches are the same. Most of the programs provide language skills development, "emergency" hotlines (call centres) which are generally available 24 hours a day and in several languages. The immigration handbook is available in many country applications. It consists of brochures explaining the country where refugees and immigrants are located and its rule. As it can be seen, there are efforts of European countries for integration policies, but it is not possible to talk about the formation of a mechanism where each system and structures fulfil a regular operation and job description.

While many countries distribute their tasks for their integration policy, they do it through local structures rather than a central system. Integration policy is carried out not at a state level but through local organizations. The success rate of the projects carried out with the efforts of institutions such as National Education, Immigration Administrations, Ministries of Labour and Social Services decreases due to their secondary functionality. The duties assigned to the Ministries in this direction are not in the main job position but in the secondary task process. Therefore, the level of effectiveness is balanced with the rate of attempt. Although these issues are important for the balanced and controlled implementation of the integration policy, they are not the only success factor. As the process of getting used to the new state society of refugees and immigrants is not a one-sided development process. The wishes of the refugees in this direction and their intention to keep up with the state society they are in are also important. In many cases, this process is caused by the refugees' attitude towards the accepting society and their inability to integrate. Although the integration policy is reflected as a state policy, it is an important process that starts with the acceptance of refugees by the local people. State policy can only be a criterion for the success of the measures to be taken to accelerate this process. In order for the refugees to be integrated, not only them but also the locals need to be ready for this. In this direction, a wide public opinion can be generated. The benefits of integrating immigrants into the local society can be disseminated and presented to the society with a wide knowledge base. The awareness that society is not built on a single order and a single culture can be spread. It can be instilled with other nations close to it that it is livable without damaging its own values. Local media and radio broadcasts may have a wide repercussion on this issue. Art and works of other cultures, other than local music, art and publications, can create a positive atmosphere in this regard. Testing many methods with a wide range of variations from sports to arts are tools that will increase the success rate of the integration policy. These attempts are important for building a bridge of trust between locals and newcomers.

# CHAPTER 12

## IDENTITY CONSTRUCTIONS OF SYRIANS IN THEIR NARRATIVES

### Güneş Koç[*]

### Introduction

In this chapter, I will discuss the role of the narratives of refugees and migrants in constructing their identity and subjectivity. My methodology involves discussing the role of the narrative which allows construction of the migrant's identity in the limbo and on the threshold. The interviewer's role will be discussed in terms of how it affects the telling of the story and in making migrants' voices heard in the country where they arrived. This work seeks to discuss the role of the narrative of refugees and migrants as discourse practices which depicts a discursive place for the construction of the identity in the limbo and on the threshold. The refugees' narratives provide an opportunity to discuss the identity construction of refugees in the foreignness and within the strangeness. According to Hannah Arendt, narratives of the stateless people serves as a tool to construct a worldliness, to be seen and to be heard.[1]

In the gaze of the other, narratives help construct the identity of refugees and migrants in the hosting countries by telling their stories and their reasons for escape and talking about racism, gender relations, family structure, and working conditions. Language is an integral part of hospitality.[2] Language is the door to the hosting state and the threshold which Derrida calls the *"first violence"*, because hospitality is often requested in a language that guests do not understand and this has to be called as symbolic violence.[3] *"Pure hospitality"* implies welcoming the unknown and the unnamed.[4]

Violence against the stranger emerges in the moment of asking the name of the other. The narrative contains a talk about the self in one's own language or in the language of other; this talk reflects the self in terms of deconstructing of the standpoint of self and of other. The narratives make

---

[*] Assist. Prof. Dr. Güneş Koç, Department of International Relations, Istanbul Arel University, Turkey. E-mail: kocgunes@gmail.com
[1] Arendt Hannah, **The human condition, London,** The University of Chicago Press, 1998.
[2] Derrida, Jacque, Hostipitality, **Angelaki Journal Of The Theoretical Humanities,** Vol.5, No. 3, 2000a, pp. 3-18.
[3] Kevin D. O'Gorman, Jacques Derrida's philosophy of hospitality, **Hospitality Review 50,** 2006, p. 54.
[4] Derrida, Jacque, Différance, **Identity: A reader,** 2000b, pp. 87–93.

the self familiar.[5] to the/in the gaze of the other. Telling the story makes it known for the gaze of other and offers a representation throughout the storytelling. The narratives within the camps of refugees and stateless people, the narratives of the migrants in the mass media give a voice to situate their standpoint on the threshold and to make them heard and seen. The migrants in the camps are unseen for the rest of the society so they are unseen and unheard. In terms of Arendt's perception of worldliness, they become worldly in the moment in which they talk about their self, their standpoint, and their gaze. In the narratives and in the stories, they construct their identity. The urban districts with a dense population of migrants are places with a lot of violence against migrants. The news about the hate crimes, racist attacks, and hate murders against migrants and mainly against Syrian migrants show that the prejudices against migrants make the hatred causing violence.

Narratives of migrants and refugees make them seen and recognized in the gaze of the other, and also make their voices heard. The interviewer provides space for the refugees and migrants to be heard and seen. Under the interviewer's gaze, the interviewee tells his/her story and makes him/herself heard and seen for the gaze of the other. In this paper, I will discuss the theoretical background of the researcher's hermeneutical position in interpreting the narratives in terms of self-technologies or strategies of constructing subjectivities in the limbo and on the threshold. Derrida (2000)[6] describes "threshold" as a category of hospitality between hospitality and hostility. This is reflected in the migrants' narratives and understood as their self-technologies to construct their subjectivity in the state of hospitality related to laws, racism, xenophobia, structural and symbolic violence, and precarious living conditions.

### The role of language within the narrative and the paradigms of narrative studies

Narratives are discourse practices in which language plays a central role within the *"formation, establishment, and negotiation of personal and group identity"*[7]. In the narrative, language is articulated into discursive practices. From a post-structuralist and social constructivist standpoint, the notion of identity is informed by the *"irreducible link between the constitution of subjectivity itself and*

[5] Cavarero, Adriana, Relating Narratives: Storytelling and Selfhood, New York, Routledge, 2000, p.33, as cited in Maria, Tamboukou, Narrative Phenomena: Entanglements and Intra-actions in Narrative Research, London, Sage, 2015, p. 43.
[6] Jacques Derrida, Hostipitality, **Journal of the theoretical humanities**, Vol. 5, No. 3, 2000a, pp. 50-57.
[7] De Fina, Anna, "Orientation in immigrant narratives: the role of ethnicity in the identification of characters", **Discourse Studies**, Vol. 2, No. 2, 2000, p. 133.

*language"*[8]. Derrida (2000b)[9], approaching the subject from a post-structuralist perspective, describes it as an inscription in and function of language.

There are different discussions about and paradigms of narrative studies. According to De Fina (2003)[10], narrative studies view identity as a social construction. De Fina distinguishes two main paradigms in that body of literature: *"the tradition centreed on autobiography and based on psychological theories of identity"* and *"the conversation analytic and ethno methodological tradition"*[11]. This study will also reference social psychology[12], discourse analysis[13] , and narrative theory and analysis[14]. Narrative (e.g. autobiographical) data, comprehensively categorized by Chase (2005)[15], has certain distinguishing features that guide narrative inquiry. Important analytical focal points include the narrative whole and its immanence in the particular elements of the story, as well as attention to how, for whom, and for what purpose stories are assembled.[16] Discourse analysis focuses on the performative function of discourse[17] and integrates language and social interaction. Both structural narrative analysis (NA) and discourse analysis (DA) focus on storytelling and allow for an in-depth examination of individual cases, as well as for an interpretation of the reader's position and of the story's meaning at a micro level.[18]

There are three traditional variations of discourse analysis. In Foucault's (1981)[19] sociological perspective, discourse appears as an ideological style, a

---

[8] De Fina, Anna, "Orientation in immigrant narratives: the role of ethnicity in the identification of characters", **Discourse Studies,** Vol. 2, No. 2, 2000, p. 15.

[9] Derrida, Jacque, Différance, **Identity: A reader,** 2000b, p. 91.

[10] De Fina, Anna, **Identity in Narrative. A study in immigrant discourse,** Amsterdam/Philadelphia, John Benjamins Publishing Company, 2003, p. 16).

[11] De Fina, Anna, **Identity in Narrative. A study in immigrant discourse,** Amsterdam/Philadelphia, John Benjamins Publishing Company, 2003, p. 16.

[12] Edwards, Derek, Potter, Jonathan, Inquiries in social construction. **Discursive Psychology,** London, Sage, 1992.

[13] Potter, Jonathan, Margaret, Wetherell, "Discourse analysis", **Rethinking methods in psychology,** 1995, pp. 80-93; Wood, Linda A., Kroger, Rolf, O., **Doing discourse analysis: Methods for studying action in talk and text,** 2000.

[14] Gee, James Paul, "A linguistic approach to narrative", **Journal Of Narrative And Life History,** Vol. 1, No. 1, 1991, pp. 15-39; Gubrium, Jaber F., Holstein, James A., **Analyzing narrative reality,** 2009; Labov, William, Waletzky, Joshua, "Narrative analysis: Oral versions of personal experience", **Journal of Narrative and Life History,** Vol. 7, No. 1, 1997, pp. 1-38; Riessman, Catherine, Kohler, **Narrative methods for the human sciences,** 2008.

[15] Chase, Susan, E., "Narrative inquiry: Multiple lenses, approaches, voices", **The Sage handbook of qualitative research,** Denzin Norman K., Linkoln Yvonna S. (Eds.), London, New Delhi, Sage, 2005, pp. 651-680.

[16] Catherine Kohler, Riessman, **Narrative Methods for the Human Sciences,** CA, USA, Sage, 2008.

[17] Potter, Jonathan, Margaret, Wetherell, "Discourse analysis", **Rethinking methods in psychology,** 1995, pp. 80-93.

[18] Carole Peterson, Allyssa Mccabe, Extending Labov and Waletzky, **Journal of Narrative and Life History,** Vol. 7, No. 1-4, 1997, pp. 251-258; Catherine Kohler, Riessman, **Narrative methods for the human sciences,** CA, USA, Sage, 2008.

[19] Foucault, Michel, The order of discourse, **Untying the text: a post-structural anthology,** 1981, pp. 48- 78.

way of speaking. T.A. van Dijk (1989)[20] conceives of discourse as the structuring principle of all communication. Finally, for Bourdieu (1991)[21], discourse is a medium in which power and language operate.

The researcher's hermeneutical perspective outlines identity as the situated outcome of a rhetorical and interpretative process bearing upon the narrative. Both the storyteller and the audience (in this case including the interviewer) make *"situationally motivated selections from socially constituted repertoires of identification and affiliation resources and craft these semiotic resources into identity claims for presentation to others"*[22]. Narrative research is not about linear temporalities; *"but rather about time contractions and rhizomatic formations, stories that contract the past that have made them what they are, starting from the middle, going back and forth, making connections with other stories of other times and other places"*[23]. The chronotope, as conceptualized by Bakhtin (1981)[24], designates the spatio-temporal matrix that underlines all narratives and other linguistic acts. The term itself can be literally translated as "time-space"[25].

The interviews with refugees and stateless people reflect parts of the participants' group identity. These narratives are expressions of identity shaped through social and discursive practices. Fairclough (1989)[26] describes narration as a social discursive practice that reflects social relations and subject positions shaped in other practices and discourses. Telling is a shared linguistic, rhetorical and interactional narrative resource, through which the storyteller reveals their subject positions and how they construct their identity. The specific narrative resources available to a group allows it to articulate, in terms of nationality, gender, or ethnicity, a distinct collective identity that sets it apart from other groups.[27] Discursive practices circumscribe social relationships and sociocultural constructs.[28] Discourses are *"socially marked"*[29] and have the capacity to mirror and modify contexts.[30]

---

[20] Teun A., Van Dijk, Structures of Discourse, **Structures of Power.Communication Yearbook**, Vol. 12, 1989, pp. 18-59.

[21] Bourdieu, Pierre, **Language and symbolic power**, Cambridge, Polity, 1991.

[22] Anna, Defina, **Identity in Narrative. A Study of Immigrant Discourse**, Georgetown, John Benjamins Publishing Company, 2003, p. 18.

[23] Maria, Tamboukou, Becomings: Narrative Entanglements and Microsociology, **FQS. Forum: Qualitative Social Research. Sozialforschung,** Vol. 16, No 1, 2015 p. 44.

[24] Bakhtin, Mikhail, **The dialogic imagination**, Austin, University of Texas Press, 1981.

[25] Morris, Pam, The Bakhtin reader. Selected writings of Bakhtin, Medvedev and Voloshinov, 1994, pp. 180-187.

[26] Fairclough, Norman, **Language and power**, 1989.

[27] Anna, Defina, **Identity in Narrative. A Study of Immigrant Discourse**, Georgetown, John Benjamins Publishing Company, 2003, p. 19.

[28] Foucault, Michel, The order of discourse, **Untying the text: a post-structural anthology**, 1981, pp. 48- 78.

[29] Bourdieu, 1982, p. 16, as cited in De Fina, Anna, "Orientation in immigrant narratives: the role of ethnicity in the identification of characters", **Discourse Studies**, Vol. 2, No. 2, 2000, p. 133.

[30] De Fina, Anna, "Orientation in immigrant narratives: the role of ethnicity in the identification of characters", **Discourse Studies**, Vol. 2, No. 2, 2000, p. 133.

## Stories in Narratives

De Fina (2003)[31], describes the story as a particular kind of narrative that relates past events in a manner constrained by social rules, and that conveys a specific message about (or interpretation of) those events and/or the characters involved in them. Within narratives, stories reflect the macro context.[32] They reveal the position of the storyteller in the way in which they reflect aspects of other people's identities.[33]

The memory revealed by stories should not be understood simply in a psychological, individual sense. Dias (2019)[34] describes Pêcheux's (1999) notion of memory as *"a structuration of complex discursive materiality, understood in a dialectic of repetition and regularization"[35]*. Such a discursive understanding of memory comprises many other dimensions besides individual recollection: mythic memory, memory inscribed in social practices, and the constructed memory of the narrator proper.[36]

Paul Ricoeur's account of narrative emphasizes the relation between narrative and time, and the way in which this relation shapes human experience.[37]

There is a vigorous debate on how to define and examine a narrative.[38] Frank (1998)[39] and Polkinhore (1988)[40] draw attention to the fact that the narrative told in an interview structures personal stories in a particular way in view of the relational context of the narrative act and emphasize the importance of paying attention to this structure. Stories are to be interpreted with reference to larger socio-cultural dynamics and discourses.[41] In the

---

[31] De Fina, Anna, "Orientation in immigrant narratives: the role of ethnicity in the identification of characters", **Discourse Studies,** Vol. 2, No. 2, 2000, p. 13-14.

[32] De Fina, Anna, "Orientation in immigrant narratives: the role of ethnicity in the identification of characters", **Discourse Studies,** Vol. 2, No. 2, 2000, p. 133.

[33] Davies and Harré, 1990, as cited in De Fina, Anna, "Orientation in immigrant narratives: the role of ethnicity in the identification of characters", **Discourse Studies,** Vol. 2, No. 2, 2000, p. 134.

[34] Ricardo Henrique Almeida, Dias, Samsara documentary: narrative and discourse analysis and a possible interpretation, **CINEJ Cinema Journal,** Vol. 7, No. 2, 2019, p. 134.

[35] Ricardo Henrique Almeida, Dias, Samsara documentary: narrative and discourse analysis and a possible interpretation, **CINEJ Cinema Journal,** Vol. 7, No. 2, 2019, p. 134.

[36] Pêcheux, 1999, as cited in Ricardo Henrique Almeida, Dias, Samsara documentary: narrative and discourse analysis and a possible interpretation, **CINEJ Cinema Journal,** Vol. 7, No. 2, 2019, p. 134.

[37] Ricoeur, 1997, as cited in Ricardo Henrique Almeida, Dias, Samsara documentary: narrative and discourse analysis and a possible interpretation, **CINEJ Cinema Journal,** Vol. 7, No. 2, 2019, p. 134.

[38] Chase, Susan, E., "Narrative inquiry: Multiple lenses, approaches, voices", **The Sage handbook of qualitative research,** Denzin Norman K., Linkoln Yvonna S. (Eds.), London, New Delhi, Sage, 2005, pp. 651-680; Catherine K., Riessman, **Illness Narratives: Positioned Identities,** Wales, U.K., Health Communication Research Center, 2002.

[39] Frank, Arthur, W., "Just listening: Narrative and deep illness", **Families, Systems, & Health,** Vol. 16, No 3, 1998, pp. 197–212.

[40] Polkinghorne, Donald, E., Narrative knowing and the human sciences, 1988.

[41] Frank, Arthur, W., "Just listening: Narrative and deep illness", **Families, Systems, & Health,** Vol. 16, No 3, 1998, pp. 197–212.

context of the interviews with refugees and stateless people, themes and storytelling strategies articulate and distinguish, often in terms of ethnicity, the collocutors' group and gender identity in the host country. As this dimension comes to the fore in the narratives, stories are told that reveal collocutors' subject positions in the symbolic and direct violence that they encounter as *"others"* in the host country and the structural violence to which they are exposed by virtue of class and ethnicity. These stories also relate the precariousness of a life constrained by the legal and social status accorded to Syrian refugees in Turkey, articulating this existence in the limbo and on the threshold in relation to nationhood, experiences of war and loss, xenophobia, structural and symbolic violence, precarious living conditions, and imaginings of the future. Schiffrin's (1996; 2000)[42] work on stories told by Jewish women and O'Connor's (1994)[43] account of prisoner narratives reflect the dimension of the narratives.

Polanyi (1985)[44] proposes a "cultural reading" and argues that the way in which a story evaluates characters and events reflects the cultural and societal milieu in which the story is told. Ochs and Lisa (2001)[45] also emphasize the cultural dimension, focusing on the socially accepted conventions and stereotypical representations that pervade the way in which the storyteller articulates the events in a story. Linde (1993)[46] concentrates on how stories are a means for reflection on individual life stories and on the beliefs held by members of various social groups. Narratives reflect communal identities and negotiate and express membership in these communities. The narrators evaluate themselves and other members of the group with reference to moral values and social norms, either upholding or rejecting them. These representations of self and others built into the process of storytelling are dynamic rather than static constructs. The narrators reflect on mainstream social characterizations, discuss them, approve or oppose them, thus negotiating their own ways of looking at themselves and others.[47] A common representation of self and others becomes possible at the confluence of group identity and of a shared representational space.

Narratives are discursive practices that *evaluate* actions and identities and

---

[42] Schiffrin, Deborah, Narrative as self-portrait: Sociolinguistic constructions of identity, **Language In Society**, Vol. 25, No. 2, 1996, pp. 167–203; Schiffrin, Deborah, "Mother/daughter discourse in a Holocaust oral history: 'Because then you admit that you're guilty'", **Narrative Inquiry 2000**, Vol. 10, No. 1, pp. 1-44.

[43] O'Connor, Patricia, E., "'You Could Feel It through the Skin': Agency and Positioning in Prisoners' Stabbing Stories", **Text**, Vol. 14, No. 1, 1994, pp. 45-75.

[44] Polanyi, Livia, Telling the American story: A structural and cultural analysis of conversational storytelling, 1985.

[45] Ellinor, Ochs, Lisa, Capps, **Living Narrative, Discourse analysis, Narrative**, United States of America, Harvard University Press, 2001.

[46] Linde, Charlotte, Life Stories: The Creation of Coherence, 1993.

[47] Anna, Defina, **Identity in Narrative. A Study of Immigrant Discourse**, Georgetown, John Benjamins Publishing Company, 2003, p. 140.

contribute to their reproduction or change. In narratives, categories such as race[48], gender (Kiesling, 2001)[49], and ethnicity (De Fina, 2000)[50] are constructed as individual or group identities and are used as the basis for assigning group membership. Stories involve discursive practices through which identities are constituted and negotiated. This negotiation articulates community membership and projects, while representing and re-elaborating social roles and relationships.

The common uses of narrative resources by the collocutors point to shared ways of telling and of constructing personal experience. Intertextuality[51] is a useful concept to explore how the stories in the interviews connect not only to other narratives of migration, but also to other discourses, such as the dominant images of immigrants that are disseminated by the media and other institutions. The collocutors' stories are often designed to counter such negative images. As they rework their own negative experiences and position themselves against exclusionary or demeaning social practices and discourses, they rearticulate their identities as migrants, refugees or stateless people, in a sense, taking ownership of the aforementioned extraneous structures and appropriating them. The stories flesh out a shared field of experience and of constitutive practices, forging a link between local expressions and group representations of identity.

**The Positioning of the Interviewer and of the Storyteller within the Narratives**

Analyzing the interviews allows the adaption of the notion of positioning to the examination of storytelling.[52] Positioning takes place at three levels:

1. The positioning of the characters with respect to each other in the reported events.

2. The positioning of the speaker with respect to the audience.

3. The positioning him/herself with respect to the flux of questions.

The listener/interviewer is located between the teller and the listener in

[48] Bucholtz, Mary, Kira, Hall, Gender articulated: Language and the socially constructed self, New York, Routledge, 1999.

[49] Kiesling, Scott, F., "Hegemonic identity-making in narrative", **Discourse and Identity**, 2001.

[50] De Fina, Anna, "Orientation in immigrant narratives: the role of ethnicity in the identification of characters", **Discourse Studies**, Vol. 2, No. 2, 2000.

[51] Kristeva, Julia, Desire in language: a semiotic approach to literature and art, 1980; Bakhtin, Mikhail, Speech genres and other late essays, Austin, University of Texas Press, 1986;

[52] Bamberg, Michael, "Emotion talk(s): The role of perspective in the construction of emotions", **The Language of Emotions**, Niemeier, Susanne, Dirven Rene (Ed.), Duisburg, Gerhard Mercator University, 1996a, pp. 209-225; Bamberg, Michael, "Perspective and agency in the construal of narrative events", **Proceedings of the 20th annual Boston conference on language development**, Vol. I, 1996b, pp. 30-39; Bamberg, Michael, "Language. concepts, and emotions. The role of language in the construction of emotions", **Language Sciences**, 19(4), 1997, pp. 309-340.

the dialogic process.[53] Meaning is constructed inter-subjectively. From this perspective, meaning in storytelling is in constant flux, never fully complete or determined.[54] Consequently, the researcher must consider the narrator's interpretation of the context of interaction with the reader.[55]

### Women's Narratives as a Political Standpoint

The feminist researcher Cavarero (2000)[56] sees narration as a discursive register that does not focus on the traditional philosophical question of what man is, asking instead who they are in their unrepeatable uniqueness. Narrative research is very much driven by an interest in singularities, differences, and the relationship between the two. Cavarero's statement about narrative relations opens up political spaces *"wherein storied selves are being exposed, transformed, ultimately deterritorialized"*[57]. With reference to feminist literature, I will make use of theoretical concepts developed by Spinoza, Foucault, and Deleuze. In *Difference and Repetition*, Deleuze (1994)[58] emphasizes the singularity of the unique existent and writes about the struggle of the unrepeatable to *"break away with the tyranny of representation"*[59]. According to Arendt (1968)[60], narrative is a political concept whose modes par excellence *"in which human beings appear to each other"*[61] are speech and action. The worldlessness[62] of refugees, migrants in limbo, as the constitutive moment of their subjecthood, is articulated in a unique way within each narrative, with reference to group identities that affect this act of constitution through *"technologies of the female self"*[63].

Women tell stories in other ways than men, as their stories reflect their differential access to power in the real social world.[64]The migrant and refugee women' stories of emancipation from patriarchal structures within the family, of resistance against racism, and of their fight against gender-based violence

---

[53] Clark, Jack, A., & Mishler, Elliot, G., "Attending to patients' stories: Reframing the clinical task", Sociology Of Health And Illness, Vol. 14, No 3, 1992, pp. 344-370.
[54] Bakhtin, Mikhail, **The dialogic imagination**, Austin, University of Texas Press, 1981.
[55] Sutherland, Olga, Breen, Andrea V., Lewis, Stephen P., Discursive narrative analysis: A study of online autobiographical accounts of self-injury, **The Qualitative Report**, Vol. 18, No. 95, 2013, pp. 1-17.
[56] Cavarero, Adriana, **Relating Narratives: Storytelling and Selfhood**, New York, Routledge, 2000, p.33.
[57] Maria, Tamboukou, Narrative Phenomena: Entanglements and Intra-actions in Narrative Research, London, Sage, 2015, p. 42.
[58] Deleuze, Gilles, **Difference and Repetition**, New York, Columbia Univ. Press, 1994.
[59] Maria, Tamboukou, Narrative Phenomena: Entanglements and Intra-actions in Narrative Research, London, Sage, 2015, p. 43.
[60] Arendt, Hannah, The origins of totalitarianism, New York, Harcourt, 1968.
[61] Arendt, Hannah, **The human condition**, London, The University of Chicago Press, 1998, p. 177.
[62] Arendt, Hannah, The origins of totalitarianism, New York, Harcourt, 1968.
[63] Tamboukou, Maria, Writing feminist genealogies, **Journal of Gender Studies**, Vol. 12, No. 1, 2003.
[64] Tannen, Deborah, **Gender and conversational interaction**, 1993, p. 67, 68.

can be seen as statements of *"the world-creating power of discourse"*[65].

Acting as the author/teller of its own story, the self *"transgresses power boundaries and limitations following lines of flight in its constitution as a political subject"*[66]. The political dimension of narrative research is the researcher's emancipatory task of giving voice to the research participants. Narrative research constitutes a nomadic self which, according to Arendt and Cavarero, traces the constitution of the narratable self.[67] The narratable self is thus constituted within collectivities and out of culturally marked differences. It is therefore discursive, provisional, inter-sectional, and unfixed. It is a nomadic becoming.[68] In Cavarero's articulation of the narratable self, the auto/biographical exercise of memory renders the self-narratable and therefore familiar.[69] The absolute stranger, the other, become familiar through these stories, even as the anonymity of each particular storyteller is protected. For the storyteller, the narrative process involves imagining an anonymous *"host"* listener that is making sense of the narrative. In a sense, the story is told under the gaze of the listener, to whom the storyteller is making herself familiar. This double role of the stories told during the interviews – of becoming familiar with the host country and of making oneself familiar to the host listeners – is crucial to collocutors. The stories become a means of overcoming their appearance as strangers in the gaze of the host.

The notion of *feminist imaginary*[70] suggests a construction of self and identity that is embedded within a narrative containing *"the 'truths' and fictions of the mind, memory, and imagination of embodied human beings"*[71]. It "creates conditions of possibility for the actual and the virtual to be brought together in the understanding of how *realities* – be they social or personal, past or present – are being constructed"[72].With reference to Deleuze and Guattari's (1987)[73] concept of nomadism, identity is a nomadic construction. In the collocutors' narratives, their identities reveal many dimensions of their

---

[65] Tannen, Deborah, Gender and conversational interaction, 1993, p. 76.

[66] Maria, Tamboukou, Narrative Phenomena: Entanglements and Intra-actions in Narrative Research, London, Sage, 2015, p. 43.

[67] Maria, Tamboukou, Narrative Phenomena: Entanglements and Intra-actions in Narrative Research, London, Sage, 2015, p. 43.

[68] Maria, Tamboukou, Narrative Phenomena: Entanglements and Intra-actions in Narrative Research, London, Sage, 2015, p. 43.

[69]Cavarero, 2000, p. 33, as cited in Maria, Tamboukou, **Narrative Phenomena: Entanglements and Intra-actions in Narrative Research**, London, Sage, 2015, p. 43.

[70] Maria, Tamboukou, Power, desire and emotions in education: revisiting the epistolary narratives of three women in apartheid South Africa. **Gender And Education**, Vol. 18, No. 3, 2006, pp. 231-250.

[71] Maria, Tamboukou, Narrative Phenomena: Entanglements and Intra-actions in Narrative Research, London, Sage, 2015, p. 44.

[72] Maria, Tamboukou, Narrative Phenomena: Entanglements and Intra-actions in Narrative Research, London, Sage, 2015, p. 44.

[73] Deleuze, Gilles, Guattari, Felix, **A Thousand Plateaus**, London, Minnesota Press, 1987.

nomadic being as they go through disruptions due to war in their home country and migration, as they experience a transition in their *"female"* and *"male"* identity in a context that provides some avenues for emancipation from patriarchal bounds, as they rearticulate their sense of self in resistance to the racist discourses to which they are exposed, and as they develop strategies of self-empowerment in opposition to racist hate speech.

## Examples of narratives with Syrian migrants living in Turkey

I will focus on two surveys with narratives of Syrian migrants living in Turkey. The first survey includes narratives of 20 Syrian migrants living in Esenyurt, the district with the highest number of Syrian migrants in Istanbul. The second survey includes 55 Syrian adolescents between 12 and 20 years old living in Mersin.

The survey conducted by Sarıoğlu (2019)[74], *"Media Analysis of Syrians in Esenyurt"* presents an analysis of narratives with 20 Syrian migrants living in Esenyurt. Istanbul hosts the highest number of Syrians (510,341)[75] but has a lower density of Syrians than ten other cities. According to the migration centre's data in 2016, the six districts on the European side of Istanbul (Küçükçekmece, Bağcılar, Fatih, Sultangazi, Esenyurt and Esenler) have the highest number of Syrian migrants; on the Anatolian side, the Ümraniye district has the highest number of Syrian migrants. Esenyurt has 58,342 Syrian migrants.[76] The survey had the following questions: 1) How was the time you have spent in Turkey? 2) How are your living conditions here? 3) What are the problems you experienced in Turkey? 4) Are you satisfied with your working conditions? 5) Do you meet your relatives in Syria? 6) How are your relations with people living in our country? 7) Do you think of returning to Syria? 8) What do you expect from future?

Seventeen narratives of the interviewees have been selected and discussed considering different dimensions of the stories they told. The gender of the interviewees is not mentioned. Three of the interviewees are teenagers.

## The narratives of the interviewees[77]

**Participant 1** – "We saw a lot of things, we suffered from bombs, our house is destroyed". We were living in Aleppo, in Syria. When we were at school, bombs were thrown on us, my leg was injured. We saw a lot of things.

---

[74] Sarıoğlu, Gülsün, "İstanbul Esenyurt'taki Suriyelilere İlişkin Medya Analizi", (Media analysis of Syrians in Esenyurt, Istanbul), **Uluslararası Yönetim Akademisi Dergisi**, Vol. 2, No. 1, 2019, pp. 201-204.
75 https://multeciler.org.tr/turkiyedeki-suriyeli-sayisi/ (Access 28.10.2020)
76 https://www.haber3.com/guncel/ilce-ilce-iste-istanbuldaki-suriyeli-siginmaci-sayisi-haberi-5084943 (Access 28.10.2020)
[77] Sarıoğlu, Gülsün, "İstanbul Esenyurt'taki Suriyelilere İlişkin Medya Analizi", (Media analysis of Syrians in Esenyurt, Istanbul), Uluslararası Yönetim Akademisi Dergisi, Vol. 2, No. 1, 2019, pp. 201-204.

Our house was destroyed, we had a kiosk and it was destroyed. There were a lot of people among my friends. We illegally arrived here in 2013. We walked in water for four kilometers. As we arrived here, everything was very bad. Then we saw a nice world. We were together. When I arrived, I was eight years old, now I'm twelve years old. As I came here, I learned Turkish. I have started working. I'm working in an auto repair shop from 8:30 until 1:00 o'clock. I like everything in Turkey. I like all the nations, the whole world."

**Participant 2** – "We were living in Aleppo. We didn't have any problems and then war happened. We never thought about leaving Syria. Then we were stuck within the war, they threw bombs on us. Our relatives died; our house is destroyed. Syrian soldiers came and they have very badly threatened us and we were supposed to leave Syria. We still have relatives there. We want to work, spend money, and want to return to Syria. We want to take our relatives, friends, and families to Turkey."

**Participant 3** – "We came in winter, there was snow and rain. It was very difficult. My older daughter was sick. We took her to the doctor. They told us because we don't have an identity card, that they can't treat her. They wanted to send us back. Our daughter was near death. Our arrival was very difficult. The children became sick, we became sick."

The central themes of the collocutors are losses, war, destruction of the home, and the difficulties when arriving in Turkey. The arrival in Turkey is difficult because of complications from poverty and lack of the belonging to a nationality (lost identity). At the same time, Turkey is recognized as a safe place which seems to have a possibility for establishing a new life. Despite the difficulties of living in Turkey, some want to bring relatives to Turkey because they perceive Turkey as a safe place. These narratives reveal the precariousness at many levels such as poverty, lack of identity (national belongingness, lack of passport, and so on).

The participants living within the informal sector shared their views on the living conditions in Turkey. Some interviewees said that the working conditions in Turkey are bad and they do not have the chance to survive while some others were satisfied.

**Participant 4** – "We run behind our bread. I'm 30 years old. I'm working in the textile workshop as 'ortacı' (doing any kind of low-profile work). I earn 600 TL monthly. I wasn't working in Syria. It's difficult to live in Turkey. The rents are expensive, the owner of the house always threatens us and increases the rent. I can't send my children to school, I have four children and they help us by working. Here there is no work, no school."

**Participant 5** – "I feel that I'm free by working. I wasn't working in Syria. The living conditions in Turkey are difficult. I started to search for work on the second day when I arrived here. I very easily found a job. First I worked at the patisserie. Then I worked as tea man. We were not needing anybody. My wife found also a job. We just had troubles like paying the bill, rent, and the school fees for the children. Now I have to think of all that. I have to work more to make it possible for my children to have better living conditions. I can stay on my feet and I feel free by working. I'm very happy that it was possible that my children could go to the school. We even bought a car. Everything turned to the good. I'm happy to live in Turkey and I want to return to Syria."

**Participant 6** – "We even couldn't pass by the rubbish, now we collect our bread from the rubbish. We were living in Sham and our job was very hard. We run to survive, we do whatever we can do. I'm the only one who works, I collect cardboard cartons. We are six people including three children, my mother, and my wife. In Sham, we even didn't pass by the rubbish but now we collect our bread from the rubbish. It is very hard for us but I hang my head down and cry. I want to have a good job; my children shouldn't be so needy. Our children should have the chance to go to school, shouldn't remain illiterate. Should learn language, everything, become wise, and their life should be good."

These narratives mention the poverty and the hope for progress but at the same time they have at their centre the struggle to advance because of the difficulty of finding a job, living in very hard conditions "such as collecting bread from the rubbish". The second participant feels free by work and has the feeling of providing a possibility for the family to survive and to integrate into society. Participant 4 also emphasizes the difficulty of sending children to school, of providing better living conditions for the children and the pressure when their apartment's owner increases the rent. The narratives of Participant 4 and Participant 6 note the difficulties of settling down because of the difficult living conditions in Turkey.

The children who participated in the interviews said that they had the chance in Syria to go to school but because of money issues in Turkey they have difficulty in going to school.

**Participant 7** – "I wanted to go to the school but I couldn't. I've been living here for three years. We came here as the war started. I want to go to school but I can't because there is war and we don't have money. For that we have to work. We stayed in Syria within the war for one year under the bombs. We came here because of that. No one else is able to work. I'm the only one who works and I can't go to school."

**Participant 8** – "I'm 12 years old, I'm coming from Aleppo. Here, I'm selling tissue. People treat me good but not all of them. In my country, I was going to school and I want to go to school even here."

**Participant 9** – "I was a law student in Sham. I wanted to continue with the university here but I couldn't continue because I didn't have an identity card. My only hope is to have a good future. I want to go to the university. I don't want more than this, neither a villa nor treasure."

The main reasons for not being able to go to the school are told as poverty and the lack of an identity card (Turkish legal status). This uncertain status limits integration into the education system. Still the teenagers' narratives state that they hope to have an education and a better future resulting from that education.

**Participant 10** – "We have troubles because we don't have our identity cards. I don't have an identity card. I want to go to the hospital, but they don't allow me to enter because of the lack of my identity card. Our passport has disappeared during the war. As we went to the hospital, they didn't provide us any treatment."

**Participant 11** – "My son İbrahim has a congenital heart defect. We took him to the hospital, they suggested not to operate on it and ordered us some medicine. We can't buy medicine because we don't have identity cards, we ask mostly our neighbours for their help."

The lack of the identity card (national identity card versus passport) is the main reason, besides poverty, that limits integration into the educational and health care system.

**Participant 12** – "We experience the language problem. We have a language problem in Turkey. They teach Europe languages or support people to learn other languages, but we must try on our own to learn Turkish."

**Participant 13** – "I came two years ago from Sham, where I was going to the university. The situation in Syria is very bad, that's why we came here. However, since I came here, my situation is still very bad. To have an education you need money. I still couldn't find any job, and there is also the language barrier and the state doesn't help us on this issue."

Participants 12 and 13 note the lack of language skills as the main barrier for integrating into society and finding a job. Other interviewees also noted this when comparing Turkey's failing politics to Europe. Language has been emphasized as a main tool of integration.

**Participant 14** – "People here treat us sometimes good, sometimes bad. They try to make us leave Turkey, like 'go away'."

**Participant 15** – "Here we have good people, also bad people. Turks think that Arabs are rich and have good living conditions. They think that Arabs work, enjoy travelling, to eat… They see me and no one understands that I'm Syrian. My neighbours, everybody is very satisfied with me and I'm satisfied with them."

**Participant 16** – "We feel ourselves here like being in our country, we are not refugees here, we feel like guests. Our neighbours are very good, and they are polite people. Allah should have mercy with everybody."

More or less all of the participants said that they want to return to their country as soon as the war has finished. They said that even if they feel very good here, no place is so safe as their own land.[78]

The prejudices against Syrians and the *jealousy* such as they have better living conditions here than Turkish citizens is another dimension of the xenophobia emphasized by the interviewees and results from the assumptions about the Syrian migrants such as that they exploit the Turkish state.

**Participant 17** – "Allah should throw water on the war so we can return to our homes. We left our home and our dead in our country. We want to return, that land is our own. There is no place like our home even if they treat us here so good. Our house is destroyed, nothing is left behind, everything is totally destroyed. Allah should throw water on the war and should give us patience until this war ends and we return to our home. We want to have a country; we want to return. We want it for our children and for everybody."

**Participant 18** – "Wherever I go, no place can be better than my land. Before war has started in Syria, we were together with our brothers in Syria. After the war, all of them have escaped to another place. My little brother has left for Iraq, the bigger one left to Denmark. One of my daughters is in Germany, the other one is in İzmir. We all want to live together, see each other but it's very difficult. We wished to see each other. We hope to return all together."

The escape from home, from the country and being spread throughout different countries is the central point of the narratives which make the interviewees focus on the lost identities and on running away from the war. Loss is a central theme transmitted and told to the gaze of the reader and to the hosting country.

Another study conducted by Kanak Mehmet and Özen Mustafa (2018)[79] interviewed 55 Syrian teenagers between 13 and 19 years old in the temporary protection centre in Mersin in 2016 and 2017. This survey asked about the Syrian teenagers' hope for their future. The semi-structured interviews

---

[78] Sarıoğlu, Gülsün, "İstanbul Esenyurt'taki Suriyelilere İlişkin Medya Analizi", (Media analysis of Syrians in Esenyurt, Istanbul), **Uluslararası Yönetim Akademisi Dergisi**, Vol. 2, No. 1, 2019, pp. 201-204.
[79] Kanak, Mehmet, Özen, Mustafa, "Türkiye'de geçici koruma altında bulunan Suriyeli ergenlerin geleceğe dair umut düzeylerinin incelenmesi", **Manas Journal of Social Studies**, Vol. 7, No. 1, 2018, pp. 455-476.

discussed living conditions, desired changes in the coming year, expectation about their life for the coming year, ideas about the importance of their personal influence, and ideas about what the next generation should do to have a better life.[80]

In response to the question "What do you think about your living conditions?" forty-three people stated very good, I'm very happy with my life; nine people stated that it's passable, three people stated bad, people treat us bad.

Some participants stated: "The place where I'm staying is very safe, the life here is very nice and easy." "It's a good place but we are very badly threatened by some Turks." "It's good here but I want to return to Syria." "It's not too bad." "It's neither bad nor good." "Life in Turkey is very expensive and life here is very difficult. It's also difficult to have a place at the university because YÖS (the university exam for the foreign students) is very difficult." "The place where I live is nice, but the neighbours are always disturbing but it's safe." "It's very nice, very safe. It's better than in Syria." "Our living conditions are decent but some Turks threaten us in a bad way." Two participants said "It is a good environment but we are threatened by some Turks in a bad way." "It is neither good nor bad but we are threatened by some Turks in a bad way."

Of the fifty-five Syrian teenagers, forty-three are happy about their living conditions, nine find it not too bad and three think that the living conditions are bad. The idea to return and to study at the Syrian schools shows that the teenagers hope that the war in Syria will end and they will be able to return to their schools. The findings show that the teenagers believe that they can shape their future and will work for it.

They answered the question about what they want to change in the coming year: "Becoming a Turkish citizen (4 people)", "Learning Turkish and other languages (6)", "Enrolling in a university (4)", "The racial conflicts should end (4)", "Syria must become liberated (2)", "Return to Syria in safety (4)", "Improve our material conditions (2)", "Be successful at school and in life (10)", "Get married (1)", "Go to a better university (1)", "Do not want any change (17)".

The findings that the biggest number of the Syrian teenagers do not want to have any change in their life and want to assimilate and become successful within the Turkish society.

Some participants state: "I want to become an important person in life

---

[80] Kanak, Mehmet, Özen, Mustafa, "Türkiye'de geçici koruma altında bulunan Suriyeli ergenlerin geleceğe dair umut düzeylerinin incelenmesi", **Manas Journal of Social Studies**, Vol. 7, No. 1, 2018, pp. 464-473.

and scientific opportunities should be provided to shape the future." "I want to become successful in my life and my life should be good in future." "I want Syria to become a free country." "I want the treatment of Syrians to be improved." "I want to become a Turkish citizen".

They answered the question about expectations in the next year as: "Returning to Syria and continuing with the school in Syria (9)", "Not being separated from friends (13)", "Going to a Turkish university (2)", "Having a profession (13)", "Learning a language (4)", "Acquiring the Turkish citizenship (4)", "Being successful at school (3)", "Fulfilling my dreams (1)", "Getting married (1)", "That Syrians are respected (10)", "Not having any expectations (10)".

Some participants stated: "I want to have a scholarship at a university but if it doesn't work out I want that my results in the YÖS exam (the exam for foreign students) should be good enough so that I can go to any university." "I want to go to a university about football which includes students with ability and talent." "Learning Turkish, becoming successful, developing the skills, fulfilling the dreams". Most of the participants want to visit a Turkish university and learn the Turkish language.

They responded to the question about their ability to shape their future with: "Yes, I believe that I can do things to shape my future (51)." "I don't know what I have to do (1)." "I don't know how to shape my future (3)."

Some participants stated: "I will do everything to fulfil my dreams and I will fight all handicaps in front of me. The most important thing is to have the right to continue with school because to have an education is my right." "I will do everything to have a good future." "I have to learn a lot and I have to be successful in life, but I don't know what I will be." "No, I don't believe I can change my future because I don't have the determination."

Most participants believe in the possibility of shaping their future and only a few participants think that they will not be able to shape their future. They answered the question about future expectations with: "Education will enable us to achieve our dreams (32)." "To handle the big troubles and to fulfil the big responsibilities (1)", "They should listen to the experience of adults (7)."

Some participants stated: "I will tell them the importance of their dreams and that the dreams will become bigger with us… Our dreams can be destroyed with the problems we encounter. The doors in front of us will be closed (as in the rainy days) but we are committed to our aims and dreams. We will make the dreams which seem not to be possible, become possible and open all the doors. You should love your dreams and believe in your dreams so that the power of your dreams brings you to a good future. (Your success is up to you, it's not about people or about your current situation.)

Don't forget that the biggest weapon you have in your hand is science." Two participants emphasized, "the role of education and school because it is the only weapon they have in their hand." "I will tell them the traditions and the customs because if the person is not educated, morals can't deal with important problems and the person can't have the success he/she wants to have." "I will educate them about the importance of the school." "I will tell them to search for the future and happiness because future generations will be shaped by them. It is important that they know to carry that responsibility." "You have to work a lot to teach in Syria again because you have to return to Syria and will construct Syria again."

Most refugees in the survey have a positive expectation of the future; they believe in education's role in building a good future and also they see how they could be strengthened to deal with big problems and to fulfill big responsibilities. In their answers, the Syrian teenagers placed importance on their dreams and goals. This shows they hope to achieve these goals and dreams in their future.

They answered the question about what should the next generation do to achieve a better life with: "They should work a lot (19)." "They should focus on school and education (13)." "They should achieve their dream and their purpose (13)." "They should listen to advice (7)." "They should take marriage seriously (1)." "They should learn Turkish (7)." "I don't know (62)."

Some participants stated: "They have to work a lot." "I would tell them to work a lot and to strengthen their will." "They should work a lot because their future is more important than anything because if they really want to be successful, it wouldn't be a handicap that they had some failures." "I would say that they have to pay attention to their lessons and moral because that's the most important thing in life. They have to choose an aim for their self because life without purpose is very unsuccessful. The more important thing is to achieve their goals." "They shouldn't ignore their studies because that is the most important thing. The most important thing to build our country again is education. That's why they have to work with a strong will. If they have a desire, nothing can stay in front of their way." "They should have an ambition and a target to follow, should do anything to realize their purpose, should take their adults as an example, should try to fulfil their aim." "They should do everything to fulfil their dreams." Most participants said that they should work a lot. The second largest group said "they should pay attention to their schools and education;" "should believe in their dreams and their aims;" "they would suggest they work on their education, starting from zero and become successful. That they become successful in the society, they live in and shape their future, improve themselves."

The Syrian teenagers living in Turkey believe in a better future that includes life in Turkey. Most stated that they believe that they will achieve their goals and dreams with education and will progress in their life via education. The findings show that despite the difficulties, the Syrian migrants are satisfied with their living conditions in Turkey. They believe that working hard, having an education, learning Turkish can be their individual contribution to constructing a better future. Despite their current difficult conditions, they dream of what future generations should and should not do.

## The narratives of self technologies

Seventeen interviewees stated that they were not welcomed in Turkey. Although escaping from Syria saved their life, their arrival in Turkey was difficult because of many reasons such as language barrier, lacking a national identity card, and precarious working conditions, which includes the lack of a daily salary and fighting for daily survival. The narrative about the *"good neighbours"* states that the district is not an inhospitable place to live. However, three narratives note that district residents stated that they are not happy to live with Syrians. The statements about the *"good neighbours"* are questionable statements including the gaze of the hosting country. Many hate murders and different forms of hate crime and xenophobia happen in the districts with high numbers of Syrians.[81] The central narratives still focus on the losses, the hope for returning to Syria, and the feeling of being on the threshold. The hostility of the gaze of the other does not come into foreground in these narratives because the main identity construction focuses on the survival of the migrants.

To settle down and live in Istanbul is not easy because of the precarious living conditions and includes the existential issues of survival such as having a job, living conditions, housing, and lack of legal status; these are also handicaps when facing health problems. The narratives had the central themes of racism, making the arrival in Turkey more difficult and the losses resulting from the war such as losing their home and relatives. In the gaze of the reader and in the gaze of the *native,* the narratives reflect the interviewee telling about the central dimensions of the vulnerability of survival on the threshold. The term threshold means the place between the exit of the country in war and the arrival in Turkey, in this sense in Istanbul. It is on the threshold, a situation surrounded by precarious existence, such as the marginal economic situation, precarious housing situation, alienation because of the lack of the identity card and passport, thus the lack of Syrian or Turkish identity. This alienation also resulted from the xenophobia and the racism encountered at the border with others.

---

[81] Many diverse news sources about the hate crimes against Syrians state that hate crime happens in those cities and districts hosting the biggest number of Syrians.

Some narratives describe the neighbours as friendly and the arrival in Turkey makes the interviewees feel safe and wanting to belong. That is a part of the identity construction connected to recognizing Turkey as a potential home and transmits to the gaze of the host, the arrival as a potential place of home. In the host's gaze, threshold is a place with a potential of hospitality in which the host can be both hospitable and hostile. Even if some interviewees emphasize that they encountered a safe and good environment upon arriving in Turkey, most said they faced a hostile environment because of racism and precarious conditions.

In the second survey with Syrian teenagers, the interviewees see their living conditions in different forms such as between hostility and hospitality. Safety is emphasized as a dimension of security and escaping from the war which puts distance to the war but also to the xenophobia experienced in Turkey. They described the main tools towards integration into the culture and a better future as becoming a Turkish citizen, learning Turkish, and having an education. At the same time, they emphasized their hope of returning to Syria when the war is over. This comment shows the identity constructed on the threshold has the idea of belonging as constructed in the aim of learning Turkish, having an education, and also achieving a better future via education.

They mentioned their hopes for the future included that the Syrians should not be threatened with hostility but be respected. They also believed in shaping their own future and the power of education, and learning languages. Their advice to the younger generations emphasized dreaming about the future. The dreams or wishes of some Syrian young adults and teenagers included the role of Turkish language, education as a *"weapon"*, the role of traditions and customs, and possessing good skills to rebuild Syria after the war.

## Conclusion

The narratives of teenage and adult Syrians centre on the construction of identity and their perception of the other. They mainly focus on existential questions such as education, learning Turkish, having a job, having good housing conditions, and dealing with xenophobia or racism. The narratives include the gaze of the hosting country such as Turkey which is a threshold. They hope to survive in Turkey while being recognized and to have a better future. This has the potential to turn their threshold status into a state of belonging in Turkish society. In some narratives, the identity construction of Syrian migrants emphasizes belonging in terms of the arrival in the host country Turkey. In other narratives, Turkey is seen as a threshold country because of the hope to return to Syria when the war is over. This mainly results from the inhospitable life in Turkey and the continuing experience of xenophobia and precarious living conditions. These narratives share the voices of Syrian migrants and tell stories to the hosting country. They state how migrants develop ways to create belonging and construct their identity on the threshold.

# CHAPTER 13

# REFUGEES, INTEGRATION AND POLITICAL-DEMOGRAPHIC CONCERNS IN TURKEY AND THE WORLD

Asena Boztaş[*]

## Introduction

Migration is an important phenomenon that humanity has lived through throughout history and guides humanity. In the modern world, the phenomenon of immigration is shaped within itself and migrants are also classified within this transformation. In this context, the main focus of the part will be the refugees, who are among the immigrants, who migrated to other countries due to war and political difficulties and are accepted by the states. Integration process of refugees facing in the international system and in Turkey, political demographic concerns experienced in host countries will form the main themes of the study.

Based on the perception that refugees in the international system are more fortunate than other immigrants, it is known that refugee populations live in many countries of the world, especially in developed countries. And again, it is known that migration demands of the developed countries are satisfied by the underdeveloped country populations for various reasons (war, unemployment, hunger, health problems, etc.). In this study that will be examined with historical data analysis with reference to the international refugee perception, "refugee" perceptions of Turkey and Turkish society. The focus will be on "Syrian Migration", one of the largest migration experiences historically.

The first convoy of Syrian refugees coming from Syria to Turkey had entered through Cilvegözü border gate in Yayladağı district of Hatay. Then, camps were established in many cities for Syrian refugees, whose numbers gradually increased, and some were settled in these camps. In addition, Turkey, in 2014, due to the DAEŞ attacks, also exposed to sudden and large inflows of refugees.[1] Since 2011, a large part of the growing number of Syrian refugees in Turkey, outside the camps, began to live in different cities. 'Syrian refugee problem' perception in Turkey has emerged and grown exactly after

---

[*] Assoc. Prof. Dr., Sakarya University of Applied Sciences, Faculty of Applied Sciences, International Trade and Finance Department, Turkey. E-mail: aboztas@subu.edu.tr, ORCID: 0000-0002-3216-3010.
[1] K.B. Kanat ve K. Üstün, "Turkey's Syrian Refugees: Toward Integration", SETA Report, 2015, pp. 11-12.

that.

Perceptions and concerns about the Syrian refugees in Turkey are similar to other refugees in the international system. This is due to both the differences in the characteristics of the refugee community and the characteristics of the host society. The refugees were accepted firstly by the "hospitable" nature of Turkish society and "our guest" approach of the Turkish government. Later, it caused "othering" and the formation of a "foreigners" perception in Turkey by the policies and practices of European states that do not accept refugees, the perception of "permanents" in Turkish society, and negative impact of the media.

The situation and perceptions of Syrian refugees in Turkey are different from Turkey's historical experience with immigrants (i.e. Turkic ethnic origins or foreign but demographically few). In this context, firstly I will look into refugees in the international system and political and demographic concerns. Then I will discuss the refugees in Turkey and political and demographic concerns along with the host society's concerns.

## Refugees in the world

Migration and immigrants, one of the biggest challenges of the international system, have always existed historically. Faced by all states in the international system, it has a human-based solution. Migration can be subjected to various classifications according to their motivations, goals and objectives. It is possible to define compulsory and voluntary migration according to reasons, or distinguish work-oriented from asylum seeker, or divide in accordance with different criteria such as legal and illegal. Different disciplines (economy, sociology, demography, geography, history, psychology, international relations, political science, etc.) address migration-related issues from different perspectives.[2] People migrate to improve their quality of life due to war, exile, natural disaster or political and economic reasons. In the process of migration, people sometimes reach worse conditions than they have left behind, they may be exposed to abuse and sometimes risk their lives. Only some of those who flee can gain refugee status. Refugees can gain some rights as individuals who migrate to other countries due to the war and political difficulties in their own countries.[3] Refugees are defined and protected in the international law. *The 1951 Refugee Convention* is a key legal document and defines a refugee as:[4] "Someone who is unable or unwilling to return to their country of origin owing to a well-

[2] A. İçduygu and İ. Sirkeci, "Migration Movements Republican Period in Turkey", **75th year From Villages to Cities**, Oya Baydar (Ed.), History Foundation Publication, 1998, p. 249.
[3] Zhanadilova Aigul, "The Problem of International Migration in the Framework of Different Theories", **Muhakeme Journal**, Vol. 1, No. 2, 2018, pp. 116-122.
[4] UNHCR, "What is a refugee?", https://www.unhcr.org/what-is-a-refugee.html (Access: 02.11.2020).

founded fear of being persecuted for reasons of race, religion, nationality, membership of a particular social group, or political opinion."

Therefore, the situation of the refugees, their problems, integration processes and most importantly, the negative reflection of the political demographic concerns in the countries they migrated to are very important issues. There are international organizations as well as national organizations for refugees that concern the whole world, and the best example is the United Nations International Organization for Migration (IOM), which brings up the problems of migrants and refugees with its annual report.[5] (IOM, 2020). The UN Refugee Agency (UNHCR) is another organization that regularly prepares reports on refugees and raises awareness in the international community.

In this context, the comparison of UN IOM, which includes a 20-year process in the 2020 World Migration Report, where the current situation and problems of refugees in the international system can be analyzed with numbers, is a very interesting determination reflecting the transformation and development of the phenomenon of migration in the international system.[6]

**Table 1.** Key facts and figures from the World Migration Reports, 2000 and 2020[7]

|  | 2000 Report | 2020 Report |
|---|---|---|
| Estimated number of international migrants | 150 million | 272 million |
| Estimated proportion of world population who are migrants | 2.8% | 3.5 % |
| Estimated proportion of female international migrants | 47.5 % | 47.9 % |
| Estimated proportion of international migrants who are children | 16 % | 13.9 % |
| Region with the highest proportion of international migrants | Oceania | Oceania |
| Country with the highest proportion of international migrants | United Arab Emirates | United Arab Emirates |
| Number of migrant workers | - | 164 million |
| Global international remittances (USD) | 126 billion | 689 billion |
| Number of refugees | 14 million | 25.9 million |
| Number of internally displaced persons | 21 million | 41.3 million |
| Number of stateless persons | - | 3.9 million |
| Number of IOM Member States* | 76 | 173 |
| Number of IOM field offices* | 120 | 436* |

---

[5] IOM, https://www.iom.int/ (Access: 11.10.2020).
[6] IOM, "World Migration Report 2020", 2020, p. 10,
https://publications.iom.int/system/pdf/wmr
_2020.pdf (Access: 09.11.2020).
[7] IOM, 2000 and the present edition of the report for sources. Notes: The dates of the data estimates in the table may be different to the report publishing date (refer to the reports for more detail on dates of estimates); refer to chapter 3 of this report for regional breakdowns;* indicates the data was not included in the report but is current for that year; as at 28 October 2019.

According to the 2020 report of the IOM, it is seen that only 14 million of the 150 million immigrants in 2000 were able to gain refugee status, by 2020, 25.9 million out of 272 million immigrants could become refugees. When we evaluate it as a ratio, the number of refugees in the immigrant population in 2000 increased from 9.3% to 9.5% in 2020. Although this development over a period of 20 years is not great, it can still be considered positive.

**Table 2.** All populations of concern* by region, 2019-2020[8]

| | |
|---|---|
| Africa | 33,351,734 |
| Americas | 15,650,382 |
| Asia and the Pacific | 9,505,943 |
| Europe | 12,085,455 |
| Middle East and North Africa | 15,938,155 |
| Total (2019) | 86,531,669 |
| Total (2020) | 82,466,625 |

Considering the 2019 data of UNHCR, another organization that carries out important studies on refugees as "Refugees, refugee-like situation, asylum-seekers, IDPS, returned IDPS, returned refugees, stateless and others of concern" in the international system, it is seen that the highest number of refugees emigrated from the African continent and the least refugees from the Asia and Pacific region, as in Table 2. In 2020, the total number of refugees decreased by about 4.7% compared to 2019.[9]

Those who try to gain a place for themselves in the dynamics of the international system and who can achieve refugee status in another state continue their great struggles within the state and society they are in, but this time without worrying about being stateless. Refugees, who immigrate from their own countries and try to adapt to the conditions of the country they have settled in, face similar problems in all countries of the world. Although these integration processes differ according to the characteristics of each individual, first of all, from a general perspective, the adaptation processes that refugees experience in the international platform will form the next part of the study.

### Integration processes of refugees in the world

Although they have conceptually different definitions, in short, *refugees* who have been displaced due to war and disaster are people who have lost everything they have. This loss includes not only the loss of property, but also the more important individual talents and social status closely related to

---

* Refugees, refugee-like situation, asylum-seekers, IDPS, returned ıdps, returned refugees, stateless and others of conce.

[8] UNHCR, "Populations", 2020, https://reporting.unhcr.org/population (Access: 01.11.2020)

[9] UNHCR, ibid; UNHCR, "Global Focus", 2020, https://reporting.unhcr.org/ (Access: 01.11.2020).

those capabilities. It is important to remind displaced refugees of the importance and function of their individual abilities, to allow them to survive in new social conditions and acquire new social status. Providing this opportunity to refugees also forms the basis of integration policies.[10]

In this context, the concept of *integration* is also important. Integration can be defined as the material and mental adaptation of individuals and groups who are permanently moved from one place to another to the living conditions in the new place.[11] Ager and Strang working on refugee integration state that the integration classify as determinants (work, housing, education, health), social relations (social bridges, social ties, social connections), facilitators (language and cultural knowledge, security and stability) and foundations (rights and citizenship) is not possible unless access is granted.[12] However, as well as access to rights, secure legal status is one of the important factors for integration.[13]

Integration processes of migrants and refugees also differ due to the difference in their status.[14] Integration processes of immigrants with insecure status progress slower than refugees with secure status. Because it is difficult for them to make future plans for settling in the country they migrated to. Unfortunately, while developed countries extend the process of granting refugee status to asylum seekers in the international system, access to shelter, employment, education and health rights of asylum seekers is restricted and integration becomes difficult.[15] The results of many studies on immigrants and refugees reveal that refugee integration is possible with access to fundamental rights and secure legal status.[16]

From this point of view, the policies aiming to control the migration flow after the 1990s are that immigrants are not temporary; It really involves

---

[10] Hak-iş, "Social Integration Guide", Social Integration Project for Refugees Via Vocational Educational Training (SIPRVET), 2020, pp. 21-22, https://www.hakis.org.tr/uploads/yayinlar/yayin-pdf-28.pdf (Access: 01.11.2020).
[11] Ibid.
[12] A. Ager and A. Strang, "Understanding Integration: A Conceptual Framework", **Journal of Refugee Studies**, Vol. 21, No. 2, 2008, pp. 166–191.
[13] S. Da Lomba, "Legal Status and Refugee Integration: a UK Perspective", **Journal of Refugee Studies**, Vol. 23, No. 4, 2010, pp. 415- 436; D. Şimşek, "Transnational Activities of Syrian Refugees in Turkey: Hindering or Supporting Integration", **International Migration**, Vol. 57, No. 2, 2018, pp. 10-14.
[14] J. Phillimore, "Implementing integration in the UK: lessons for integration theory, policy and practice", **Policy and Politics**, Vol. 40, No.4, 2012, pp. 525–45.
[15] G. Loescher, Beyond Charity: International Co-Operation and the Global Refugee Crisis, New York, Oxford University Press, 1993, pp. 45-48.
[16] Hak-iş, op.cit.; M. Mckeary and B. Newbold, "Barriers to Care: The Challenges for Canadian Refugees and their Health Care Providers", **Journal of Refugee Studies**, Vol. 23, No. 4, 2010, pp. 523- 545; M. Valenta and N. Bunar, "State Assisted Integration: Refugee Integration Policies in Scandinavian Welfare States: the Swedish and Norwegian Experience", **Journal of Refugee Studies,** Vol. 23, No. 4, 2010, pp. 463-483; N. Vrecer, "Living in Limbo: Integration of Forced Migrants from Bosnia and Herzegovina in Slovenia", **Journal of Refugee Studies**, Vol. 23, No. 4, 2010, pp. 484- 502.

refugee integration, taking into account the existence of the second and third generations. However, many asylum seekers and refugees are excluded from the society and exposed to racism because most integration policies push refugees into an isolated life from society.[17] However, a good integration policy means that the host community to the refugee community; Likewise, the refugee community promotes the host community and ensures that both sides live in peace and harmony. If refugee communities are not successfully and healthily integrated into the new social life some negative consequences occur such as; isolation, marginalization-ghettoization, breaking away from social reality / being out of social reality, radicalization, social tensions, threatening social peace, etc. Thus, immigrants do not know the culture, political and social structure of the society they settled in after migration, public perception, access ways to public services, work ethics, ways and methods of acquiring a profession, developing skills, getting education and finding a job, and they are deprived of their ability to access related resources. As a result, immigrants cannot develop healthy ties with the new society. However, for a successful and healthy integration process, it is of utmost importance to resolve existing social conflict areas, prevent potential tension and conflict areas, and create opportunities for both the immigrant community and the host society.[18]

Integration processes for refugees in the international system may differ from country to country. The main reason for this is the domestic and foreign policy practices of states. However, regional organizations, especially UNHCR and UN IOM, make great efforts to act jointly within the framework of international law and international human rights. In this context, considering the studies conducted in Europe, the region that receives the most immigration, it is concluded that although laws are enacted for immigration control, preventing the entry of asylum seekers and refugees living in Europe is the main goal. The most important reason for this is that refugees are perceived by developed Europeans as a threat to nation-states and a problem to be solved.[19] The decisions taken and policies implemented in this direction actually reflect the European states' perspective on the refugee and immigrant problem.[20] The perspective of the developed Western societies towards refugees and immigrants triggers the exclusion of refugees from the society and the increase of campaigns organized for the expulsion

[17] D. Şimşek, "Refugee Integration, Migration Policy and Social Class: The Case of Syrian refugees in Turkey", **Journal of Social Policy Studies**, Vol. 18, No. 40/2, 2018, pp. 369-370.
[18] Hak-iş, op.cit.
[19] P. Nyers, **Rethinking Refugees: Beyond States of Emergency**, Abingdon, Routledge, 2008, pp. 56-59.
[20] N. De Genova, "Migrant 'illegality' and deportability in everyday life", **Annual Review of Anthropology,** vol. 31, 2002, p.1; J. Hampshire, "Regulating migration risks: the emergence of risk-based border controls in the UK", **Sussex Centre for Migration Research Working Paper**, School of Oriental and African Studies, London. 2008, pp. 14-20.

of asylum seekers.[21]

Developed states aim to control the refugee and immigrant populations with their immigration policies. But they fail at the point of social transformation. It is possible to observe this problem in the examples of developed countries such as the USA and Austria. The US immigration policies aim to stop illegal entries, asylum seekers and refugees from working. However, migrant workers are the choice of employers as they work cheaply. Therefore, despite the sanctions imposed on employers and illegally working refugees and asylum seekers, their numbers are increasing.[22] Similarly, although Australia has arranged its post-war immigration policy for the country's population to consist of whites and British people, it has turned into a multicultural structure with its economy including immigrants and asylum seekers from different national and ethnic origins, starting from the 1970s.[23]

The vast majority of international research and studies emphasize the insufficiency of state policies on refugee integration applied to refugees and criticize this deficiency in the international system. Criticizing national and international refugee and asylum policies, these studies agree that policies do not take the human factor into account adequately. For example, Bloch stated that asylum seekers and asylum seekers in England do not feel safe because they do not have an immigrant status, and that they cannot find a place in the society they take refuge in both emotionally and structurally, they cannot find a job and have difficulty in establishing their lives. For example, Bloch stated that asylum seekers and asylum seekers in England do not feel safe because they do not have immigrant status. However, he emphasized that the immigrants could not find find a job and a place in the society both emotionally and structurally and they had difficulty in establishing their lives. So he emphasized that the UK should develop its *"refugee 373 policy"*.[24] Lloyd stated that France's asylum policy is not sufficient for similar reasons.[25] As can be seen, the international migration and asylum policies led by developed countries, which are heavily influenced by immigration and flooded by refugees, have focused on controlling the borders of nation-states, protecting their national identities, their citizens, and limiting their access to accommodation, education and health rights they offer to asylum seekers,

---

[21] A. Bloch and L. Schuster, "At the extremes of exclusion: deportation, detention and dispersal", **Ethnic and Racial Studies,** Vol. 28, No. 3, 2005, pp. 491-512.
[22] S. Castles and M. Miller, **The Age of Migration: International Population Movements in the Modern World**, Basingstoke, Palgrave-Macmillan, 2003, pp. 115-133.
[23] D. Şimşek, "Refugee Integration, Migration Policy and Social Class: The Case of Syrian refugees in Turkey", p. 372.
[24] A. Bloch, "Refugee settlement in Britain: The impact of policy on participation", **Journal of Ethnic and Migration Studies,** Vol. 26, No. 1, 2000, pp. 75-88.
[25] C. Lloyd, "Anti-racism, racism and asylum-seekers in France", **Patterns of Prejudice**, Vol. 37, No.3, 2003, pp. 323-340.

although they vary from country to country.[26]

## Political-demographic concerns of refugees in the world

Differences in geostrategic locations, state structures, development levels and demographic factors, etc. Considering the factors and their unique nature, there are no common migration and refugee policies for all states in the international system. However, it is obvious that while determining and implementing policies for refugees and immigrants, universal ethical elements on the basis of human rights may come to the fore. In this respect, it is possible to say that the policies of states towards refugees are shaped in the axis of national interests and society expectations. Because political-demographic concerns within the country shape the policies towards refugees as well as the society's perspective towards refugees.

On the other hand, there are also political-demographic concerns that arise in the migrating refugee society. Concerns arise regarding the security of the cultural and national identity of the migrant society.[27] Especially legal and illegal immigration can threaten the identity of the society with sudden changes in the characteristics of the population as ethnic, religious and minorities, causing a change in the composition of the population.as a result of refugee problems and displacement of people. At this point, a marginalization in the form of "us" and "them" may be the case in both segments (the immigrant society and the society that lives in the country).[28]

In this regard, the most important factor in the creation of a threat perception in the refugee society and host society is the state of the past and present relations of the two parties. When the refugee community strives to integrate with the lifestyle of its community, it can be seen as less threatening by the indigenous community. However, if it does not attempt to integrate and does not respect the way of life of the indigenous community, the presence of the refugee community may be perceived as a threatening factor by the indigenous community.[29]

However, when evaluated from a refugee perspective, most of the refugees, especially women and children, who constitute an average of 80% of the refugee population,[30] generally concentrate in low social status business

---

[26] L. Schuster, "Common sense or racism? The treatment of asylum-seekers in Europe", **Patterns of Prejudice,** Vol. 37, No. 3, 2003, pp. 233-256.

[27] S. Bali, "Population Movements,", P. Williams (ed.), **Security Studies: An Introduction**, London, Routledge, 2008, pp. 468-482.

[28] B. S. Ağır, "Kosovo Issue at the Crossroads of Security and Migration", **Ankara University Faculty of Political Sciences Journal**, Vol. 69, No. 3, 2014, p. 458.

[29] Y. A. Stivachtis, "International Migration and the Politics of Identity and Security," **Journal of Humanities and Social Sciences,** Vol. 2, No. 1, 2008, p. 4.

[30] Simurg, "Immigration, Woman and Body", 2007, Psychiatry-Psychotherapy, http://www.psikiyatri psikoterapi.com/travma_8.asp. (Access: 11.11.2020).

lines in the countries they go to and live separately from the society in places where people in the low income group live.[31] Despite this, it shows that especially refugee women prefer to stay permanently in the country they see a future because they do not like the uncertain environment, when they stay in a place for a certain period of time, when their children start school and find a job, they do not easily return to their countries, they settle in the country they migrated to and form an ethnic minority in the new country.[32]

In this context, it can be stated that the situation of refugees who had to leave their homeland as a result of political reasons and civil wars, such as the forced migration of Albanian immigrants after the Kosovo crisis, the immigration of African slaves to the American Continent, the immigration of Iraqis and Syrians due to the civil war, the migration of the civil wars and terrorism in the African Continent, the immigration of Bosniaks and Macedonians, etc. that are different parts of the world, show similarities and differences.[33] But on the other hand, integration problems in host countries have also diversified. Another interesting point is that the same host society can take different approaches to different refugee groups. For example; Turkish society, which is more moderate towards immigrants from Europe, may take a less moderate approach towards refugees from the Middle East such as Iraq and Syria. This is based on the characteristics of the migrating refugee society and its adaptation to the host society, as mentioned earlier. This is based on the characteristics of the migrating refugee society and its adaptation to the host society, as mentioned earlier.

Therefore, the capacity of social, economic, political and administrative institutions to integrate refugee communities and refugee communities opposition to assimilation affects the stability of the society in which they live, and hence the state. This effect is more intense in states with important economic problems, ineffective administrations, deep political polarization or rapid social changes.[34] Therefore, immigrants create important problems for weak states, especially with their effects on economic, social and political relations. Under certain circumstances, the presence and activities of immigrants can adversely affect the stability of these countries to the extent that they increase the likelihood of domestic violence. For example, it has been suggested that the efforts of immigrant communities to protect their identity may be the cause of internal conflicts in the states they are in.[35] Apart

---

[31] S. Castles and J. M. Miller, **Age of Migration, International Migration Movements in the Modern World**, İstanbul, Bilgi University Publications, 2008, p. 18.

[32] M.M. Erdoğan, **Syrians in Turkey: Social Acceptance and Adaptation Research**, Hacettepe University Migration and Politics Research Center, Ankara, 2014, pp. 18-30.

[33] B. S. Ağır, op.cit., p. 460.

[34] J. Huysmans, The Politics of Insecurity, Fear, Migration and Asylum in the EU, London, Routledge, 2006, pp. 56-70.

[35] Y. A. Stivachtis, op.cit., p. 10.

from this, immigrants can carry out terrorist acts, engage in activities such as illegal arms smuggling or cooperate with ethnic, religious, class or political opposition groups operating in the country where they are accepted.[36] As a result, states hosting immigrants can also increase their internal security regulations. Eventually, the ethnic, religious or cultural identity of immigrants may increase problems in weak states with low socio-political cohesion. The fact that weak states are dragged into instability due to the phenomenon of immigration can create problems in terms of regional security.[37]

Cause of these problems are foreseen by the societies and states in the international system, they generally do not take a very mild attitude towards refugees either as a state or socially. Therefore, refugees also attract the strong reactions of certain sections of the receiving communities. Because migration mainly manifests itself as *multidimensional social change* and *economic restructuring*. The widespread perception of society towards refugees is that these people are taking away their professions, driving up home prices in the country and placing an excessive burden on social services. In addition, refugees are seen by the host community as the cause of unemployment, illness and crime.[38]

As a result, migration causes different cultures to come across and it creates an obligation for people from different cultures to live together. In this process, *the policy and bureaucratic structuring* that will manage the harmonization process between the host society and the refugee society are of great importance. Intercultural harmony will also prevent possible internal and external conflicts. Adaptation problems arising from cultural differences, Communication barriers and ways to overcome these obstacles are among the priority issues of many immigration communities today. One of the most important problems caused by the phenomenon of international migration globally; People from different cultures living together, coping with differences and overcoming communication barriers, in short, comes the *problem of integration*.[39] Correct management of the integration process will ensure the happiness of both the host and the refugee community by bringing social harmony and peace with it.

### Refugees in Turkey

Historicallys and today, Turkey known as a "hospitable country" hosts the largest refugee population globally. As of 2020, the number of people

---

[36] M. Weiner, "Migration and Security," Hughes, C. W. and Meng, L. Y. (ed.), **Security Studies: A Reader,** London, Routledge, 2011, pp. 253-264.

[37] Y. A. Stivachtis, Y. A., op.cit., p. 16.

[38] S. Castles and J. M. Miller, Age of Migration, International Migration Movements in the Modern World, pp. 18-21.

[39] A. Ş. Tunç, "Refugees Behavior and Social Impacts: An Evaluation of the Syrians in Turkey", **Turkish Journal of TESAM Academy,** Vol. 2, No. 2, 2015, p. 35.

forcibly displaced due to conflict, violence and persecution reached record levels globally; Turkey has been hosting over 4 million in the last seven years as the top country with the highest number of refugees in the world. Approximately 3.6 million registered Syrian refugees are in Turkey; more than 98% of Syrian refugees live across 81 provinces in the country[40] as well as 400,000 Afghan, Iranian and Iraqi nationals.[41]

Turkey saw three major mass migrations in the last three decades. There have been mass inflows of Northern Iraqi Kurds in 1988, Bulgarian Turks in 1989 and Syrians since 2011. However, Syrian migrations since 2011 are clearly different from the migration flows of Northern Iraqi Kurds in 1988 and Bulgarian Turks in 1989 in terms of their effects on Turkey's domestic and foreign policy, the total number of migrants and the duration of their mass influx.[42] Therefore, they are prioritized in this study.

**Table 3.** Syrians under temporary protection in Turkey per year[43]

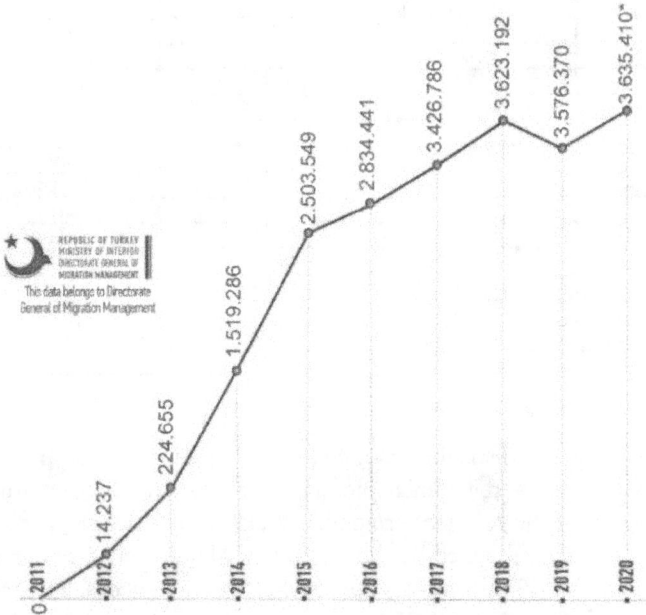

Source: Directorate General of Migration Management, 18.11.2020

[40] UNHCR, "UNHCR Turkey Statistics", 2020, https://www.unhcr.org/tr/unhcr-turkiye-istatistikleri (Access: 02.11.2020).
[41] ILO Turkey Office, "ILO Turkey Refugees and Host Communities Support Program", 2020, https://www.ilo.org/ankara/projects/WCMS_702144/lang--tr/index.htm (Access: 23.09.2020).
[42] A. Kaya and M.M. Erdoğan (ed.), **Turkey's Immigration History: 14th Century 21st Century Turkey Migrations**, İstanbul, Bilgi University Publications, 2015, pp. 298-299.
[43] The Directorate General of Migration Management, "The Directorate General of Migration Management Statistics-Temporary Protection", 2020, https://www.goc.gov.tr/gecici-koruma5638 (Access: 24.11.2020).

In this respect, the first convoy of refugees came to Turkey on April 29, 2011. The number of Syrian refugees between 2011 and 2020 has increased with each passing year.[44] The reason is that Turkey adopted an "open door" policy. According to this policy, no Syrian who entered the border without discrimination of religion, language and race[45] were sent back and they were given "temporary protection status". Turkey's welcomed "guests" from that time are still refugees in Turkey.

**Table 4.** Age and gender distribution of Syrians under temporary protection[46]

| AGE | MALE | FEMALE | TOTAL |
|---|---|---|---|
| TOTAL | 1.955.807 | 1.679.603 | 3.635.410 |
| 0-4 | 256.382 | 247.871 | 504.253 |
| 5-9 | 283.345 | 260.304 | 543.649 |
| 10-14 | 203.881 | 185.425 | 389.306 |
| 15-18 | 142.612 | 119.287 | 261.899 |
| 19-24 | 287.302 | 213.398 | 500.700 |
| 25-29 | 203.495 | 148.636 | 352.131 |
| 30-34 | 159.602 | 116.417 | 276.019 |
| 35-39 | 119.724 | 97.436 | 217.160 |
| 40-44 | 85.312 | 76.398 | 161.710 |
| 45-49 | 60.805 | 57.604 | 118.409 |
| 50-54 | 50.125 | 49.104 | 99.229 |
| 55-59 | 38.396 | 38.385 | 76.781 |
| 60-64 | 28.725 | 29.534 | 58.259 |
| 65-69 | 20.478 | 20.936 | 41.414 |
| 70-74 | 7.824 | 8.804 | 16.628 |
| 75-79 | 3.834 | 4.696 | 8.530 |
| 80-84 | 2.210 | 2.938 | 5.148 |
| 85-89 | 1.094 | 1.524 | 2.618 |
| 90+ | 661 | 906 | 1.567 |

Source: Directorate General of Migration Management, 18.11.2020

Considering the age distribution of Syrian refugees in Turkey it can be said that the world showed a similar picture with the refugees. Accordingly, while the majority of the refugees are children and young people, according to the age range table published by the Migration Management; Syrian male refugees make up 53.8% of the total number of Syrian refugees. The rate of Syrian women refugees is 46.2%. The number of Syrian refugees under the age of 10 is 1 million 45 thousand 622 people (28.8%). According to the table, the number of Syrian male refugees is 276,177 more than the number of

---

[44] E. Özdemir, "Perception of Syrian refugees in Turkey", **The Journal of Defense Sciences**, Vol. 16, May 2017, p. 117.
[45] S. Bidinger et al, Protecting Syrian Refugees: Laws, Policies, and Global Responsibility Sharing, Boston University School of Law, USA, 2014, p.96.
[46] The Directorate General of Migration Management, "The Directorate General of Migration Management Statistics-Temporary Protection", 2020, https://www.goc.gov.tr/gecici-koruma5638 (Access: 24.11.2020).

Syrian female refugees, and the biggest difference between the number of males and females is between the ages of 19-24 with 73,891 people. It is observed that the number of female refugees in the age range above 55 is higher than the male refugees.[47]

The goal of the majority of Syrian refugees constitute the largest segment of refugees in Turkey to immigrate to Europe via Greece, though it is known that the cuts reached the target in the minority. The reason for this process and the implementation of immigration policies in Greece and other European countries are not open until Turkey. However, Turkey to voluntarily or involuntarily (due to the realization of the dream of Europe) the integration of Syrian refugees settled is very important. National and international efforts and studies carried out in this process will be included in the next part of the study.

**Integration processes of refugees in Turkey**

Turkey itself also has an immigrant background due to the ethnic structure, opened its doors to immigrants and refugees throughout history and, both as a state and as a society, it has always been hospitable and continues to do. Despite being the country with the largest number of Syrian refugees today, both as a society and as a state, continuing this attitude, Turkey stands with all the oppressed in the international system.

Regarding both 1951 Geneva Convention and the 1967 Protocol, Turkey carries out legal and institutional reforms in order to build an effective national asylum system to meet international standards. In April 2013, Turkey's first asylum law in the Foreigners and International Protection Act, was approved by the Grand National Assembly of Turkey and entered into force on April 11, 2014. The law put forward the basic foundations of Turkey's national asylum system, immigration policy making and administration of the process; and as the main institution responsible for all foreigners in Turkey, Directorate General of Migration Management was established.[48] However, the problems of refugees in the integration process in Turkey basically shows similarities with other refugees in the international system. Due to the size of Syrian refugee population in Turkey, they are given priority in this section.

The immigration of Syrian refugees is one of the largest mass population movements in world history. In this context, the importance of the integration process of Syrian refugees in Turkey is clear. As a result of the

---

[47] **Refugees Association,** "Number of Syrians in Turkey in October 2020", 28 October 2020, https://multeciler.org.tr/turkiyedeki-suriyeli-sayisi/ (Access: 01.11.2020).
[48] UNHRC, "Refugees and Asylum Seekers in Turkey", 2020, https://www.unhcr.org/tr/turkiyedeki-multeciler-ve-siginmacilar (Access: 15.10.2020).

war in Syria, large refugee movement has emerged and European countries started closing their borders to prevent the entry of refugees. It has become clear at this point that Syrian refugees in Turkey as Lebanon and Jordan to be remain as long term immigrants. Western countries have preferred to provide financial support to neighbouring countries with large numbers of refugees rather than taking refugees into their countries. This has made resettlement more complex for refugees than in the past. On the basis of problems in improving the refugees' settlement, Turkey needed urgently to strengthen the critical process. It is based on the integration of refugees with their newly immigrated society or remedying inequalities for resettlement in a third country, access to essential services, acquisition of qualifications in the fields of education and economic life. Accordingly, for the integration processes of refugees to be successful, policies need to be based on a long-term framework that balances the concerns of both refugees and their communities. Therefore, a sound plan for refugee settlement should be presented, with actionable, inclusive and open policies. This plan should also take into account the gender and age perspectives of refugees.[49]

Turkey is implementing the "open door" policy with social and political integration efforts as shown in the reports of research centres such as IGAM, together with the data of international and national official institutions such as the Directorate General of Migration Management and the Ministry of Internal Affairs such as UNHCR and IOM. IGAM's report named "Examples of good practices in refugee hosting in Turkey" in February 2020, jobs and livelihoods, education, social cohesion and protection programs in the scope of the project implementation of the social integration of immigrants in Turkey were mentioned.[50]

Although basic perception of Syrian refugees who have migrated to Turkey between 2011-2020 regarded to Turkey is a "transit route" through to Europe, with the European states closing their doors to Syrian immigrants in the process, Turkey has become, now, Syrian immigrants "target country". Thus, Turkish society's perception of them has changed from "guest" to "permanent". In this process, the positive perceptions in the host society started to turn negative over time. Therefore, both political-demographic concerns of the refugees and the political-demographic concerns of the Turkish society have intensified.

---

[49] D. Şimşek, "Integration of Syrian Refugees in Turkey: Challenges and Opportunities", **Journal of Research in Economics, Politics & Finance**, Vol. 4, No. 2, 2019, pp. 172-187.
[50] İGAM, "Good Practice Examples in Refugee Hosting in Turkey Survey Report", February 2020, https://igamder.org/uploads/belgeler/Report_Good%20Practice%20Examples%20in%20Refugee%20Hosting_Final_20%2002%202020.pdf (Access: 10.11.2020).

## Political-demographic concerns of refugees in Turkey

Migration inflows to Turkey is not new. When we examine international migration movements towards Turkey in the process of building the nation-state, we can see that the migration of ethnic groups from neighbouring countries, and those with Turkish ethnic origins adapt easily to Turkey. However, Turkey in recent years witnessed the influx of immigrant groups who are various in terms of ethnic and religious origins and they come from a wide variety of countries, for different purposes, and therefore are often described as "foreigners".[51]

Turks who migrated to Western Europe in the 1960s, today, has seen a constant influx of Syrian refugees[52]. While Syrian refugees are perceived as "guests" by the Turkish community, as these guests become "permanent", they are now perceived as "foreigners" and being marginalized as a result of these concerns in the host society. At this point, two options come to the fore. The first is that the refugee can establish himself with his individual characteristics. S/he achieves this through its communication skills as well as its adaptation to society. The second option is that the refugee community-host society adaptation policies and practices facilitate the integration in the host country. At this point, Turkey is no longer a "transit country" but a "target destination".

The main concerns of war-displaced Syrians and other refugee communities are security, adaptation to a new place, communication, housing, health, education (especially the education of their children), gaining a profession to earn a living, being able to participate in the host society, etc. The concerns of the Turks, the host society, came to light when of these refugees became permanent. In this context, due to the increase in the refugee population and the unqualified workforce, and concerns that they may turn to crime, etc., the security threat concerns also arise in the Turkish society which affects the direction of the perception. Then the refugees are compared to the host society who suffers from unemployment and the refugees are seen a burden on the economy. In this regard, especially perception management in the media is important as it can affect both societies positively or negatively.

In this context, the Refugee Association's Administrative Coordinator P. Erçoban points out that some news about refugees as "poor people, fugitives,

---

[51] A. İçduygu, S. Erder and Ö. F. Gençkaya, "Turkey's International Migration Policy, 1923-2023: From the Nation-State Bodies of the Trans-national transformation", MIREKOÇ Research Reports 1/2014 Tübitak 1001_106k291, September 2009, Ocak, 2014, İstanbul, Migration Research Center, 2014, p. 222.
[52] S. Ünal, "Turkey's Unexpected Guests: Foreign Immigrants And Refugees Experience In The Context Of 'Other'", **Zeitschrift für die Welt der Türken**, Vol. 6, No. 3, 2014, pp.69-70; A. İçduygu, **International Migration Debates in the Context of European Union Relations**, İstanbul, TÜSİAD-T/2006-12/427, 2006, p. 70.

those involved in crime, problematic people, distressing the country, raising crime rates, murderer, rapist, thief" are discriminatory, xenophobic, anti-refugee discourses.[53] With news like this, exclusionary and marginalizing discourses in Turkey may lead and strengthen the "Syrian refugees should go home" perception.[54] Prejudices are the basis of the discriminatory language used in the media. In this context, it can be said that mental representations of Syrian refugees are made visible, formulated and legitimized with metaphors through discourses.[55] According to field studies conducted in the provinces of the region where Syrian refugees are concentrated,[56] it is noteworthy that although the refugees have a very close cultural identity to the region, they express that there are serious cultural differences between the people of the region and the refugees and at this point they describe them as incompatible. In addition, the perception of Syrians who do not pay attention to cleanliness, who are lazy, who do not keep their promises, who make a lot of noise and who are rude prevails in the people of the region.[57] Furthermore, from the date of Syrian refugees arrived in Turkey that they are responsible for the increases in house rents and prices in the country, the statements that men in Turkish society to have a religious marriage with Syrian women as a second or even third wife, allowing some Syrians to beg for the entire Syrian refugee community or perceptions that Syrians have a high criminal potential, promotes the marginalization of the refugee society by the host society.[58]

Another factor driving the perception of both Syrian refugees and Turkish society is the refugee policies and media of European states.[59] The main policy of European states, which are the primary targets of Syrian refugees, is to not let Syrian migrants in. European states in this regard, both by land and sea was closed all the way, even the transition has raised the level of security on the border with Turkey to prevent inflow of refugees. However, European countries targeted by Syrian immigrants do not want them, instead they provide financial support for refugees in Turkey. Syrian refugees in Turkey who give up on Europe and do not return to Syria become

---

[53] E.C. Dağlıoğlu, "Turkey to shelter the Syrians, not guests", (**Refugee, Interview with P. Erçoban**), 11.01.2014, http://www.agos.com.tr/haber.php?seo=turkiyeyesiginan-suriyeliler-misafir-degil-multeci&haberid=6419 (Access: 06.11.2020).

[54] S. Ünal, op.cit., p. 81.

[55] H. Ç. Keneş, "The Role of Metaphor in the Construction of Discriminatory Hegemony: Using Metaphors in Communication of Syrians", **Gaziantep University Journal of Social Sciences**, Vol. 15, No. 2, 2016, p. 263.

[56] R. Yaşar, "Refugee Perception in Kilis Social Autism and Initial Views of Othering", **Field Research**, Kilis 7 December University, 2014, pp. 1-70.

[57] M.M. Erdoğan, **Suriyeliler Toplumsal Kabul ve Uyum**, İstanbul, Bilgi University Publications, 2015, p. 117.

[58] E. Özdemir, op.cit., pp. 123-127.

[59] A. Eşigül et al., "Information from Perception: Refugees in Turkey, Immigration and Refugee A Study of Perception", PS: EUROPE, Friedrich-Ebert- Stiftung, July 2017, p. 5.

"permanent". Hence the perceptions of Turkish society and Syrian refugees changed.[60] Turkish society knows that have to adapt to this society that can no longer be guests, but resist because of its concerns and then marginalizes Syrian refugees. The Syrian permanent refugee community, on the other hand, is aware of the high level of hospitality of the Turkish society, especially with the reactions of European states and societies against them and knows that it has to adapt to the Turkish society and makes an effort for this.

### Conclusion and recommendations

This study examined political-demographic concerns of the refugees who have legal rights and political-demographic concerns of the host society in the context of the migration and immigration problems in the international system, sociological factors.

First part of the study explored the situation and political-demographic concerns of refugees in the international system drawing on various reports and the literature. In the second part, the situation of refugees in Turkey regarding political and demographic concerns were discussed.

The main challenge regarding refugees is integration. Therefore, the host country's policies and practices towards refugees are very important, as well as refugees' relations and interaction with the host society. For the full integration of the refugee community with the host society, the concerns of both communities should be minimized.

Considering the history of refugees in Turkey, Syrian immigration in the last decade is different. Turkey used to receive refugees and immigrants of the same – Turkish- ethnicity. Nowadays, Turkey is in the centre of one of history's greatest migration crisis and has been seen as a "transit" country for Syrian refugees. But at the face of rejection by Europe characterised by stricter immigration policies and practices, Syrian immigrants gave up their hopes of migration to Europe and began to see Turkey as a "target country". This has caused differences in perceptions of both Syrian refugees and Turkish host society. While the media and integration problems of the refugee society mostly affect the perception of Turkish society, the perception of Syrian refugee society is affected by social acceptance, livelihood, health and education, etc.

In this respect, the acceptance of refugees by host communities and their adaptation in the country of migration depends on appropriate migration policies and mutual interactions of societies. The same is true for Syrian refugees in Turkey. However, there is also a great need for local governments'

[60] D. Tümeğ, "Turkish People's Perception of Syrian Asylum / Refugee Current Situation, Fieldwork and Policy Recommendations", Report, TÜRKSAM Publications, Ankara, April 2018, pp. 20-21.

involvement and a conscious host society as much as the central government to raise awareness of the refugee community.

# CHAPTER 14

# INTEGRATION POLICIES OF THE EUROPEAN UNION
# AND TURKEY TOWARDS REFUGEES

## Cemal Kakışım[*] and Ozan Selçuk[**]

## Introduction

Being a complex, multi-dimensional and multi-layered concept, integration is not a new term in refugee studies. The Refugee Convention of 1951 and its 1967 Protocol about the status of refugees is the basis for the protection and the integration of refugees. Being a centrepiece document for refugees, the convention is part of initiatives for the advancement of universal human rights.

Integration of refugees into host societies is the most lasting solution in the developed world. Having the same level of integration services as refugees, United Nations High Commissioner for Refugees (UNHCR) is the lead spokesperson for beneficiaries of subsidiary security within the European Union (EU). A study carried out recently by the UNHCR in several EU countries involving refugees, men, women, boys and girls has found that refugees are viewed as main barriers to integration by the lack of local language skills and culture. On the other hand, host societies lack an understanding of the specific situation of refugees, according to the report. According to the study, host communities lack an understanding of the particular refugee situation.

Over the past 20 years, the integration of refugees has been on the policy agenda of the EU and Turkey. However, this phenomenon has become one of the high politics of those countries since the Arab Spring broke out as a series of anti-government protests, uprisings against oppressive regimes. Egypt, Libya, Tunisia and Syria are affected socially and politically from the uprising, which brought about negative global results. One of the results is human flow affecting the EU countries and Turkey. Since 2011, more than five million people majority of whom are from Syria, Iraq and Afghanistan arrived Turkey in less than 5 years. On the other hand, in 2015, the influx of more than one million people heading for European countries has created a migration crisis, which has forced Turkey and the EU into a social, political, and economic trouble.

[*] PhD, Recep Tayyip Erdogan University, International Relations, cemal.kakisim@erdogan.edu.tr
[**] PhD, Recep Tayyip Erdogan University, Social Work, ozan.selcuk@erdogan.edu.tr

Created under the umbrella of the United Nations (UN), the International Organization for Migration (IOM), sees integration as a part of migration management policies (IOM Turkey, 2020). From this point of view, integration is one of the goals to be achieved in migration policies. States with different institutions (for example, Turkey, the Ministry of Internal Affairs Immigration Administration General Directorate, Ministry of Education, Red Cross, IOM Turkey) policies are producing. However, in the policy-making process, states can take different attitudes at the same time. Therefore, integration is a goal not only for society but also for states. As can be seen in the example of the IOM, international organizations are important actors of the integration process. This process can be strengthened with the participation of international organizations with a supranational effort.[1]

The strategy of integration seeks to carry society's results for all over time convergence. Both people and residents, with and without a history of immigrants, must actively be interested. They will contribute through their skills and competencies to the social, economic, cultural and civic life of society. In this discussion paper, by using the concept, refugee is defined as someone who is unable or unwilling to return to their country of origin owing to a well-founded fear of being persecuted for reasons of race, religion, nationality, membership of a particular social group, or political opinion.[2]

Migration resulted in turbulence and challenges in the host societies of Turkey and the EU, which has remained high on the agenda. The reactions of the host societies forced the politicians to take measures to eliminate drawbacks of the migration crisis. On the other hand, the current integration policies were found to be insufficient and did not meet the needs of both the host societies and the refugees themselves. This situation has led to the questioning and radical change of existing policies. Turkey and the EU States have made significant changes in the integration and immigration policies, and have created new institutions since 2013 and 2015, respectively.

In this chapter, the transformed integration policies of Turkey and the EU was discussed through a holistic approach. To this end, this chapter is divided into two sections which are (1) Integration Policies of Turkey, (2) Integration Policies of the EU. In order to discuss integration policies comprehensively, each section is addressed in six different topics: (1) Citizenship, (2) Housing, (3) Healthcare, (4) Education, (5) Employment, (6) Social Cohesion.

This chapter discussed the integration policies of Turkey and the EU in order to provide an overview of existing policies towards refugees and to

---

[1] Ayhan Kaya, **İslam, Göç ve Entegrasyon**, İstanbul, İstanbul Bilgi Üniversitesi, 2016.
[2] Paul Weis, "The refugee convention, 1951", The Research Centre for International Law Cambridge University, **Cambridge International Document Series**, Vol. 7, 1995, pp. 533-558.

evaluate the pros and cons of the actions taken by the States.

## Integration policies of Turkey

Turkey's geographical location has been a natural transit route for migrating from east to west for hundreds of years. For this reason, it has been both a transit country for refugees and a refugee-hosting country. Turkey has made many regulations for refugees and immigrants because of migration and human mobility. With its impact on human mobility in the 1920s and 1930s, the Settlement law of 1934, the first legislation for refugees and asylum-seekers, entered into force. The individuals of Turkish descent and culture were accepted as immigrants in this law.[3] Turkey was a State party to the 1951 Geneva Convention relating to the Status of Refugees and its 1967 Protocol. However, Turkey has put a geographical reservation to the contract. According to the reservation, Turkey only accepted people as a refugee coming from the European Council countries.[4] Later, due to immigration from Iraq and Iran, Turkey passed the 1994 Regulation on Asylum.

In 2011, the civil war in Syria had begun, and Syrians took refuge in Turkey. The number of Syrian refugees increased in a short time and reached millions. Turkey has followed an "open door" policy towards asylum seekers from the beginning and hasn't forcibly returned. Turkey was thus forced to make more comprehensive legislation in compliance with the international standards. In 2013, Turkey enacted the Law on Foreigners and International Protection (LFIP). The geographical limitation in the Geneva Convention has also been preserved in the new regulation. In LFIP, international protection is defined as four different the status granted for refugees, conditional refugees, subsidiary protection, and temporary protection. In LFIP, Turkey's main asylum legislation, international protection defined as four different the status granted for refugees, conditional refugees, subsidiary protection, and temporary protection.[5] In 2014, the Temporary Protection Regulation (TPR) entered into force, and Syrians are accepted as asylum seekers within the status of temporary protection.[6] In this regard, integration policies of the Turkey offer priorities for successful and healthy integration, which are (1) citizenship, (2) housing, (3) education, (4) healthcare, (5) employment, (6) social harmony. In the following sections, the integration policies in Turkey will be discussed along with these priorities.

---

[3] Doğuş Şimşek, "Göç Politikaları ve İnsan Güvenliği: Türkiye'deki Suriyeliler Örneği", **Toplum ve Bilim Dergisi**, Sayı 140, 2017, p. 17.
[4] Dilek Latif, "Refugee of the Turkish Republic", **The Turkish Yearbook of International Relations**, Vol. XXXIII, 2002, p. 20.
[5] İbrahim Kaya ve Esra Yılmaz Eren, "Türkiye'deki Suriyelilerin Hukuki Durumu: Arada Kalanların Hakları ve Yükümlülükleri", **Siyaset, Ekonomi ve Toplum Araştırmaları Vakfı**, 2015, p. 25.
[6] ibid, p. 30-32.

## Citizenship

One of the most important goals of immigrants and asylum-seekers who have lost their sense of belonging to the country of their citizenship because of endless wars, political instability, human rights violations, and economic crises is to gain the country's citizenship where they refuge in. Syrian asylum seekers in Turkey seek to gain Turkish citizenship. However, granting citizenship to Syrians is one of the most controversial topics in Turkish society. It is causing profound disagreement about the cultural, political, and social sense in society.

The gain citizenship of Turkish was organized by the Turkish Citizenship Law No 5901. According to this law, Turkish citizenship is acquired by birth or meeting certain conditions.[7] Turkish citizenship by birth shall be automatically acquired on the basis of descent or place of birth. Outside of birth, Turkish citizenship is acquired through adoption, the decision by the competent authority, and the acquisition of the right to choose.[8] The right of citizenship granted by an authorized competent authority depends on many conditions; be able to speak a sufficient Turkish level, be a good moral character, reside at least 5 years in Turkey, become adults, have adequate income, etc.[9]

In this context, Turkish authorities' grantees citizenship rights to immigrants who meet these conditions, provided that they do not pose an obstacle to public order and national security.[10] For this reason, Turkish citizenship is not granted to Syrian because they have had temporary protection status. They need to gain one of the statuses of refugee, conditional refugees, and subsidiary protection for obtaining citizenship. Moreover, Syrians don't apply for other statuses as their temporary protection status continues.[11] According to the LFIP, since Syrians are not given refugee, conditional refugee, and secondary protection status, they don't gain citizenship.

However, Syrians may gain the right to apply for Turkish citizenship through marriage and adoption. It is also possible to gain citizenship for Syrian children who were born in Turkey. In this context, a Syrian who marries a Turkish citizen may obtain the right to apply for Turkish citizenship if they meet other conditions such as being married for at least 3 years and

[7] **European Convention on Nationality,** Council of European Portal, https://www.coe.int/en/web/conventions/full-list/-/conventions/treaty/166 (Access 11.12.2020).

[8] **Türk Vatandaşlığı Kanunu,** https://www.mevzuat.gov.tr/MevzuatMetin/1.5.5901.pdf (Access 11.12.2020).

[9] Türk Vatandaşlığı Kanunu, ibid.

[10] Türk Vatandaşlığı Kanunu, ibid.

[11] Kaya ve Eren, op.cit., p. 62-63.

living in family unity.[12] Underage Syrian children may also apply for citizenship if a Turkish citizen adopts them.[13]

Based on these conditions, many Syrian asylum seekers gained Turkish citizenship. According to the Migration and Integration Report prepared in the Grand National Assembly of Turkey, nearly 30.000 Syrian refugees were granted Turkish citizenship.[14] The Ministry of Interior officials announced that 110.000 Syrians were granted Turkish citizenship in 2019, and 53,000 of them are adults, and 57,000 are children.[15]

## Housing

Since 2011, Turkey has opened its doors to thousands of Syrians who have fled their home country's violence. Except in exceptional circumstances, none of them has been forcibly returned to Syria. Temporary accommodation centres (TAC) in regions close to the border have been first established to meet the need for food and housing for the first refugees who reached Turkey. The first Syrian groups were placed in TAC. The first Syrian groups were placed in these centres. However, because of the migration flow reaching millions quickly, the Syrian refugees spread to the provinces outside TAC. According to the Directorate General of Migration Management statistics, 59.645 Syrians have lived in 7 TAC in 5 provinces as of 2020. 3,571,057 Syrians live outside of TAC.[16] According to the statistics, nearly 98% of Syrians have spread various provinces and have lived together with the Turkish people.[17]

International organizations evaluate the conditions of tACs in Turkey. According to the UN 2012 Syrian Refugees Report, Turkey provided high standards of service to asylum seekers. Also, TACs in Turkey was called the best refugee camps worldwide in the International Crisis Group 2013 Report.[18] Health, cleaning, food, and education services for Syrian in TAC provide. These services are pretty limited for Syrians live in out of TAC. Although they significantly benefit from education and health services, they

---

[12] Ali Kemal Nurdoğan ve Mustafa Öztürk, "Geçici Koruma Statüsü İle Türkiye'de Bulunan Suriyelilerin Vatandaşlık Hakkı", **Süleyman Demirel Üniversitesi İktisadi ve İdari Bilimler Fakültesi Dergisi,** Cilt 23, Sayı 3, 2018, p. 1171.
[13] Nurdoğan, ibid. p. 1171.
[14] Hakan Bostan, "Geçici Koruma Statüsündeki Suriyelilerin Uyum, Vatandaşlık ve İskan Sorunu", **Göç Araştırmaları Dergisi,** Cilt 4, Sayı 8, 2018, p. 62.
[15] Mülteciler Derneği, Türkiye'deki Suriyeli Sayısı Ekim 2020, https://multeciler.org.tr/turkiyedeki-suriyeli-sayisi/ (Access 11.12.2020).
[16] T.C. İçişleri Bakanlığı Göç İdaresi Genel Müdürlüğü, Geçici Koruma, 2020, https://www.goc.gov.tr/gecici-koruma5638 (Access 10.12.2020).
17 2016 Türkiye Göç Raporu, Yayın No: 40, **T.C. İçişleri Bakanlığı Göç İdaresi Genel Müdürlüğü,** 2017, p. 80, https://www.goc.gov.tr/kurumlar/goc.gov.tr/YillikGocRaporlari/2016_yiik_goc_raporu_haziran.pdf (Access 10.12.2020).
[18] Kaya ve Eren, op.cit., p.68.

do not have a regular income and shelter.[19] However, Syrian prefer mostly big cities to live by taking poor living conditions. Although Syrians have spread all provinces in Turkey, the four provinces where they most live are Istanbul, Gaziantep, Hatay, and Şanlıurfa, respectively.[20]

Turkey is planning to build permanent collective housing for Syrian in Turkey's territory and the safe areas close to the Syrian border. It is aimed to settle Syrians living in the temporary container in the collective housing.[21] Syrians living out of TAC have accommodation options under quite different conditions depending on their financial means and close connections. For example, Syrians who have economic mean to buy a house or have Turkish relatives live in comfortable housings. However, millions of Syrians who have limited financial means live in basements, warehouses, and slums created under very primitive conditions.[22]

## Education

Education is one of the most important steps in the integration of Syrian refugees into Turkish society. According to statistics of the Immigration Administration General Directorate of Statistics, the number of Syrian refugees in Turkey, 224.655 in 2013 raised to 3.576.659 in January 2020. With the increase, the number of Syrians in the 5-17 age range who are in school-age reached 1.082.172.[23]

Educational services offered by Turkey for Syrians launched firstly in the camps. However, in a short time, it expanded to include educational institutions across the country. The lessons for Syrian children in the camps were conducted in Turkish, and so Syrians were supported to learn Turkish. With the TPR published in 2013, Syrians were provided with temporary protection status and the services of employment, health, education, interpretation, and social assistance. Within the scope of education services, Syrians have been given the right to studying and receive a diploma in public schools.[24] However, a new education policy was preferred taking into account some problems encountered in practice until 2016. It was preferred inclusive education that is *"a process of addressing and responding to the diversity of needs of all learners through increasing participation in learning, cultures and communities, and*

---

[19] Hacı Yunus Taş ve Selami Özcan, "Suriyeli Göçmen Sorunlarının, Sosyal Politikalar Bağlamında Analizi", **Hak-İş Uluslararası Emek ve Toplum Dergisi**, Cilt 7, Sayı 17, 2018, p. 42.

[20] T.C. İçişleri Bakanlığı Göç İdaresi Genel Müdürlüğü, ibid.

[21] **Hürriyet**, Suriyelilere Kalıcı Konut, 03.02.2018, https://www.hurriyet.com.tr/gundem/suriyelilere-kalici-konut-40729951 (Access 10.12.2020).

[22] **Housing- Turkey**, The Asylum Information Database (AIDA), 2020, https://www.asylumineurope.org/reports/country/turkey/housing-1 (Access 10.12.2020).

[23] T.C. Milli Eğitim Bakanlığı, Hayat Boyu Öğrenme Genel Müdürlüğü, https://hbogm.meb.gov.tr/meb_iys_dosyalar/2020_01/27110237_OCAK_2020internet_BulteniSunu.pdf (Access 10.12.2020).

[24] Abdullah Said Özcan, "Çokkültürlülük Bağlamında Türkiye'nin Suriyeli Öğrencilere Yönelik Eğitim Politikası", **Pesa Uluslararası Sosyal Araştırmalar Dergisi**, Cilt 4, Sayı 1, 2018, p. 25-26.

*reducing exclusion within and from education".[25]* In inclusive education, students' differences such as race, language, culture, and the different needs of them are not considered a source of problems but as an advantage in terms of multiculturalism.[26] Turkey offered Arabic and culture courses in the context of their differences as well as Turkish to Syrian students. It is trying to prevent discrimination against Syrians and consider their cultural demands.[27] In the context, an Inclusive Education Project supported by UNICEF is carried out by the Ministry of National Education. Within this project's scope, support training is provided to both Syrian teachers and Turkish teachers who teach Syrian students.[28]

Language deficiency is one of the most common problems for Syrian children in education. While Arabic education is offered to temporary education centres, Turkish education is only provided in public schools. Turkish language education is offered by various organizations, especially municipalities, but these courses are insufficient in terms of the number of students. Also, public schools haven't adequate infrastructure to provide Turkish education.[29] Language deficiency is causing children to be affected differently according to age categories. Younger Syrian children adapt to schools easier because of the ability to learn languages quickly.[30] Adult children with more difficult language learning are isolated in classrooms or are not accepted to the school. Therefore, most adult children who need to study are forced to join the labour force with low wages.[31]

## Healthcare

Asylum-seekers face serious healthcare problems due to the adverse conditions of the country they left and the difficulties during migration. Children and older people, the most disadvantaged of refugees, are at serious risk. Turkey's healthcare services are a critical issue for Syrians traumatized by war and injured during the escape process. Healthcare services had been provided for Syrians at the border when the first Syrian groups arrived at Turkey's border. Then healthcare services have provided in TACs. However, with the camps' insufficiency and Syrians' spread throughout the country,

---

[25] **Guidelines for Inclusion: Ensuring Access to Education for All,** UNESCO, p. 13.
https://unesdoc.unesco.org/ark:/48223/pf0000140224 (Access 10.12.2020).
[26] Hilal Kazu ve Emrah Deniz, "Kapsayıcı Eğitim Bağlamında Öğretmenlerin Mülteci Öğrencilere İlişkin Tutumlarının Çeşitli Değişkenler Açısından İncelenmesi", **Uluslararası Toplum Araştırmaları Dergisi,**Cilt 14, Sayı 20, 2019, p. 1340.
[27] Özcan, ibid. p. 27.
[28] Kazu ve Deniz, ibid. p. 1340.
[29] Maurice Crul, Elif Keskinler, Jens Schneider, Frans Lelie, and Safoura Ghaeminia, "No Lost Generation? Education for Refugee Children. A Comparison Between Sweden, Germany, the Netherlands and Turkey", **The Integration of Migrants And Refugees,** Rainer Bauböck and Milena Tripkovic (Ed.), European University Institute, 2017, p. 68.
[30] ibib. p. 69
[31] idib. p. 69.

health services have been expanded to cover 81 provinces.[32] Syrians recorded in Turkey and have the temporary identification number benefit freely from healthcare services such as emergency medical treatment, preventive and primary health care. Syrians who have not the temporary identification number benefit only from healthcare services of combating infectious diseases, immunization, and emergency health.[33] Moreover, 112 emergency services, primary preventive, diagnostic, curative health services, and secondary and tertiary health services are provided for millions of Syrians living out of TAC and TAC.[34] Community Health centres in TACs are providing primary preventive, diagnostic, and curative health services. In out of TACs, these healthcare services are freely provided by Immigrant Health centres, Family Health centres, and voluntary health institutions.[35]

The diseases such as polio, measles, mumps spread in Turkey when Syrians who are not vaccinated against these diseases come to Turkey. Therefore, Syrians were involved in Expanded Programme on Immunization, and in this context, Syrian children in the age range 0-5 and 0-15 are vaccinated and added vaccination schedule of Turkey.[36] Thus, it aimed at Syrians' compliance with public health and the Turkish health system as in many areas.

Syrians language deficiency is one of the most important problems encountered in healthcare. They are troubling to express the health problem. Series of measures have been taken to overcome this problem in Turkey. Interpreters were employed in healthcare services, and an interpreter line was established for international patients.[37] Nurses, doctors, and interpreters who provide health services to refugees have been trained by UNHCR, World Health Organization (WHO), Disaster and Emergency Management Authority (AFAD).[38] Additionally, Syrian healthcare workers are employed. Syrian health workers whose profession is approved by the Ministry of Health are employed in Immigrant Health centres or health centres in TACs.[39]

Improving the Health Status of the Syrian Population Under Temporary

---

[32] Nagihan Önder, "Türkiye'de Geçici Koruma Altındaki Suriyelilere Yönelik Sağlık Politikalarının Analizi", **Göç Araştırmaları Dergisi**, Cilt 5, Sayı 1, 2019, p.135-136.

[33] **Sıhhat Projesi**, https://www.sihhatproject.org/proje-faaliyetleri_0-657 (Access 10.12.2020).

[34] Ergun Demir, Işıl Ergin, A. Öner Kurt, Nilay Etiler, "Sığınmacıların/Geçici Koruma Altına Alınanların Sağlık Hizmetlerinden Yararlanmasında Mevcut Durum ve Yaşanan Sorunlar", **Engeller, Savaş, Göç ve Sağlık**, Işıl Ergin (Ed.), Türk Tabibler Birliği Yayınları, 2016, p. 85.

[35] ibid. p. 86.

[36] Aylin Sinem Gültaç ve Pınar Yalçın Balçık, "Suriyeli Sığınmacılara Yönelik Sağlık Politikaları", **Sakarya Tıp Dergisi**, Cilt 8, Sayı 2, 2018, p. 197.

[37] ibid. p. 198.

[38] ibid. p. 198.

[39] Ahmet İçduygu and Doğuş Şimşek, "Syrian Refugees in Turkey Towards Integration Policies", **Turkish Policy Quartely**, Vol. 15, No. 3, 2016.

Protection and Related Services Provided by Turkish Authorities (SIHHAT I) project funded by EU was implemented to develop the health care infrastructure for asylum seekers and eliminate the problem of compliance in health care. The first phase of the project started in 2016, is expected to be completed in 2020.[40] Within the project's scope, it aims to support Immigrant Health centres, create new centres, and employ Syrian health workers to serve in these centres.[41]

### Employment

Syrians integrate into the labour market as every area of social life in Turkey. Syrians living out of TACs have to work as unregistered in unqualified jobs to meet their vital needs such as shelter, food, and health. However, Syrians' unregistered work has gradually caused serious problems, and it has made it necessary to make a legal regulation on this issue. With the legal regulation enacted in 2016, Syrians under temporary protection status were legally allowed to work in the provinces where they are registered. However, considering the impact of this decision on the labour market, the number of Syrians employed in an enterprise is limited not to exceed 10% of the total number of personnel.[42] According to the Ministry of Family, Labour, and Social Services, 31 thousand 185 Syrians have been given work permits as of 2019.[43] This number is well below the number of Syrians who can work. There are 1,651,831 Syrian men and 945 337 Syrian women in the 15-64 age range can working in Turkey.[44] According to these numbers, the vast majority of Syrians are employed in unregistered work in Turkey.

While Syrians, more qualified and educated, prefer European countries to work and live in, their unskilled and less educated remain in Turkey. Consequently, Syrians in Turkey work as unregistered in low-paid jobs that do not require any qualifications.[45] Because of language deficit, low education level, lack of an official diploma, financial impossibility, Syrian turn to socioeconomically unqualified jobs.[46] Most are employed in the

---

[40] **Sıhhat Projesi,** https://www.sihhatproject.org/proje-faaliyetleri_0-657 (Access 10.12.2020).
[41] Önder, op.cit., p. 148.
[42] **Geçici Koruma Sağlanan Yabancıların Çalışma İzinlerine Dair Yönetmelik,** 2016, https://www.mevzuat.gov.tr/MevzuatMetin/3.5.20168375.pdf (Access 10.12.2020).
[43] Mülteciler Derneği, Türkiye'deki Suriyeli Sayısı Kasım 2020, https://multeciler.org.tr/turkiyedeki-suriyeli-sayisi/ (Access 10.12.2020).
[44] Şeyda Nur Koca, "Suriyeli Sığınmacıların Türk Emek Piyasasına Katılım Süreçlerinin Toplumsal Boyutları", **Göç Araştırmaları Dergisi,** Cilt 5, Sayı 2, 2019, p. 327.
[45] Ahmet Tayfur Akcan, "Türkiye İşgücü Piyasasında Suriyeli Sığınmacıların Yeri ve Etkileri", **Sosyal Güvenlik Dergisi,** Cilt 8, Sayı 2, 2018, p. 64.
[46] Esra Özpınar, Yasemin Satır Çilingir ve Ayşegül Taşöz Düşündere, "Türkiye'deki Suriyeliler: İşsizlik ve Sosyal Uyum", **Türkiye Ekonomi Politikaları Araştırma Vakfı,** 2016, https://www.tepav.org.tr/upload/files/1461746316-7.Turkiye___deki_Suriyeliler___Issizlik_ve_Sosyal_Uyum.pdf (Access 10.12.2020).

manufacturing, construction, and service sectors.[47] Nevertheless, Syrians who obtain a work permit receive at least the minimum wage. Syrians, who obtain a work permit, are directed to vocational courses by Turkey Business Association to integrate into the labour market and make more qualified jobs, and so they gain work experience.[48]

Moreover, Syrians could build a business and become employers in Turkey. Syrians with sufficient financial means establish their own businesses under the Turkish Commercial Code and employ Syrian refugees there.[49] In 2017 and 2018, most of the foreign companies starting up in Turkey was established by Syrians. The Ministry of Commerce announced that the number of businesses with at least one Syrian partner in 2019 was 15,159.[50]

## Social cohesion

The first groups of Syrian asylum-seekers arrived in Turkey about nine years ago. During this time, the political authority could not be established in Syria and could not be a serious step taken to the return of asylum-seekers from Turkey to Syria. This adventure approaching ten years has created the impression is gradually began the Syrians, initially accepted as guests, to be permanent in Turkey. Thus, Syrians cohesion to Turkish society came to the fore among the topics of the agenda. Education and healthcare, employment, housing, and ultimately citizenship, which are mentioned above, are actually the basic building blocks of the social cohesion process.

LFIP includes harmonization activities for immigrants. In LFIP, with the contributions and suggestions of non-governmental organizations, universities, local administrations, and public institutions, it is stated that the social harmonization activities of the protected persons will be planned. Harmonization and Communications Department under Directorate General of Migration Management was established.[51] In LFIP, the adaptation of protected persons to Turkish society is not defined as assimilation or integration. Harmonization (cohesion) is defined as the process of understanding between immigrants and society voluntarily.[52] In this context, instead of Syrians' assimilation, it aims to make them compatible with Turkish society with their own culture.[53]

"Turkish society assumes the most important role and responsibility

---

[47] Murat Erdoğan, Suriyeliler Barometresi-2019: Suriyelilerle Uyum İçinde Yaşamın Çerçevesi, Orion Kitabevi, 2020, p. 41.
[48] Koca, ibid, p. 333.
[49] Erdoğan, ibid. p. 44.
[50] Erdoğan, ibid. p. 44.
[51] Sinem Yıldırımalp, Emel İslamoğlu ve Cemal İyem, "Suriyeli Sığınmacıların Toplumsal Kabul ve Uyum Sürecine İlişkin Bir Araştırma", **Bilgi**, Sayı 35, 2017, p.111.
[52] Erdoğan, op.cit., p. 17.
[53] Bostan, op.cit, p. 53.

for Syrians. The arrival of millions of refugees to the country in a short time, unprecedented even in the history of the world, created a "social shock" in the society. Turkish society's solidarity and sacrifice in this process have enabled many probable problems to be eliminated automatically or negativities to be limited. Despite the increasing concern, anxiety, and objections in recent years, Turkey's level of social solidarity and social acceptance are still at extremely high levels. This is a precious situation both for the Turkish community and for the Syrians."[54]

Although lifestyle and cultural differences make the cohesion process between Turkish society and Syrians difficult, the social acceptance and adaptation process has begun for Syrians in Turkey. The increasing number of Syrian babies born in Turkey and Syrians who married Turks contributes positively to harmony and cohesion between Syrians and Turkish people.[55] Also, various activities are carried out to normalize Syrians and their cultural adaptation to Turkish society. Turkish education, vocational and hobby courses, information activities, psychosocial support services, and training activities stand out among these activities.[56]

However, despite all these activities, the desired success in social cohesion and social acceptance has not been achieved yet. In a study, it has been questioned that the adapts of Syrians to Turkish society and Turkey. According to the study results, while most Turkish people (64.4%) clearly state that they do not adapt, Syrians think that they are adapting contrary.[57]

## Integration policies of the European Union

More than a million refugees' crossing the Mediterranean Sea for Europe in 2015 was a turning point for the available integration policies of Europe and marked a paradigm shift for migration literature in Europe's history. Conceptualized as migration crisis, the notion of integration and related policies were being questioned. The migration crisis has led to radical changes in the integration policies implemented in European countries. With the motto of "Inclusion for All", the European Union sets the new agenda for the 2021-2027 period. The new agenda entails a whole European-wide approach to integration with its institutions, citizens, and residents.

The successful integration of migrants and refugees will warrant a better, prosperous, and wealthy Europe and will contribute to the coherence of its societies. The European Union (EU) supports national and local initiatives

---

[54] Erdoğan, op.cit, . p. 57.
[55] Yıldırmalp, İslamoğlu ve İyem, op.cit., p. 35.
[56] Bostan, op.cit., p. 58.
[57] Erdoğan, op.cit., p. 104.

and policies, whilst the Member States bear the primary responsibility for integration. In this regard, integration policies of the EU offer priorities for successful and healthy integration, which are (1) citizenship, (2) housing, (3) education, (4) healthcare, (5) employment, (6) social harmony. In the following sections, the integration policies will be discussed along with these priorities through best practices drawn from the experiences of states across Europe.

## Citizenship

Today, citizenship is understood primarily as an opportunity and obligation to participate in a contemporary democratic society. These rights and responsibilities include privileges such as voting, being in various units in the community, military service, taxing and serving in similar ways, as well as rights and responsibilities such as compliance with the law. All of this means joining the basic elements of the political system that the individual is a member of, which is identical to citizenship. However, in the global reality of the 21st century, which we call the age of globalization or immigration, both the concept of nation state and the concepts of classical citizenship in some way threatened by new geopolitics and, paradoxically, they are returning to have a certain importance.

Acquiring citizenship is one of the main pillars for the successful integration of refugees and migrants, providing them with a sense of identity and a wide range of rights. Overall, the policy for granting citizenship plays a significant role in the management of migration processes. It helps governments to prevent actions posing a threat to national security.

The Czech Citizenship Act explicitly states that apart from the statutory requirements for the grant of Czech citizenship, Czech citizenship may be granted to the applicant if it is incorporated into Czech society, particularly where the integration relates to family, work or society[58].

The term citizenship indicates the relationship between an individual and the national state; it is a status to which the legal system links the fullness of civil and political rights. Many migrants and international protection holders face difficulties related to insufficient knowledge of the services offered, the lack of homogeneity of administrative procedures and the lack of knowledge of the functioning of the public administration.

Refugees, having a well-founded fear of persecution, cannot ask for documents and certificates to prove personal states and facts to the authorities of their country of origin, including consular representations

---

[58] **Granting Czech Citizenship**, http://obcanstvi.cestina-pro-cizince.cz/index.php?hl=en_US&p=zadost-o-udeleni-statniho-obcanstvi-cr (Access 11.12.2020).

abroad, and this can lead to significant problems in some administrative procedures, since the lack of such documentation could prevent the exercise of fundamental rights.

The social inclusion process must make access to information on individual rights and duties and on the services available, as well as an adequate orientation towards their use and, indeed, one of the declared objectives of the National Integration Plan is to enhance the information of international protection holders about their rights and duties.

## Housing

The living environment and living conditions in terms of housing are key to the integration of refugees and migrants. Integration can only flourish by making housing fairly available to immigrants, migrants and national residents, as well as by stimulating multicultural living environments.[59] In view of this, Justice and Home Affairs Council of European Union adopted "The Common Basic Principles (CBP) for Immigrant Integration Policy" in 2004 to lay down a common agenda for EU initiatives in the field of integration. CBP 6 reads as:

> "Access for immigrants to institutions, as well as to public and private goods and services, on a basis equal to national citizens and in a non-discriminatory way is a critical foundation for better integration."[60]

EU member states with its many actors (NGOs, regional and local authorities) should involve in providing accommodation for refugees for the realization of this priority above. However, depending on their legal status, gender, civic status and nationality, refugees face social disadvantages to acquire a decent housing. Scarce housing, living conditions available for refugees are important risk factors for refugees. Such factors create further risks such as having to live in deprived areas with limited sources and employment opportunities. These conditions contribute to re-marginalization of refugees.

It is evident that an adequate and accessible housing without adopt crucial for the refugees and migrants and also their families, and it is an important factor in the process of successful integration. However, transition from the reception centres which accommodate the refugees during the proceedings for granting protection to housing facilities after receiving a refugee status is a path filled with many administrative obstacles, financial and language

---

[59] NGO Network of integration Focal Pointp. (2019). Policy Briefing on Housing for Refugees and Migrants in Europe. https://ec.europa.eu/migrant-integration/?action=media.download&uuid=2A9D0 F59-D323-7D0D-32AF0093CD9B9031. (Accesp. 5.12.2020).
[60] **Common Basic Principles,** European Economic and Social Committee, https://www.eesc.europa. eu/resources/docs/common-basic-principles_en.pdf (Access 11.12.2020).

difficulties and cultural problems. The refugees and beneficiaries of international protection have access to housing under the same conditions as other third country nationals legally residing in a European state.

For example, in Bulgaria, a person who granted international protection may be provided with financial support for up to six months under the established terms and procedures but in practice, refugees tend to settle down in the larger cities where they may have more opportunities for accommodation and employment. However, due to lack of available number of houses and discriminatory legislation, it is hard for refugees to find accommodation in Bulgaria, but it may conclusively be said that refugees in Bulgaria are solely responsible for their own housing by renting private properties. In Czech Republic case, integration asylum centres are available for refugees for which they pay for rent and utility fees. Maximum of 12 months for housing is funded under certain conditions this is considered to be the initial adaptation to the live in Czech Republic.

On the other hand, there are good practices of accommodation policy for integration. Casa Amica, a social housing agency in Italy, promotes housing project with various stakeholders (NGOs, regional and local authorities) in order to offer housing services to those who are unable to satisfy their housing needs on the market for economic reasons or for the absence of an adequate offer. trying to strengthen their condition.[61] Dutch Council for Refugees struggle to empower refugees to access to adequate housing in the Netherlands. Being an independent and non-governmental organization, A member of the European Council on Refugees and Exiles (ECRE), Dutch Council for Refugees (DCR) warrants just refugee policies through proactively advocating the refugees' rights.[62] The project "Kosmopolis" has been built in Austria for private housing. Some of the apartments for refugees who already are working are reserved in a newly developed city. An information centre has been built in the vicinity to prevent misunderstandings between refugees and those living there. A Protocol in Portugal between the Municipality of Lisbon and Portuguese NGOs has provided refugees with accommodation and access to training, education and labour market integration services in the Municipality of Lisbon.[63]

---

[61] **Casa Amica Fondazione,** http://www.fondazionecasaamica.org/fondazione/housing-sociale/ (Access 11.12.2020).
[62] **Dutch Council for Refugees,** VluchtelingenWerk Nederland, https://www.vluchtelingenwerk.nl/ artikel/dutch-council-refugees# (Access 11.12.2020).
[63] Christa Schweng and Panagiotis Gkofas, "(SOC/532) Integration of Refugees in the EU", **European Economic and Social Committee,** 2016, http://edz.bib.uni-mannheim.de/edz/doku/wsa/2016/ces-2016-0262-en.pdf (Access 11.12.2020).

**Education**

The 26th Article of Universal Declaration Queens that every human being has right to education, as an empowering right. This right is also supported by the international Covenant on Economy, Social and Cultural Rights and the Convention on the Rights of the Child. The "education" dimension of integration in Europe as discussed in this context. Another principle set forth by Justice and Home Affairs Council of European Union in its common basic principles for refugees regarding the access to quality education is that "efforts in education are critical to preparing immigrants, and particularly their descendants, to be more successful and more active participants in society"[64]. This universal and indispensable right is undoubtedly an integral part of a successful integration of refugees. In this regard, European Union offers concrete policies and action to support the integration of refugees. On the other hand, the high-quality education offered across Europe is among the key factors shaping the refugees' decision to reach Europe.[65]

According to a report published by UNHCR, refugees in the world are five times more likely to have education opportunities than the global average. Compared to the 92% global average, only 61% of refugee children have access to primary education. Moreover, this gap gradually increases as the age gets older. Compared to the 84% global average, only 23% of adolescent refugees attend secondary education. In higher education, while the global average is 34%, less than 1% of refugees go to university. Refugee children, young and adults must have access to education programs in order to work in high-skilled professions and make a great contribution to the communities in which they live.[66]

The migration crisis of 2016 has dramatically changed the education policies of European states. As a result, each state provided opportunities for children of refugees to go to school. In Bulgaria Greece and Serbia, for example, between 50% and 62% of all school-age refugee and migrant children were integrated into education system.[67] In Sweden, a child has right to education if s/he is registered to stay in the country. Aliens and Borders Service in Portugal raise awareness among refugees to encourage them to send their children to school. Greece established reception classes for refugee children, whereas Bulgaria strengthens their teachers' capacity to best educate

[64] NGO Network of integration Focal Pointp. (2019). Policy Briefing on Housing for Refugees and Migrants in Europe. https://ec.europa.eu/migrant-integration/?action=media.download&uuid=2A9D0 F59-D323-7D0D-32AF0093CD9B9031. (Access 10.12.2020).
[65] UNHCR. (2019). *Access to Education for Refugee and Migrant Children in Europe.* Retrieved from https://reliefweb.int/sites/reliefweb.int/files/resources/5d774e3e4.pdf (Access 10.12.2020).
[66] UNHCR. (n.d.). *Education.* Retrieved from https://www.unhcr.org/tr/en/education (Access 10.12.2020).
[67] UNHCR. (2019), op. cit.

and integrate those children. On the other hand, the Netherlands has policy of observing early school leaving issue among refugees to ensure these people have access to education.

In addition to country specific policies, European Union supports the integration of refugees through range of programs such as online linguistic support[68] to providing the opportunity to learn the local language, and Erasmus projects.[69] European Commission funds many inspiring projects to help refugees successfully integrate into local community.

However, there are many obstacles that need to be improved to access to education. Refugees under 1951 convention and subsidiary protection have access to education within the same conditions as their peers. However, they cannot enjoy this right automatically,[70] which makes it hard to receive quality education. While discussing the very issue, one should consider that there is no common regulation encompassing all European states. Therefore, there are disparities between the countries. This is partly caused by the available figures provided by the countries, in which some countries record data based on status of the children (Bulgaria), whereas others record based on citizenship and/or language skills (France, Italy, Sweden). However, some countries record data of the refugee children regardless of their legal status (Greece, Serbia).

## Healthcare

The effective access to healthcare services of refugees and migrants is one of the most important factors for their successful integration in the host country. The healthcare policy for refugees and migrants is closely connected with the policy on social cohesion, sustainable development and intercultural dialogue.

Depending on the entry, transit or destination targets, European countries were affected differently by the 2015 migration crisis. Similarities exist however, in that the access to appropriate health care facilities of refugees and migrants has always been hampered. Some of the barriers to access to health care, language and cultural obstacles have already been established, including information on where and how to receive healthcare, economic obstacles and cultural incompetence among health providers.[71] Nevertheless, the lack of policies to ensure health care rights still applied for a majority of EU countries, as stated in the 2015 Migrant Integration Policy Index

---

[68] Online Linguistic Support, https://erasmusplusolp.eu/en/ (Access 11.12.2020).
[69] Erasmus Project Results Platform, https://ec.europa.eu/programmes/erasmus-plus/projects/ (Access 11.12.2020).
[70] UNHCR (2019). op. cit.
[71] Maarie Norredam, "Migrants' Access to Healthcare", **Danish Medical Bulletin,** Vol. 58, 2011.

(MIPEX), despite the fact that the level of implementation of the EU national policies to resolve those barriers was particularly low in Eastern Europe.[72]

Entitlement to healthcare services varies widely among the European countries, even though the right to health and, thus the right to health services should be universal. However, entitlement to services to meet the unmet needs of the refugees differs from state to state. Regardless of its universal character, the right to healthcare is undermined by enforcement of policies in certain states across Europe.[73]

For all asylum seekers, Spanish legislation allows for complete access to the public health system. By means of this legal provision, they shall be entitled to health services at the same level as citizens and third countries legal residents in Spain, including the access of individuals with torture, serious physical or psychological violence or traumatizing conditions to specialized treatment. This provision shall apply.[74]

Any asylum seeker and refugee in Greece is entitled to free access to primary, secondary and tertiary health care. If a refugee has a medical condition and needs prompt and urgent health treatment, he will have access to medical facilities from the hospital's Emergency Department.[75]

The key challenges to obtaining healthcare for refugees and migrants were the lack of equitable policies and efficient administrative processes to achieve entitlement.[76] In insurance schemes where the enrollment process can be more complex than in tax-funded systems, this is more troublesome. Exemption from limitations in many countries is possible for the most vulnerable migrant groups in many countries (e.g., infants, pregnant women, victims of violence...). However, there are still obstacles to access specialized health services, such as clinical and psychiatric services for specialists; care for women; childcare and care for victims of abuse. The explanations vary from country to country and are often dictated by the inconsistencies between what the legislation says and what the authors say is applied in

---

[72] David Ingleby and Thomas Huddleston, "The MIPEX Health Strand: A Longitudinal, Mixed-Methods Survey of Policies on Migrant Health in 38 Countries", **The European Journal of Public Health**, Vol. 29, No. 3, 2018. 458–62.

[73] **Report on the Health of Refugees and Migrants in the WHO European Region,** World Health Organization, 2018, https://appp.who.int/iris/bitstream/handle/10665/311348/9789289053785-eng.pdf?sequence=1&isAllowed=y (Access 11.12.2020).

[74] **Country Report: Spain,** Asylum Information Database (AIDA), 2017, http://www.asylumineurope.org/sites/default/files/report-download/aida_es_2017update.pdf (Access 11.12.2020).

[75] Access to Healthcare Services for Refugees and Asylum Seekers in Greece, The UN Refugee Agency, https://help.unhcr.org/greece/living-in-greece/access-to-healthcare/ (Access 11.12.2020).

[76] Chiarenza A., Dauvrin, M., Chiesa, V., Baatout, P., § Hans Verrept, "Supporting Access to Healthcare for Refugees and Migrants in European Countries Under Particular Migratory Pressure" **BMC Health Services Research,** Vol. 19, No. 513, 2019, https://doi.org/10.1186/s12913-019-4353-1 (Access 11.12.2020).

practice.[77]

### Employment

Justice and Home Affairs Council of European Union adopted "The Common Basic Principles (CBP) for Immigrant Integration Policy" in 2004, which lays down a common agenda for EU initiatives in terms of integration of refugees into labour market.

> "Employment is a key part of the integration process and is central to the participation of immigrants, to the contributions immigrants make to the host society, and to making such contributions visible" (CBP 3).

> "Frequent interaction between immigrants and Member State citizens is a fundamental mechanism for integration. Shared forums, intercultural dialogue, education about immigrants and immigrant cultures, and stimulating living conditions in urban environments enhance the interactions between immigrants and Member State citizens" (CBP 7).

As can be inferred in the basic principles above, the receiving country has to perform a facilitator role for refugees to allow them to succeed in the labour market. But it also has to decide on additional qualifications the refugee may need to acquire if he/she is to succeed in the labour market.[78] In addition to this document, European Commission adopted "Action Plan on the Integration of Third-Country Nationals" in 2016, which emphasizes that "employment is the main part of the integration process". Therefore, the primary task of the European states is to accelerate the access of refugees to labour market.

Another important document prepared by Committee on Employment and Social Affairs of European Parliament is about refugees' social inclusion and integration into the labour market. The resolution contains recommendations to EU member states regarding access of migrants to housing, education, health services and the labour market. In this regard, the policies available for employment stress that the combination of learning the local language with vocational training; recognition of skills and qualifications including informal; resettlement of refugees, taking into account their skills and local labour markets are key to integration.

There are now numerous integration schemes and services at national level whose primary aim is to speed up access to the job market for refugees and asylum seekers. The key obstacles facing refugees are language barriers,

---

[77] Chiarenza et al. op.cit.
[78] Schweng and Gkofas, op.cit.

diploma and qualification difficulties as well as extended access to work. In integrating this migrant group, the Nordic countries and Germany were the most effective.[79] Many policies are available for integration into labour market, one of them which is OECD's "Making Integration Work" series published in 2016. The study demonstrates how policymakers can promote the integration of humanitarian migrants and eliminate obstacles in the course of that aim through examples of good practice.[80]

## Social cohesion

The so-called refugee crisis of 2015 made nations reconsider their approach to integration of refugees into their societies. Social cohesion requires the states think beyond the sole refugee-host society interaction. A precondition for social coherence and economic development is the effective absorption of immigrants.[81] As discussed in previous section, employment may serve as a catalyst contributing the successful integration of refugees.

Adaptation of the human being to the environment and society, which is defined as a social cohesion, is one of basic needs and features of human being. What connects human beings to the life is the cohesion they provide to the environment and society they live in. This issue has become increasingly important in migration studies in recent years, is dealt with under the headings of social cohesion.

Social cohesion is also closely related with cultural diversity and social development. As stated in the Common Basic Principles below, basic knowledge of the host society's cultural codes is part of the process.

"Basic knowledge of the host society's language, history, and institutions is indispensable to integration; enabling immigrants to acquire this basic knowledge is essential to successful integration" (CBP 4).

However, this does not necessarily mean that cultural characteristics of refugees and migrants is to be undermined. It should be kept in mind that cultural diversity is one of the main factors that have to be taken into account for social cohesion to be possible in Europe.[82]

---

[79] Valentina Vedeneeva, "Integration of Refugees in Europe: Employment as a Priority", **Mirovaya Ekonomika i Mezhdunarodnye Otnosheniya,** Vol. 63, No. 1, 2019, pp. 103-111. https://doi.org/10.20542/0131-2227-2019-63-1-103-111 (Access 11.12.2020).

[80] Making Integration Work: Refugees and Others in Need of Protection, OECD Publishing, 2016, Paris, https://read.oecd-ilibrary.org/social-issues-migration-health/making-integration-work-humanitarian-migrants_9789264251236-en#page4 (Access 11.12.2020).

[81] **A New Strategy for Social Cohesion: Revised Strategy for Social Cohesion,** Council of Europe, 2004, p.3, https://www.coe.int/t/dg3/socialpolicies/socialcohesiondev/source/RevisedStrategy_en.pdf (Access 11.12.2020).

[82] **White Paper on Intercultural Dialogue "Living Together as Equals in Dignity",** Council of

European Union has highlighted its cohesion policy as an important funding source to support effective integration policies covering education, employment, housing and non-discrimination policies.[83] This entails that social cohesion is one of the last building blocks in the life of the refugees and migrants. It determines how well they are integrated and accepted by the local community. Cohesion policy has the potential to support long term integration of refugees. In view this, the European Commission supports many actions[84] for social cohesion.

## Conclusion and recommendations

Refugees face important challenges in exercising fundamental and universal rights in their host societies. The migration crisis of 2015 has questioned the integration policies of the EU and Turkey towards refugees. Thus, the crisis paved the way for a paradigm change in a positive way. It also necessitated a closer look to this very situation. Being high on the agenda, this paper discussed the integration policies for refugees in six dimensions, which are citizenship, housing, education, healthcare, employment and social cohesion. These dimensions are prerequisites for successful integration.

Turkey's policies towards refugees and asylum seekers, starting with the Settlement Act of 1935, have been adapted to the present conditions with the enactment of LFIP and the Temporary Protection Directive published in 2013 and 2014, respectively. Also, various institutions have been established to manage and plan activities for the target group. These institutions and regulations have been shaped by the massive migration of Syrians, which started in 2011, then rapidly reached millions onwards. According to regulations, Syrians are not accepted as immigrants and are only provided with temporary protection.

However, in this process, various steps have been taken to integrate Syrians into Turkish society, under different titles, especially in terms of education, health, citizenship, housing, employment, and social cohesion. The main problem in cohesion policies is the lack of a basic approach to whether Syrians are to be provided with permanent or temporary. Thus, current policies do not be considered as a pre-stage by which Syrians will ultimately be offered citizenship. However, it is targeted to meet the humanitarian needs such as education and health especially during their stay

Europe, 2008, https://www.coe.int/t/dg4/intercultural/source/white%20paper_final_revised_en.pdf (Access 11.12.2020).
[83] **Cohesion Policy Support for Migrants and Refugees,** European Parliamentary Research Service Blog, 2016, https://epthinktank.eu/2016/05/06/cohesion-policy-support-for-migrants-and-refugees/ (Access 11.12.2020).
[84] **Inclusion of Migrants and Refugees in Cities,** European Commission, https://ec.europa.eu/info/eu-regional-and-urban-development/topics/cities-and-urban-development/priority-themes-eu-cities/inclusion-migrants-and-refugees-cities_en (Access 11.12.2020).

in Turkey. One of the major difficulties encountered in this context that Turkey failed is the language of the Syrians. Lack of knowledge of Turkish language makes it difficult for Syrians to benefit from various services, particularly from education, healthcare and employment. This negatively affects social acceptance and social cohesion of Syrians.

As discussed, the 2015 immigration crisis has resulted in paradigmatic change in integration policies of the EU. This called for a proactive integration policy for refugees in the host societies. It is no doubt that in the absence of ensuring participation of both the host society and the refugees, the integration process will not be successful as a whole. The new policies of the EU aimed to empower the newcomers, whereas it also encouraged "being self-sufficient and going back" policies.

The dimensions discussed in each section aimed to contribute to added value of the topics discussed. The dimensions of integration of the EU discussed in this chapter imply that they still depend mostly on national milieu. Despite the Common Basic Principles (CBP) for Immigrant Integration Policy of the EU, the differences in integration policies still exist between the EU States. However, agreeing on the common principles regarding the integration is of utmost importance to be considered between the States. Common principles will help the EU countries share the burden fairly and overcome the crisis. Social innovative approaches are required immediately, and such approaches will contribute to long term success of integration policies for the EU.

# CHAPTER 15

# LOCAL INTEGRATION OF SYRIAN REFUGEES IN LEBANON, JORDAN, AND TURKEY

## Hekma Wali[1]

## Introduction

From the very onset of the forced displacement engendered by the war in Syria, the neighbouring countries, namely Lebanon, Jordan, and Turkey (LJT), opened their doors to the Syrian refugees. However, after mid-2013, incessant mass-influxes of refugees compelled governments of Lebanon and Jordan to shift their initial open-door policy and impose some restrictive measures on refugee's entry to their territories. Turkey, conversely, has retained such a policy and attempted to manage the major arrivals. These three countries have welcomed Syrian refugees as temporary guests until a durable solution would be found, that is either to be returned to their country of origin when repatriation is sustainable or be resettled to a third country by United Nations High Commissioner for Refugees (UNHCR).

Local integration of refugees in these countries as a third durable solution is conventionally inconceivable. It is evident that Jordan and particularly Lebanon are not asylum countries since they are not state parties to the 1951 Convention; both are rather signatories to Memoranda of Understanding. Turkey, on the other hand, is a state party to the Convention, yet under other conditions adopting its geographical limitation upon acceding to the 1967 Protocol, hence restraining applications only to European asylum seekers. Therefore, LJT governments do not provide prospects for local integration of Syrian refugees, particularly when considering that they represent the first three countries hosting refugees worldwide.

Considering the existing parameters along with unfeasible repatriation and scarce resettlement opportunities, LJT governments in coordination with UNHCR have differently handled the issue of refugee social inclusion. This essay examines the main features of such integration focusing on the policies implemented by LJT governments. More specifically, it concentrates on the question of whether refugees are welcomed or rejected by the hosting governments and communities. Both aspects are considered according to the response introduced to Syrian refugees.

This research also digs into the question of whether LJT governments

---

[1] Dr., Postdoctoral Researcher in Migration and Asylum Studies.

provide any initiatives to include refugees within their societies. It attempts to scrutinise the plans proposed mainly in the fields of employment, education, and healthcare. It examines the attempts of social inclusion of refugees in the host countries which seem to be feasible to an extent in Jordan and Turkey, rather than in Lebanon. In addition, challenges to refugee integration in these countries are briefly considered and some policy recommendations for better response to social inclusion are also suggested.

### Local integration process of Syrian refugees

Finding a home in the country of asylum and integrating into the hosting community might represent a durable solution to refugees' plight and an opportunity to build a new life, in cases where repatriation is not an option. Local integration is defined by UNHCR as "a complex and gradual process with legal, economic, social and cultural dimensions", which "imposes considerable demands on both the individual and the receiving society". This process ends with acquiring the nationality of the country of asylum, in many instances. According to UNHCR, ca. 1.1 million refugees around the world obtained the citizenship of their country of asylum over the past decade.[2]

It is crucial to consider Syrian refugees' numbers and shares in neighbouring countries, mainly in Lebanon, Jordan, and Turkey (LJT) as they are the first three countries hosting the largest number of refugees in the world. As demonstrated in the table below, Turkey has the highest percentage of share with ca. two thirds of the refugees (64.4%) in major refugee-hosting countries in the region, followed by Lebanon (16.3%) and Jordan (11.8%). Accordingly, local integration of refugees in LJT is apparently an apposite solution considering the inappropriate conditions of return and the paucity of resettlement opportunities.

**3RP** Regional Refugee and Resilience Plan

**AFAD** Afet ve Acil Durum Yönetimi Başkanlığı (Disaster and Emergency Management Presidency)

**CBP** Community-Based Protection

**CCTE** Conditional Cash Transfer for Education

**DGMM** Directorate-General for Migration Management (Göç İdaresi Genel Müdürlüğü)

**GCR** Global Compact on Refugees

**GoJ** Government of Jordan

---

[2] https://www.unhcr.org/local-integration-49c3646c101.html (Access 10.05.2020).

**GoL** Government of Lebanon

**GoT** Government of Turkey

**ILO** International Labour Organisation

**LFIP** Law on Foreigners and International Protection

**LJT** Lebanon, Jordan, and Turkey

**MHCs** Migrant Health Centres

**MoH** Ministry of Health

**MoI** the Ministry of Interior

**MoL** Ministry of Labour

**MoSA** Ministry of Social Affairs

**NGOs** Non-Governmental Organisations

**TACs** Temporary Accommodation Centres

**TECs** Temporary Education Centres

**TEPAV** Economic Policy Research Foundation of Turkey

**TGNA** Grand National Assembly of Turkey (Türkiye Büyük Millet Meclisi)

**TOBB** Union of Chambers and Commodity Exchanges of Turkey (Türkiye Odalar ve Borsalar Birliği)

**TPR** Temporary Protection Regulation

**UNDP** The United Nations Development Programme

**UNHCR** United Nations High Commissioner for Refugees

**UNICEF** United Nations Children's Fund

**UNRWA** The United Nations Relief and Works Agency for Palestine Refugees

**WFP** World Food Programme Syrian Refugee Numbers and Shares in Countries of Asylum in the Region (2020)[3]

It should be also argued that local integration is a solution not only for resolving the protracted situation of Syrian refugees in LJT, but also for the resilience of hosting communities there. These two elements are completely intertwined, in that no one could be achieved without the existence of the

---

[3] https://data2.unhcr.org/en/situations/syria (Access 12.05.2020).

other. The interests and needs of the host country are as substantial as the resolution of the protracted situation of hosted refugees. For that reason, "while donor decisions on funding areas have a major impact on which policy options can be implemented, the interests and needs of the host country should remain paramount".[4]

| Major refugee-hosting countries in the region | Syrian refugees | Share of displaced Syrians (%) |
|---|---|---|
| Turkey | 3,579,008 | 64.4 |
| Lebanon | 910,256 | 16.3 |
| Jordan | 656,733 | 11.8 |
| Iraq | 247,440 | 4.5 |
| Egypt | 130,074 | 2.3 |
| Other (North Africa) | 31,657 | 0.6 |

## Lebanon

It is crucial to note that Lebanon continues to host the largest number of refugees according to its national population worldwide, in that 1 in 6 people is a refugee.[5] It should be mentioned that these refugees are unsheltered, in that Lebanon, unlike Jordan and Turkey, has no share of refugees in camps. Syrians were not allowed by the Government of Lebanon (GoL) to establish formal camps, unlike Palestinian refugees who fled to Lebanon during the 1948 war.[6]

The GoL and communities are the first to bear the brunt of the refugee crisis. It is conventional that the density of refugee population deepens the political, economic, social and security plights in Lebanon. This critical situation along with the growing popular hostility and restrictions on refugee entry, registration and movement have dramatically intensified the crisis of Syrian refugees in Lebanon and impeded attempts of local integration. Apart from the prevalent perception of economic burden caused by refugees, the political context is of equal importance, in that

> "fears grew that the presence of a large number of mostly Sunni Syrian refugees could be permanent, and that this will alter the demographic balance against the interests of Christian and Shia political groups in Lebanon and challenge the existing political

[4] International Centre for Migration Policy Development (ICMPD), "Policy Options for Maximising the Development Potential for Refugee Hosting Countries: Executive summary", 2019, p. 1, https://reliefweb.int/sites/reliefweb.int/files/resources/Executive_summary_policy_options_for_maxi mising_the_development_potentional_for_refugee_hosting_countries.pdf (15.05.2020).
[5] UNHCR, "Global Trends Forced Displacement In 2018", 2019, p. 3, https://www.unhcr.org/5d08d 7ee7.pdf (Access 15.05.2020).
[6] Care International, "Syrian Refugees in Lebanon Eight Years on: What Works and Why That Matters for The Future", 2018, p. 7, https://reliefweb.int/sites/reliefweb.int/files/resources/CARE International Lebanon_RefugeesinLebanon_Whatworksandwhythatmattersforthefuture.pdf (Access 20.05.2020).

order."[7]

**Figure 1.** Share of Refugees in Camps in LJT[8]

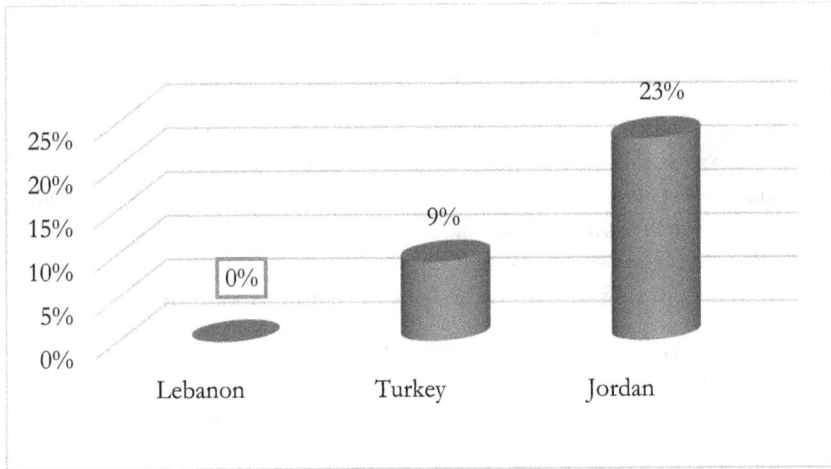

Regarding the social context, the North of Lebanon has predominantly less negative perception towards Syrians as they have common social, religious, and cultural backgrounds. However, in the other remaining parts of Lebanon, where Shiites and Christians live, Syrians are much rejected.

For that reason, return for many refugees has been the potential alternative nonetheless the unripe conditions for return in Syria. This critical situation has then led 53,286 (including only those verified by UNHCR) to return between 2014 and 2019.[9] Furthermore, return has increasingly been compelled through the political context, in that chief Lebanese policymakers have proclaimed on several occasions that return needs soon to start happening in a larger way. The latent agenda behind this debate stems partly from the momentous political and military alliance between Hezbollah and the Syrian regime, given the increasing influence of Hezbollah with their allies after the elections of May 2018. For the part of Syrian government, refugees return represents a crucial step towards the normalisation of their international relations and the demonstration of their good governance being a government embracing its citizens, hence a legitimate government in the view of the international community.[10]

---

[7] Care International, op. cit, p.4.
[8] UNDP, ILO, and WFP, "Jobs Make the Difference: Expanding Economic Opportunities for Syrian Refugees and Host Communities- Egypt - Iraq - Jordan - Lebanon - Syria – Turkey", 2017, p. 22, https://www.jobsmakethedifference.org/full-report (Access 18.05.2020).
[9] https://data2.unhcr.org/en/situations/syria_durable_solutions (Access 19.05.2020).
[10] Care International, op. cit, p.4.

Lebanon seems to be a harsh haven for Syrian refugees for the growing popular hostility towards them. The refugees' arrival changed the image of the country in ways that made many Lebanese "uncomfortable".

> "Not all refugees are poor, but it is the poor who most decisively shape the host society's perceptions. Wealthy Syrians blend effortlessly into privileged urban quarters. Their impoverished co-nationals, on the other hand, are conspicuous as beggars and menial workers in city streets and by their squalid encampments in the country's predominantly agricultural periphery, in particular the Beqaa valley and the north. In these places, they share already inadequate public services and infrastructure with poor Lebanese and compete for jobs in the bottom bracket of the labour market."[11]

Additionally, hostility has particularly sprouted when jihadist groups such as Jabhat al-Nusra and the Islamic State (ISIS) started to clash with Lebanese security forces in border regions as, specifically, Christian Lebanese strongly reacted. Consequently, several municipalities imposed "extra-legal restrictions" on the movement of Syrian refugees.[12]

Accordingly, increasing hostility is accompanied by restrictive administrative regulations. From October 2014, the Lebanese authorities have implemented new policies regarding the reception of Syrians into its territories aiming at reducing the number of displaced Syrians and encouraging them to return.[13] To achieve these goals, the government introduced visa requirements for arriving Syrians, required UNHCR to halt the registration of refugees and ceased the extension of refugees' visas free of charge.[14] It is evident that entry restrictions reduced the influx; however, ceasing registration and ending visa extensions only increased the percentage of unregistered refugees and those without valid residency status.

Tightening residency regulations has then aggravated the status quo, in that no Syrian refugee is entitled to cross the border and come back, otherwise they would be deprived of their legal stay in Lebanon. It should be underlined that "a residency permit obtained on the basis of UNHCR registration does not allow a refugee to cross into Syria and come back to Lebanon". The GoL considers any crossing of the border a return; consequently, the right of the displaced Syrian to stay in Lebanon is inevitably

[11] **Easing Syrian Refugees' Plight in Lebanon**, International Crisis Group, Brussels, 2020, p. 4.
[12] Ibid., p. 5.
[13] Maja Janmyr, "Precarity in Exile: The Legal Status of Syrian Refugees in Lebanon", **Refugee Survey Quarterly**, Vol. 35, No. 4, 2016, p. 59.
[14] Maja Janmyr, "The Legal Status of Syrian Refugees in Lebanon", Issam Fares Institute for Public Policy and International Affairs, American University of Beirut, 2016, p. 13, https://www.aub.edu.lb /ifi/Documents/publications/working_papers/2015-2016/20160331_Maja_Janmyr.pdf (Access 10.05.2020).

ended. Lack of valid residency status per se does not expose refugees to deportation, yet it causes additional pressures, such as troubles at checkpoints and temporary detention.[15]

Furthermore, it should be accentuated that refugees have been evicted and their shelters have been demolished in late years. Since 2017 particularly, some Lebanese politicians have become increasingly strident in calling for refugees' return. More importantly, several Lebanese municipalities have engaged in "forcibly evicting them from their homes and expelling them from their localities" since 2016. At least 3,664 displaced Syrians had been evicted from at least 13 municipalities between 2016 and the first quarter of 2018. According to UNHCR, ca. 42,000 Syrian refugees were at risk of eviction in 2017. Moreover, in the same year, the Lebanese Armed Forces evicted another 7,524 near the Rayak air base in the Bekaa Valley and, according to Lebanon's Ministry of Social Affairs, 15,126 Syrian refugees near the air base had pending eviction orders.[16] Since early 2019, the Lebanese Armed Forces has launched the demolition of Syrian refugee shelters claiming, "they did not comply with long-existing, but largely unenforced, housing codes".[17] Hence, all these conditions have exacerbated the situation of vulnerable Syrian refugees and aborted the prospect of local integration.

Registered Syrian refugees were permitted to work in Lebanon until early 2015, when the government ceased such right. Syrian refugees are now required to sign a pledge not to work and can only maintain their livelihoods through humanitarian aid provided by the GoL and with support from the international community. It should be stressed that labour restrictions have been increasingly enforced since late 2018.[18] In case Syrian refugees obtain sponsorship and a work permit, their legal status is changed to "migrant workers", although UNHCR still considers them refugees. Additionally, employment of displaced Syrians is mainly restricted to "third sector jobs" in construction, agriculture and cleaning services (demonstrated in the table below), as there is a labour shortage in these sectors and as these occupations do not respond to the skills and income expectations of the majority of the native Lebanese labour force. It should be noted that bureaucratic and financial factors are steep in front of a Syrian refugee to attain a work permit in any other sector. "An employer must first prove his inability to find an adequately skilled Lebanese worker for a given job, before he can request a

---

15 Easing Syrian Refugees' Plight in Lebanon, International Crisis Group, pp. 7-8.
16 **"Our Homes Are Not for Strangers": Mass Evictions of Syrian Refugees by Lebanese Municipalities.** Human Rights Watch, USA, 2018, p. 1, https://www.hrw.org/sites/default/files/report_pdf/lebanon0418_web.pdf (Access 16.05.2020).
17 Human Rights Watch, "Lebanon: Syrian Refugee Shelters Demolished: Coercive Measures Intensify Pressures to Return to Syria", 2019, https://www.hrw.org/news/2019/07/05/lebanon-syrian-refugee-shelters-demolished (Access 16.05.2020).
18 Easing Syrian Refugees' Plight in Lebanon, International Crisis Group, p. 6.

permit for a qualified Syrian worker."[19]

According to data published by the Lebanon Ministry of Labour on the website of the Central Administration of Statistics (CAS), only 1,102 work permits were issued to Syrians in 2015, and only 200 in 2017.[20] A report published by UNDP, ILO, and WFP, entitled "Jobs Make the Difference: Expanding Economic Opportunities for Syrian Refugees and Host Communities- Egypt - Iraq - Jordan - Lebanon - Syria – Turkey", stated that only 0.5% of working-age refugees have their work permit applications submitted by employers in Lebanon.[21]

**Figure 2**. Distribution of Syrian refugees by Occupation (%)[22]

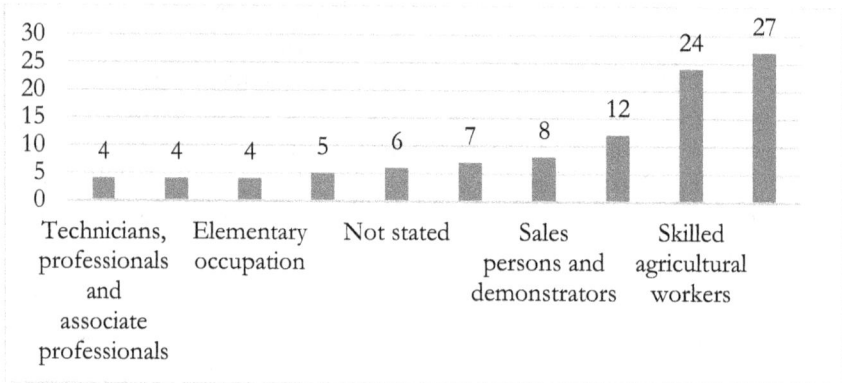

The restriction of the legal access to work for Syrian refugees in Lebanon translates their vulnerability and inability to meet their basic needs. This has certainly paved the way for the expansion of unregulated activities and informality. Equally important, "the difficulty and cost of obtaining a work permit for Syrian refugees are also harming Lebanese employers, who are facing substantial labour shortages in key economic sectors such as construction and agriculture".[23]

On the other hand, there have been several initiatives to engage Syrian refugees in labour market. Non-Governmental Organisations (NGOs), in

[19] Lorenza Errighi and Jörn Griesse, "The Syrian Refugee Crisis: Labour Market Implications in Jordan and Lebanon", 2016, p. 11, https://ec.europa.eu/info/sites/info/files/dp029_en.pdf (Access 15.05.2020).
[20] Jad Kabbanji and Lama Kabbanji, "Assessing the Development-Displacement Nexus in Lebanon: Working Paper", International Centre for Migration Policy Development (ICMPD), Vienna, 2018, pp. 14-29, https://www.syrialearning.org/system/files/content/resource/files/main/Assessing%20the%20 Development-Displacement%20Nexus%20in%20Lebanon_final.pdf (Access 14.05.2020).
[21] UNDP, ILO, and WFP, op. cit, p. 41.
[22] Assessment of the impact of Syrian refugees in Lebanon and their employment profile, International Labour Organisation, Beirut, 2014 , p. 25.
[23] Errighi and Griesse, op. cit, pp. 11-12.

collabouration with local municipalities, have implemented programmes and projects to provide labour-intensive work for Syrian refugees to improve basic infrastructure, such as clearing canals and solid local waste management projects. UN humanitarian and development agencies have also implemented programmes alike. However, these projects have been controversial despite their significance in meeting the condition of local integration. Additionally, there is no far-reaching programming underway despite the GoL's proposed five-year, multibillion-dollar infrastructure improvement and plans for development actors to fund a €22 million project to upgrade roads and agricultural lands and improve water.[24]

Regarding the impact of the Syrian refugees on the education sector, it should be noted that their presence has affected the educational system in Lebanon. The GoL has allowed the access of Syrian refugee children to schools as one measure to impede the setting up of refugee camps. By mid-2015, more than half of the students registered in Lebanese schools were Syrians.[25] However, according to the GoL's statistics for the 2016-2017 school year, their number decreased, in that Syrian children represented nearly half of the students in public schools that year.[26] It should be stressed that important strides were noted in school enrolment for children aged 6-14. According to the Vulnerability Assessment report of 2017, prepared by UNICEF, UNHCR and WFP, 70% of Syrian children aged 6-14 were enrolled in school, at the national level, compared to 52% in 2016.[27]

As demonstrated in the chart below, the share of Lebanese students in Lebanon's public schools has been nearly the half compared by non-Lebanese. To cope with this challenge, "the Lebanese government has set up second shifts at existing schools and opened new schools throughout the country". Hence, the presence of Syrian refugees has undeniably sustained the existing education system in Lebanon, in that international aid has supported the government to develop educational infrastructure and has provided temporary jobs for many unemployed Lebanese teachers. Furthermore, these efforts have increased enrolment rates of Lebanese as well as Syrian children at public school and raised the number of refugee children receiving educational certificates, as observed by Lebanon's Ministry of Education and Higher Education. However, it should be underscored that Syrian and Lebanese children do not share the same classrooms in most cases. The instruction language is the chief impediment, given that Lebanese are

---

[24] UNDP, ILO, and WFP, op. cit, p. 49.

[25] Elizabeth Ferris and Kemal Kirisci, "Syrian refugees: Challenges to host countries and the international community", 2016, pp. 51-52, https://www.jstor.org/stable/pdf/10.7864/j.cttlc2cqws.7. pdf?refreqid= excelsior%3Aae9d-5299381c3dfedfcc2ac44e18dfb0 (Access 02.06.2020).

[26] Kabbanji and Kabbanji, op. cit, p. 18.

[27] UNDP, ILO, and WFP, op. cit, p. 32.

taught in English and French, whereas Syrians are educated in Arabic.[28]

**Figure 3.** Share (%) of Lebanese and Non-Lebanese Students in Lebanon's Public Schools (2011-2017)[29]

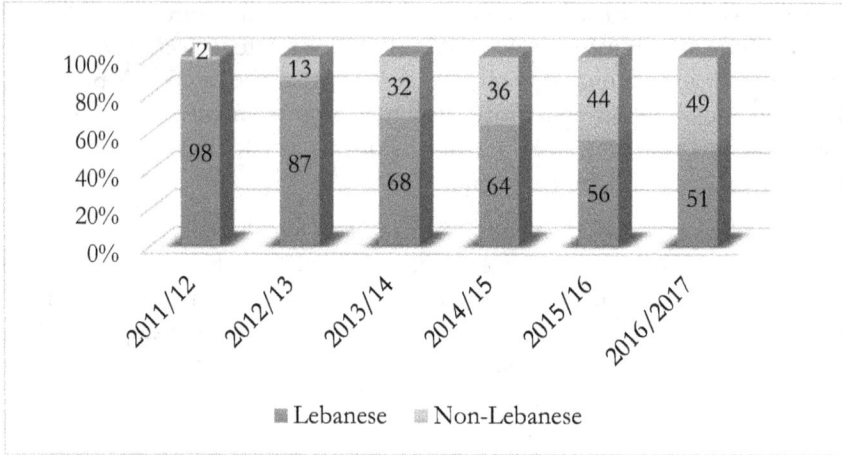

Concerning access of Syrian refugees to healthcare, it should be noted that the healthcare system in Lebanon is so fragmented that has left the majority of Syrians, along with vulnerable Lebanese, without easy access to health services. Syrian refugees, who are registered or recorded with the UNHCR, have access to 28 primary healthcare centres, primarily run by the UNHCR's NGO partners and Ministry of Social Affairs (MoSA). They can access primary healthcare in these centres for a fee between LBP 3,000 and 5,000 per consultation, while Lebanese are charged between LBP 10,000 and 15,000. Moreover, UNHCR provides vaccines, acute medication, and two ultrasounds for pregnant women free of charge; however, chronic illness medications are charged for a fee of LPB 1,000 per visit.[30] It should be argued that despite the contributions by UNHCR, 71% of Syrian refugees with chronic diseases stopped the use of medication since they could not afford its fees. Hence, despite UNHCR's provision of services free of charge, the other remaining services are not affordable to refugees. Equally important, those who fall outside UNHCR's scope of assistance for primary care are not able to pay for healthcare costs (Lebanon Support, 2016, 9).[31]

---

[28] Kabbanji and Kabbanji, op. cit, p. 19.
[29] GoL and UN, "Lebanon crisis response plan 2015-16: Year two. Beirut: Government of Lebanon and United Nations", 2015, p. 52, https://reliefweb.int/sites/reliefweb.int/files/resources/20151223_LCRP _ENG_22Dec2015-full%20version%29_s.pdf (Access 02.06.2020).
[30] UNHCR, "Health Services for Syrian Refugees in Beqaa", 2014, p. 4, https://reliefweb.int/report/lebanon/health-services-syrian-refugees-bekaa (Access 02.06.2020).
[31] Lebanon Support, "Access to Healthcare for Syrian Refugees: The Impact of Fragmented Service Provision on Syrians' Daily Lives", 2016, p. 9, https://civilsociety-centre.org/sites/default/files/resources/accesshealthcaresyrianrefugees-ls2016.pdf (Access 30.05.2020).

With reference to secondary and tertiary healthcare, in the case of life-threatening emergencies, UNHCR provides targeted assistance of 75% of the total medical cost.[32] Yet, regarding economically vulnerable refugees, UNHCR covers up to 90% of the whole cost, when funds permit.[33]

Regarding access to public hospitals, it should be noted that refugees have faced different challenges. The expensive treatments and lack of livelihoods are the leading challenges, in that hospitals stick to mischievous coping strategies so as to secure payment since Syrian refugees cannot afford the financial coverage for medical treatment. It should be underlined that hospitals which are not contracted with UNHCR are rejecting Syrians. Even the contracted hospitals face challenges concerning the payment of non-covered medical treatment. Some hospitals do not accept patients unless a guarantee that UNHCR, or any other NGO, will pay their share is provided. Another challenge is over-crowdedness, in that several hospitals usually refuse patients owing to lack of space. Rising tensions between the Lebanese communities and Syrian refugees is considered another important challenge since 85% of registered refugees (70% of whom are under the poverty line) are living in areas where 67% of the host community is under the poverty line, too.[34] Tensions have been persistent between them, particularly in the beginning of the crisis when the international community was concentrating exclusively on displaced Syrians and ignoring the other vulnerable Lebanese. Consequently, while Syrians had been subsidised for their health services, the Lebanese were required to pay higher share for the same services (Kostrz, 2015). In addition, sources of tension for Syrian patients emanate from experiencing longer waiting lines than Lebanese patients and less care by the staff.[35]

The GoL has proclaimed that the mass-influx of Syrian refugees has harmed the healthcare system in Lebanon. They partly blame UNHCR for the healthcare system crisis, in that it covers only 75% of the hospitalisation cost, accordingly 25% are to be paid by the patient's part. The government stresses that this measure has affected Syrian refugees, as well as the most vulnerable Lebanese. Additionally, the authorities argue that the healthcare system crisis has impeded public hospitals to respond and provide the necessary services to Syrian refugees, as well as Lebanese nationals.[36]

---

[32] UNHCR, "UNHCR Lebanon: Health Update", 2014, p. 2, https://reliefweb.int/sites/reliefweb.int/files/resources/10-HealthUNHCRMonthlyUpdate-September2014.pdf (Access 30.05.2020).
[33] UNHCR, "Guidelines for Referral Health Care in Lebanon: Standard Operating Procedures – Lebanon Updated June 2018", 2018, p. 27, https://data2.unhcr.org/en/documents/download/64586 (Access 29.05.2020).
[34] Lebanon Support, op. cit, pp. 18-20.
[35] Ibid., p. 21.
[36] Kabbanji and Kabbanji, op. cit, pp. 19-20.

Overall, due to several reasons, none of the durable solutions, whether that is return, integration or resettlement, are currently in sight for the majority of Syrian refugees in Lebanon. The tensions between the GoL, and UNHCR and the wider international community are described as "a catch 22", in that what is suggested by one is rejected by the other leading to a stalemate. UNHCR substantially denounces any attempt to repatriate Syrian refugees, whereas the GoL urges the prospect of return. UNHCR resolutely advocates the local integration of Syrian refugees, while the Lebanese authorities and communities have not permitted their inclusion at all levels. The initiatives of the international community to raise resettlement quotas have dwindled, in the meantime some Lebanese authorities insist that they will not allow Syrians to remain in Lebanon much longer. Accordingly, the GoL abstains from planning for longer-term solutions.[37]

To conclude, the economic and political considerations make the prospects of enhancing the inclusion of Syrian refugees into mainstream Lebanese society an even greater challenge than in Jordan and Turkey.[38]

## Jordan

Jordan continues to shoulder a disproportionate refugee burden as it is the second largest refugee-hosting country per inhabitants in the world. The majority of Syrian refugee community in Jordan live outside camps (ca. 79%) and face precarious living conditions. In order to respond to the protracted refugee situation requiring new responses to refugee integration, the government along with its partners embarked on the "Jordan Compact". It is deemed a paradigm shift in responding to the Syrian refugee crisis as it represents a roadmap for resilience of Jordanians and Syrian refugees alike by "shifting the focus from short-term aid to job creation, growth, and investment".[39]

The Jordan Compact was signed in February 2016 at the London Conference hosted by the UK, Germany, Kuwait, Norway, and the United Nations. It combines the international humanitarian and development actors under host country leadership. It raises humanitarian and development funding through multi-year grants ($700 million annually for three years) and concessional loans ($1.9 billion). The payment of these grants and loans is matched to specific targets. One main target is linked to formal labour market access. According to this Compact, Jordan is "to issue 200,000 work permits for Syrian refugees in specified sectors". Moreover, it "commits the EU to

---

[37] Care International, op. cit, p.5.
[38] Ferris and Kirisci, op. cit, p. 61.
[39] Renad Amjad, Aslan Jaafar, Emma Borgnäs, et al., "Examining Barriers to Workforce Inclusion of Syrian Refugees in Jordan", Columbia University: School of International and Public Affairs (SIPA), 2017, p. 4.

relaxing trade regulations to stimulate exports from 18 designated economic zones and industrial areas in Jordan, in return for employment quotas for Syrian refugees in these businesses". Additionally, the Compact states "Jordan will institute reforms to improve the business and investment environment and formalise Syrian businesses". Equally important, it requires Jordan to "providing school places to all Syrian children, and some vocational training opportunities".[40]

Jordan can be viewed as a crucially revealing case of "good practice" for the implementation of the Global Compact on Refugees (GCR). A "good practice" is an initiative designed and submitted by people, states, organisations and businesses across the world to be implemented in order to support and find long-term solutions for displaced communities and stateless people.[41]

In the context of the second objective of the GCR, which is to "build refugee self-reliance"[42], the right of Syrian refugees to legal work has been settled through Jordan's Labour Law 8, 1996. The Jordan Compact, sustained by concessional financing, has permitted refugees' access to work permits for specific labour sectors. Different policy decisions have been implemented to encourage labour market opportunities for Syrian refugees and Jordanians, such as a moratorium in June 2016 on new migrant workers entering Jordan. Moreover, as of April 2016, the Ministry of Labour (MoL) permitted a grace period of three months for Syrian refugees working without a work permit to regulate their employment status, which had been extended to the end of 2016. This involved waiving fees related to obtaining a permit to mobilise refugees and employers alike and the acceptance of identity card instead of a passport by the Ministry of Interior (MoI).[43] The grace period had extensively brought about the issuance of more than tenfold of work permits between January and early December 2016.44

[40] Veronique Barbelet, Jessica Hagen-Zanker, et al., "The Jordan Compact : Lessons learnt and implications for future refugee compacts", 2018, p. 2, https://data2.unhcr.org/en/documents/download/61932 (Access 17.05. 2020).

[41] UNHCR, "What is a good practice?", 2019, https://globalcompactrefugees.org/article/what-good-practice (Access 30.05.2020).

[42] https://www.unhcr.org/comprehensive-refugee-response-framework-crrf.html (Access 02.02.2020).

[43] ILO, "Results of Focus Group Discussions on Work Permits with Syrian Refugees and Employers in the Agriculture, Construction & Retail Sectors in Jordan", 2016, p. 13, https://data2.unhcr.org/en/documents/ download/43373 (Access 20.05.2020).

[44] Maha Kattaa, "Syrian Refugees' Status in the Jordanian Labour Market", **Turkish Policy Quarterly**, Vol. 15, No. 3, 2016, p. 75.

**Figure 4.** Number of Work Permits Issued for Syrian refugees Between January and November 2016[45]

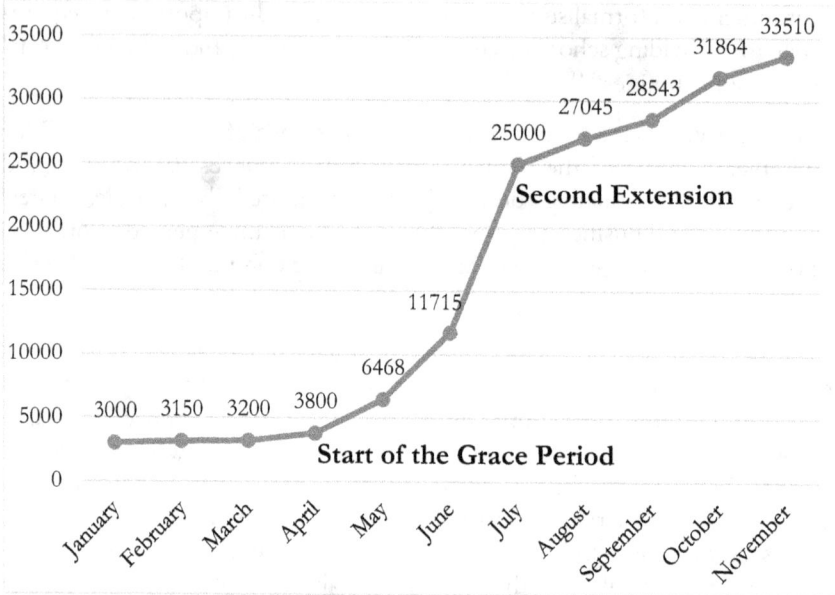

The total number of work permits issued to Syrians has amounted to almost 100,182 by May 2018.[46] Equally important, since November 2018, through a Cabinet decision, refugees have the legal right to launch home-based businesses, raising income opportunities, specifically for women.[47]

However, it should be stressed that only about 10% of the employed Syrians have formal work permits.[48] This is perceived particularly in construction sector, in that 3000 Syrians have work permits; whereas 30,000 work without permit.[49] Regarding the issuance of work permits by sector, it should be noted that the situation is partly similar to that in Lebanon. Refugees have mainly obtained work permits in the sectors of agriculture,

[45] Ibid., p. 75, (Reported from MoL).
[46] ILO, "Decent Work Country Programme: The Hashemite Kingdom of Jordan 2018-2020", (n.d.), p. 9-20, https://www.ilo.org/wcmsp5/groups/public/---arabstates/---ro-beirut/documents/generic document/wcms_656566.pdf (Access 18.05.2020).
[47] https://www.globalcompactrefugees.org/article/jordan (Access 19.05.2020).
[48] ILO and FAFO, "Impact of Syrian refugees on the Jordanian Labour Market: Findings from the Governorates of Amman, Irbid and Mafraq", 2015, p. 6, https://www.ilo.org/wcmsp5/groups/public/---arabstates/---ro-beirut/documents/publication/wcms_364162.pdf (Access 04.06.2020).
[49] ILO, "Work Permits and Employment of Syrian Refugees in Jordan: Towards Formalising the Work of Syrian Refugees", 2017, p. 32, https://www.ilo.org/wcmsp5/groups/public/---arabstates/---ro-beirut/documents/publication/wcms_559151.pdf (Access 04.06.2020).

manufacturing, trade, food services and construction.

**Figure 5.** Number of Work Permits Issued to Syrians Disaggregated by Economic Activity (up to 2015)[50]

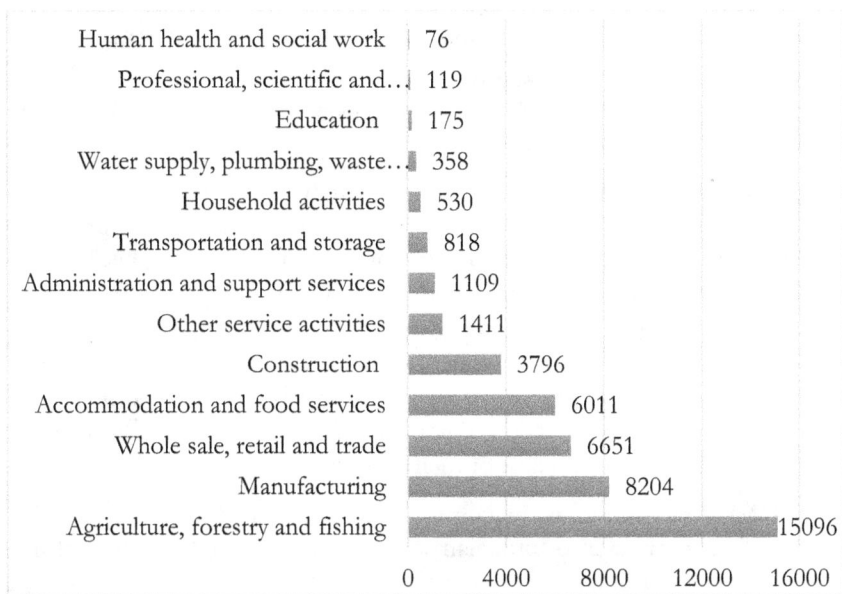

However, despite the increased incentives to enhance Syrian refugees' labour market participation in Jordan and to actively contribute to the Jordanian economy, the result is still not demonstrated to be as strong as hoped for. "Only six out of the 936 exporting companies who are eligible to apply for the relaxed rules of origin currently qualify by employing at least 15% Syrian refugees", and the number of Syrian refugees who have been issued work permits in the export industry remains restricted. This translates the presence of other barriers preventing Syrian refugees from either being able to or wishing to reach formal work in this industry, and employers from either being able to or wanting to employ Syrian refugees in their factories.[51]

Social inclusion is also upheld through the government's commitment to ensure refugees' access to education. The Government of Jordan (GoJ) has opened its schools to Syrian refugee students, in that they can access education through the following schools or programmes: The United Nations Relief and Works Agency for Palestine Refugees (UNRWA) schools, Ministry of Education (MoE) schools (in camps, single or double-shift schools in host communities), or non-formal or informal education

---

[50] ILO and FAFO, op. cit, p. 54.
[51] Amjad, Jaafar, Borgnäs, et al., op. cit, p. 57.

programmes.[52] As a response to the Syrian Crisis, the MoE established schools in camps and increased double-shifts in others in 2011.[53] It has scheduled teaching staff in double-shifts to accommodate the new children and to manage overcrowded classrooms.[54] Camps' school enrolment rate reached 67% in the Zaatari and Azraq camps as of March 2015 (Queen Rania Foundation, 2017: 2). Additionally, it should be noted that the number of enrolled Syrian refugee children in formal education increased from 61.6% in March 2015[55] to 72% in January 2017.[56]

However, despite this positive development, the number of out-of-school children is still critically elevated, in that it counted for 73,137 by April 2018, as reported by the 'No Lost Generation' initiative during the Brussels Conference.[57] Such a situation is due to certain barriers including lack of proper enrolment documentations, discouraging family registration process, lacking birth certificates, three-year-rule[58] preventing (re-) entry to formal education, financial constraints (leading to child labour and child marriage), school violence (child protection & safety concerns), school being too distant from child's residency, and lack of mental health & psychosocial support.[59]

The MoE has continued its commitment to Syrian students, despite the impact of their arrival into Jordanian schools and the burden this has placed on the human and financial resources of Jordan's education system, by dint of its "Education for All" vision supporting both vulnerable Jordanians and refugees. As an innovation in learning, initiatives supporting online learning have been introduced to both Jordanians and refugees permitting them to

---

[52] Queen Rania Foundation, "QRF Fact Sheet Refugee Education in Jordan", 2017, p. 1, https://www.qrf.org/sites/default/files/2019-05/refugee_education_in_jordan_en_condensed.pdf (Access 04.06.2020).

[53] Human Rights Watch, "Jordan: Further Expand Education Access for Syrian Refugees", 2017, https://www.hrw.org/news/2016/08/16/jordan-further-expand-education-access-syrian-refugees (Access 05.06.2020).

[54] Ferris and Kirisci, op. cit, p. 41.

[55] UNICEF, "Access to Education for Syrian Refugee: Children and Youth in Jordan Host Communities - Joint Education Needs Assessment Report - Education Sector Working Group", 2015, p. 24, https://reliefweb.int/sites/reliefweb.int/files/resources/REACH_JENA_HC_March2015_.pdf (Access 04.06.2020).

[56] UNICEF, "Every Child Reaching Their Potential Through Learning", 2017, https://www.unicef.org/jordan/5._Jordan__Every_child_reaching_their_potential_through_learning.pdf (Access 04.06.2020).

[57] No Lost Generation, "We Made a Promise: Ensuring Learning pathways and protection for Syrian Children and youth", 2018, p. 29, https://reliefweb.int/report/syrian-arabrepublic/we-made-promise-ensuring-learning-pathways-and-protection-syrian (Access 06.06.2020).

[58] "The three-year rule is a policy in place within the Ministry of Education that states that no student can enrol in Jordanian public schools if they have been out of school for three years or more." (Prabhakar R., 2018: 12)

[59] Mouna Younes and Morrice, L., "Summary of Challenges Relevant to Refugees' Education in Jordan", Centre for International Education and Development, University of Sussex, Brighton UK, 2019, pp. 9-11.

flourish alongside each other.[60]

**Figure 6.** The Number of Enrolled Syrian Refugee Children in Formal Education in Jordan (2015-2017)[61]

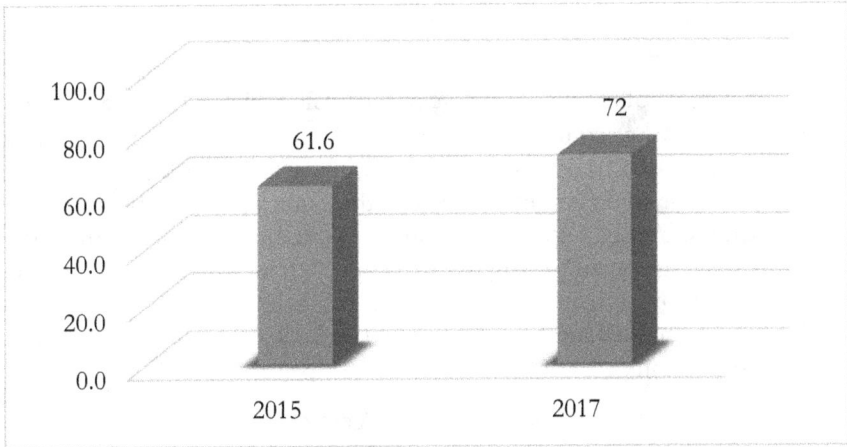

As an effort to foster social cohesion, UNHCR and partners sustain Community-Based Protection (CBP)[62] for those who are affected by the Syrian conflict. This approach depends mainly on building community centres across the country for refugees and local communities to participate in several activities together and promoting dialogue and trust, as the majority of refugees in Jordan live in urban communities.

Equally important, refugees have increasingly been included in financial life, by introducing iris-activated cash dispensers in order to facilitate cash assistance. Additionally, university students now receive their stipends through mobile wallets.[63]

Regarding access to healthcare by Syrians in Jordan, it should be stressed that it is fairly well established. Jordan has one of the most advanced health

---

[60] https://www.globalcompactrefugees.org/article/jordan (Access 19.05.2020).
[61] UNICEF, "Access to Education for Syrian Refugee: Children and Youth in Jordan Host Communities - Joint Education Needs Assessment Report - Education Sector Working Group", p. 24. UNICEF, "Every Child Reaching Their Potential Through Learning"
[62] "Community-based protection (CBP) puts the capacities, agency, rights and dignity of persons of concern at the centre of programming. It generates more effective and sustainable protection outcomes by strengthening local resources and capacity and identifying protection gaps through consultation. UNCHR takes a community-based approach in all its work with the people it serves. Through consultation and participation, communities engage meaningfully and substantively in all programmes that affect them, and play a leading role in change. UNHCR recognizes that, without the engagement of persons of concern, external intervention alone cannot achieve sustained improvement in their lives." (Source: UNHCR, Emergency Handbook. https://emergency.unhcr.org/entry/50478/community-based-protection).
[63] https://www.globalcompactrefugees.org/article/jordan (Access 19.05.2020).

care systems in the region, with both public and private sector services that can be accessed by Syrian refugees. Jordan has managed to integrate refugees into their health system so they can have access to the public services in a similar way as Jordanians. Syrians who are registered under the MoI in Jordan are provided with healthcare access and services in the governorate where they live in, as uninsured Jordanians.[64]

In the context of the first objective of the GCR, which is to "ease pressure on countries that welcome and host refugees"[65], Syrian refugees have now access to subsidised healthcare through a multi donor account, the Jordan Health Fund for Refugees, established in the Ministry of Health (MoH) to help lessen the burden on the Health infrastructure in Jordan. Another step towards meeting the objectives of the Compact in Jordan has been the issuance of Government Identity cards, facilitating refugees' access to healthcare and basic education, as well as enhancing the overall protection scope in the country.[66]

UNCHR also provides help for the refugees concerning healthcare. Free health services and resources are provided in the camps to help lessen the financial burden on Jordan in meeting the health needs of the refugees. UNHCR in its response plan has involved intersectoral working groups in an organised, systematic and specialised delivery of services in all sectors including health. Programmes, like the Mental Health and Psychological Support Sub-Working Group,[67] manage clinical psychiatric care, along with other groups responsible for psychological support.

The GoJ and UNCHR have launched comprehensive programmes to address the health needs of refugees. Some refugees have, however, failed to access these services because of their lack of knowledge about them. For that reason, the Community Health Task Group[68] was created in 2013 to raise community awareness of their rights to access health care, the nature of care services and the places of their availability. The coverage of the community health programme targets both refugees and Jordanians.

Furthermore, since 2013, the government initiated a programme labelled the Host Community Support Platform/National Resilience Plan in parallel with RRPs. This initiative was established to impede "the deterioration of development achievements in Jordan while tackling the refugee crisis". It

[64] Wireen Dator, Hamzeh Abunab and Norenia Dao-ayen, "Health Challenges and Access to Health Care Among Syrian Refugees in Jordan: A Review", **East Mediterranean Health Journal**, Vol. 24, No. 7, 2018, 684.
[65] https://www.unhcr.org/comprehensive-refugee-response-framework-crrf.html (Access 02.02.2020).
[66] https://www.globalcompactrefugees.org/article/jordan (Access 19.05.2020).
[67] https://data2.unhcr.org/en/working-group/7 (Access 20.05.2020).
[68] https://data2.unhcr.org/en/working-group/64?sv=4&geo=36 (Access 20.05.2020).

initially covered only northern Jordan, mainly Irbid, Mafraq, and Zarqa governorates, as the crisis has been intense in the northern area.[69]

However, many refugees still cannot access healthcare, particularly after the change in health policies in 2014 requiring refugees to cover the costs of medicines and consultations. Financial constraints are the first barriers for refugees to access health services, added to the far distance of clinics, especially from their camps.[70] Although UNHCR provides cash assistance to Syrian refugees both in and out of the camps and to vulnerable Jordanian nationals, the financial constraint is still reported as a barrier to health access.

It should be argued Jordan has partly managed the crisis and developed its mechanisms to sustain the welfare of Syrian refugees in the country due to its extended experience of hosting refugees.

"Despite the enormous socio-political, environmental and economic burdens of handling refugees, Jordan has remained steadfast in its humanitarian commitment to refugees despite depletion of its resources and, to some extent, deprivation of its local population of government allocations."[71]

While considerable progress has been made, several challenges remain overarching. The Compact did not integrate refugee perspectives at its inception, in that it has been slow to improve their daily lives. It is evident that financial support has raised school enrolment; however, predominant numbers of children have not joined schools owing to financial barriers and potentially to the quality of services provided. Furthermore, there has been a substantial progress regarding the issuance of work permits; yet, crucial sectors and self-employment remain closed to refugees. Additionally, concerning the indicators measuring progress, they should concentrate on the extent to which they improve life standards of refugees. Equally significant, donor governments, host governments and international organisations currently focusing on refugee compacts "should start with what refugees need and want, and be realistic about what such arrangements can achieve".[72]

Overall, it should be noted that Jordan has represented a strong model for the local inclusion of Syrian refugees through mainly its Compact and multiple initiatives encouraged by the international community enhancing the concept of burden sharing. Several conferences have been held to promote

---

[69] Dator, Abunab and Dao-ayen, op. cit, p. 684.
[70] Shannon Doocy, Emily Lyles, Laila Akhu-Zaheya, Ann Burton and Gilbert Burnham, "Health Service Access and Utilization Among Syrian Refugees in Jordan", **International Journal for Equity in Health**, Vol. 15, No. 108, 2016, p. 2.
[71] Dator, Abunab and Dao-ayen, op. cit, p. 683.
[72] Barbelet, Hagen-Zanker, et al., op. cit, p. 1.

the Jordan experience, particularly Brussels Conferences, organised by the European Union, to muster political support and humanitarian funding. Among the recent endeavours, the 2019 London Initiative is a joint action between the British and Jordanian Governments so as to support investments, growth and jobs in Jordan and to contribute to an economically strong and peaceful country.

## Turkey

From 2015, Turkish authorities shifted its policy from providing temporary protection, to promoting voluntary return of refugees and integrating them into its society.

The Turkish authorities long considered the Syrian refugee situation as temporary and provided extensive humanitarian aid to displaced Syrians seeking refuge within its territory. The Disaster and Emergency Management Authority (AFAD), Turkey's main emergency management instrument, established camps and provided social assistance to the new arrivals. However, when the refugee situation started to become protracted, given that normalisation in Syria approaches a deadlock, the government decided to make policies considering Syrians' long-term prospects in the country.

It is crucial to note that both the scale and duration of the refugee influx also compelled Turkish policymakers to back off from their initial encampment policy and, hence, to urbanise refugees in camps for the long term. Currently, ca. 98% the Syrian refugee population in Turkey live in cities. The table and the charts below demonstrate the evolution of the policies of the Turkish authorities regarding the urbanisation of Syrian refugees in camps as an initiative of local integration. According to the data published by UNHCR Turkey, the number of camps has been reduced from 24 in 2016 to only 7 in May 2020. Equally important, the number of provinces retaining camps decreased to its half from 10 provinces (2016-2018) to 5 in May 2020. Accordingly, the total number of refugees residing in camps in Turkey dropped from 262,720 in 2016 to 217,356 in 2018 to only 63,437 in May 2020.

Starting from 2018, the pace of relocation process to Temporary Accommodation Centres (TACs) has been speeded up. In that year, UNHCR helped the Directorate-General for Migration Management (DGMM) in the closure of six (TACs) hosting 51,200 persons, and the decongestion of three additional ones hosting ca. 45,200 persons. Syrian refugees residing in the TACs were given the following options: relocating to an urban area in a province of their choice, moving to another TAC identified by DGMM if their TAC was closed, or staying in their own TAC if it was decongested. UNHCR provided support for the relocation of refugees who preferred to leave their TACs. A one-off cash relocation assistance package to cover transportation, rent and immediate needs was granted and more than 65 million Turkish Liras were provided for 60,490 refugees choosing to move to urban areas. Ca. 8,685 refugees preferring to move to another TAC received transportation assistance.[73]

**Table 2.** Evolution of Encampment in Turkey (2016-2020)[74]

| Year | Number of Provinces with Camps | Total Number of Camps |
|------|-------------------------------|-----------------------|
| 2016 | 10 | 24 |
| 2017 | 10 | 22 |
| 2018 | 10 | 19 |
| 2019 | 8 | 13 |
| 2020 | 5 | 7 |

The regulation of temporary protection has been expanded over the years. The Government of Turkey (GoT) has also introduced other measures regarding refugees' access to education, health services and the labour market. Meanwhile, restrictive regulations on mobility have been enacted, owing to the government's mounting interests concerning national and regional security. It should be noted that EU concerns have played role in introducing such measures, in that the March 2016 EU-Turkey Statement required Turkey to take "any necessary measures to prevent new sea and land routes for irregular migration opening from Turkey to the EU".[75]

As an initiative to integrate Syrian refugees in the Turkish society, the Turkish authorities has enacted a regulation to grant Turkish citizenship to certain individuals. According to the data published on 30 December 2019 by the Ministry of Interior (MoI), 110,000 Syrians have been granted citizenship: 53,000 adults and 57,000 children.[76] Additionally, the State of Turkey grants citizenship to any individual who has a mother or a father with

---

[73] UNHCR, "UNHCR Turkey Operational Update, Year 2018 Highlights", 2018, p. 5, https://www.unhcr.org/tr/wp-content/uploads/sites/14/2019/02/UNHCR-Turkey-Operational-Highlights-2018-Final.pdf (Access 19.05.2020).

[74] UNHCR, "UNHCR: Syrian Refugee Camps Provincial Breakdown", 2016, https://data2.unhcr.org/en/ documents/details/51787 (Access 28.05.2020). UNHCR, "UNHCR Turkey: Syrian Refugee Camps and Provincial Breakdown of Syrian Refugees Registered in South East Turkey - May 2017", 2017,https://data2.unhcr.org/en/documents/details/569 83 (Access 28.05.2020). UNHCR, "UNHCR Turkey: Syrian Refugee Camps and Provincial Breakdown of Syrian Refugees Registered in South East Turkey - May 2018", 2018, https://data2.unhcr.org/en/ documents/details/63545 (Access 28.05.2020). UNHCR, "UNHCR Turkey: Syrian Refugee Camps and Provincial Breakdown of Syrian Refugees Registered in South East Turkey - May 2019", 2019, https://data2.unhcr.org/en/documents/details/69484 (Access 28.05.2020). UNHCR, "UNHCR Turkey: Syrian Refugee Camps and Provincial Breakdown of Syrian Refugees Registered in South East Turkey - May 2020", 2020, https://data2.unhcr.org/en/documents/details/76072 (Access 28.05.2020).

[75] European Parliament, "EU-Turkey Statement and Action Plan", 2018, p. 1, www.europarl.europa.eu/legislative-train/theme-towards-a-new-policy-on-migration/file-eu-turkey-statement-action-plan (Access 28.05.2020).

[76] Refugees and Asylum Seekers Assistance and Solidarity Association (RASAS), "Türkiyedeki Suriyeli Sayısı Mayıs 2020", 2020, https://multeciler.org.tr/turkiyedeki-suriyeli-sayisi/ (Access 28.05.2020).

Turkish nationality, or both or who is married to a Turkish national following three years of the marriage. These regulations have facilitated the issuance of citizenship to several Syrian refugees.

**Figure 7.** Total number of refugees in camps in Turkey (2016-2020)[77]

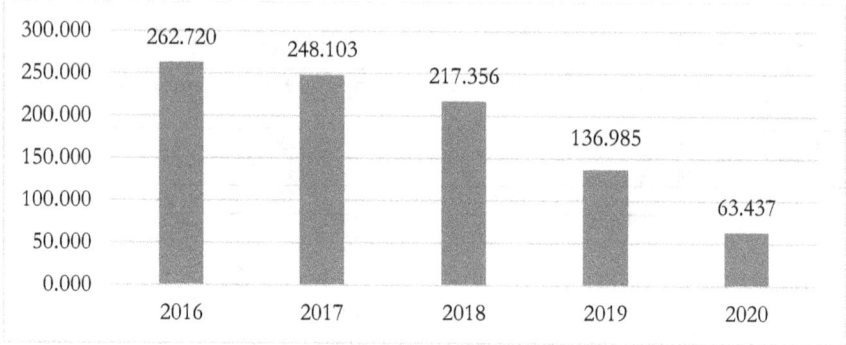

As Jordan, Turkey has significantly intended to reform work permit regulations to support Syrian refugees. It should be stressed that Turkey has been the primary to establish a formal procedure for Syrian refugees to access work permits, as the authorities issued the Regulation on Work Permits of Refugees Under Temporary Protection in January 2016. This regulation has also permitted Syrian refugees to access the government employment agency, ISKUR, which presents job matching and other services.[78] According to the data published by the MoI, 31,185 Syrians have received work permits by 31 March 2019.[79] However, it should be mentioned that the vast majority of permits have been issued to Syrians with residency permits.[80] Furthermore, the number of granted work permits remains low, particularly in comparison to the total number of working-age Syrian refugees in Turkey.

Prior to 2016 regulation, most Syrian refugees were assigned to work in the informal sector. In 2015, ca. 300,000 Syrians were employed informally, including those under 18. It is evident that working in the informal sector has exposed Syrian to exploitation, in that most of them work informally in

---

[77] UNHCR, "UNHCR: Syrian Refugee Camps Provincial Breakdown", 2016.
. UNHCR, "UNHCR Turkey: Syrian Refugee Camps and Provincial Breakdown of Syrian Refugees Registered in South East Turkey - May 2017", 2017.
UNHCR, "UNHCR Turkey: Syrian Refugee Camps and Provincial Breakdown of Syrian Refugees Registered in South East Turkey - May 2018", 2018.
UNHCR, "UNHCR Turkey: Syrian Refugee Camps and Provincial Breakdown of Syrian Refugees Registered in South East Turkey - May 2019", 2019.
UNHCR, "UNHCR Turkey: Syrian Refugee Camps and Provincial Breakdown of Syrian Refugees Registered in South East Turkey - May 2020", 2020.
[78] UNDP, ILO, and WFP, op. cit, p. 46.
[79] Rasas, op. cit.
[80] UNDP, ILO, and WFP, op. cit, p. 46.

labour-intensive, low-wage jobs in sectors such as construction and agriculture. Accordingly, the regulation introduced by the Ministry of Labour (MoL) in 2016 has been a crucial action for the facilitation of fair and legal access to the labour market for Syrians, in that they are paid at least the minimum wage.[81]

The regulation, however, stipulates some caveats and requirements. Syrians have permission to work only in the province where they are registered. Additionally, according to the Turkish law of labour, the number of foreigners employed within a business cannot exceed 10% of the number of Turkish citizen employees. Some Turkish scholars have indicated that this quota brings about impediments, particularly in the southern and south-eastern provinces, where close to half of Syrian refugees live, let alone the high unemployment levels in some of them as demonstrated in the map below, for example Kilis. Such a situation may aggravate the labour market there as it increases competition between local and Syrian labourers for low-paid informal jobs.[82]

**Map 1.** Unemployment rate (2015) and share of Syrians (2016) out of the total population of Turkey[83]

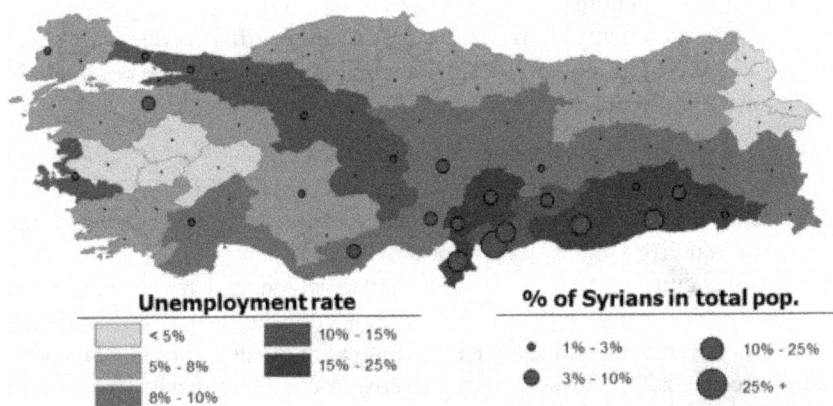

| Unemployment rate | | % of Syrians in total pop. | |
|---|---|---|---|
| < 5% | 10% - 15% | 1% - 3% | 10% - 25% |
| 5% - 8% | 15% - 25% | 3% - 10% | 25% + |
| 8% - 10% | | | |

Overall, most Syrian refugees in Turkey have then difficulties to access formal employment. This conventional sight emanates from the existed conditions of restricted number of work permits issued so far, the limited availability of job opportunities, the tribulation of finding a job that matches the skills of the refugees and the number of occupations accessible to

---

[81] Fulya Memişoğlu, "Assessing the Development-Displacement Nexus in Turkey: Working Paper", International Centre for Migration Policy Development (ICMPD), Vienna, 2018, pp. 21-22.
[82] Timur Kaymaz and Omar Kadkoy, "Syrians in Turkey: The economics of integration. Expert Brief Regional Politics", 2016, p. 4, https://www.tepav.org.tr/upload/files/1473326257-7.Syrians_in_Turkey The_Economics_of_Integration.pdf (Access 29.05.2020).
[83] Ibid., p. 4.

foreigners. Another hurdle should be underlined which is the lack of information among Turkish employers about the regular employment of foreigners and how to handle procedures for work permit applications. Overarchingly, taking these factors into account, refugees have retained their engagement in informal employment, hence being exposed to potential exploitation and discrimination.[84]

It should be underscored, however, that the existence of Syrian refugees has contributed to the Turkish economy by introducing new businesses, investments, and skills. According to the statistics published by the Union of Chambers and Commodity Exchanges of Turkey (TOBB) on their website, the number of Syrian-partnered firms established annually in Turkey expeditiously soared from 30 in 2010 before the conflict to 81 in 2011, 165 in 2012 and 489 before the mass-influx, to 1,257 in 2014, 1,599 in 2015, 1,764 in 2016, 1,202 in 2017 and 1,595 in 2018 after the mass-influx starting from 2014. It should be noted that the whole number of Syrian-partnered firms established in Turkey reached 15,159 by 26 February 2019.[85]

More importantly, as demonstrated in the chart below, these established firms have extensively contributed to the Turkish economy, in that their investment share is considerably substantial, let alone the job opportunities provided for the unemployed people. For example, their investment share was (₺) 271.093.500 only in 2018. Their total investment share counted (₺) 1.201.763.838 between 2013 and 2018 (TOBB, 2020).[86]

Regarding the classification of industries found in Syrian-owned enterprises, there is a variety of businesses, such as eatery and food, construction, textiles, property, travel, and transportation. It should be noted that Syrian enterprises are mainly located in southern parts of Turkey, for example the cities of Gaziantep and Mersin which had more than 1,000 registered Syrian enterprises each in 2016. It is important to stress the volume of trade between Syria and these cities, along with border cities like Hatay, in that it exceeded 2010 levels, given the strong connection the Syrian firms have with counterparts in Syria and in other Middle Eastern markets. Equally crucial, according to the bulletin published by the Economic Policy Research Foundation of Turkey (TEPAV) regarding the month of June 2018, Istanbul has the largest number of companies established with joint Syrian capital, followed by Mersin, Bursa and Hatay.[87]

---

[84] Memişoğlu, op. cit, p. 22.
[85] Rasas, op. cit.
The Union of Chambers and Commodity Exchanges of Turkey (TOBB), "Information Retrieval Division: Company Establishment and Liquidation Statistics", 2020, https://tobb.org.tr/BilgiErisim Mudurlugu/Sayfalar/Eng/KurulanKapananSirketistatistikleri.php (Access 30.05.2020).
[86] TOBB, op. cit.
[87] Memişoğlu, op. cit, p. 23. ; Economic Policy Research Foundation of Turkey (TEPAV), "Suriye

**Figure 8.** The number of Syrian-partnered firms established annually in Turkey and their investment share in TL (2013-2018)[88]

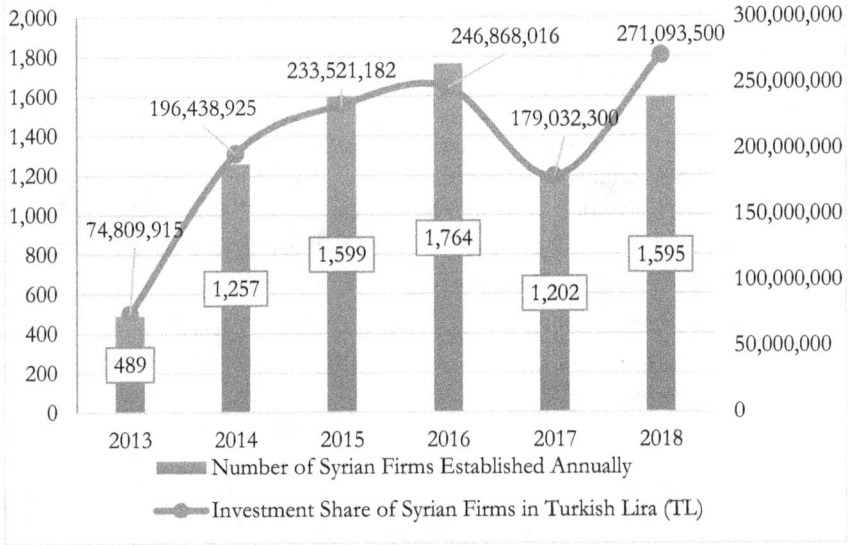

According to some studies, it should be underlined that there has been a drop in unemployment in Gaziantep, Kilis and Adıyaman. After the influx of Syrian refugees in the southern Turkey, these cities have experienced an economic revival. The Syrian labour force has increasingly contributed to the economic growth in this region. However, there has been a rise in unemployment in Şanlıurfa and Diyarbakir meanwhile. Some researchers have explicated such evolution by the downward pressure on wages following Syrians' participation in agricultural work particularly in seasonal work. Syrian labourers have considerably replaced agricultural labourers from Şanlıurfa, Adıyaman and Mardin.[89] Overall, some economists even argued that refugee influx may has been a leading factor behind Turkey's unprecedentedly high economic growth rate in 2015.[90]

Regarding the education sector, it should be stressed that half of the Syrian population in Turkey are school-age children. According to some

Sermayeli Sirketler Bülteni [Bulletin on Syrian-capital companies]", 2018, p. 2, https://www.tepav.org.tr/upload/files/1533018887-4. TEPAV_Suriye_Sermayeli_Sirketler_ Bulteni___Haziran_2018.pdf (Access 30.05.2020).

[88] Ibid.

[89] Kalkinma Atölyesi, "Bereketli Topraklar, Zehir Gibi Yasamlar: Suriyeli Gocmen Mevsimlik Gezici Tarim Iscileri Adana Ovasi Mevcut Durum", 2016, p. 9, http://www.ka.org.tr/dosyalar/file/Yayinlar/Raporlar/TURKCE/04/BEREKETL%C4%B0%20TOPRAKLAR%20ZEH%C4%B0R%20G%C4%B0B%C4%B0%20YA%C5%9EAMLAR.pdf (Access 31.05.2020). Memişoğlu, op. cit, p. 24.

[90] Nevzat Devranoğlu, "Fridges and Flour: Syrian Refugees Boost Turkish Economy", 2016, https://www.reuters.com/article/us-mideast-crisis-turkey-economy/fridges-and-flour-syrian-refu-gees-boost-turkish-economy-idUSKCN0VS1XR (Access 31.05.2020).

studies, access to education for Syrian children has been a tribulation owing to "legal, bureaucratic and language barriers; financial hardship; and lack of the required educational materials, teaching staff and public-school capacity".[91]

According to Turkish law, all children, even foreigners, have the right to access basic education free of charge in public schools. After the influx of 2014, the Turkish Ministry of National Education issued Circular 2014/21 concerning the educational services for foreigners, stipulating the establishment of Temporary Education Centres (TECs) so as to facilitate access to education for Syrian children and also introducing measures to enable them to enrol in public schools.[92]

The TECs provide Syrian curricula in Arabic and Turkish, as an attempt to remove the language barrier, upon authorisation of the provincial directorates of national education. In TECs, children are instructed by Syrian teachers of several qualification levels.[93] Children living in camps have attended TECs within the camps. Regarding urban refugee children, they can attend TECs if there is one in the city they live in; otherwise, they can attend public or private schools. After the issuance of the circular, the number of Syrian children enrolled in public schools soared from 62,357 in the academic year 2015-2016 to 201,505 in 2016-2017. The school enrolment of Syrian children in Turkey rose from 30% in 2014-2015 to 62.52% in 2017-2018 as demonstrated in the table below.

The increase of school enrolment among Syrian refugees is partly explained by the positive impact of financial support through EU-funded education projects. For example, the Conditional Cash Transfer for Education (CCTE) programme, as part of the EU Facility for Refugees, has been a sustainable instrument for promoting Syrian students' enrolment. This programme provides a monthly cash assistance sum of 35 TL for boys and 40 TL for girls in kindergarten and primary school, 50 TL for boys and 60 TL for girls at high school and additional support for families at the beginning of each school term in the form of 100 TL per beneficiary child in primary school, 200 TL in lower secondary school and 250 TL in upper secondary school. Moreover, about 83% of CCTE beneficiaries benefit from the Emergency Social Safety Net programme which provides monthly cash transfers of 120 TL per family member.[94]

[91] Memişoğlu, op. cit, p. 24.
[92] Ahmet İçduygu and Şimşek Doğuş, "Syrian Refugees in Turkey: Towards Integration Policies", Turkish Policy Quarterly, Vol. 15, No.3, 2016, 66.
[93] **Turkey's refugee crisis: The Politics of Permanence. Report No. 241.** International Crisis Group, 2016, p. 5, https://d2071andvip0wj.cloudfront.net/241-turkey-s-refugee-crisis-the-politics-of-permanence_0.pdf (Access 30.05.2020).
[94] UNICEF, "Conditional Cash Transfer for Education (CCTE) Programme for Syrians and Other

**Table 3.** Number of Syrian children enrolled at school in Turkey (2014-2018)[95]

| School Year | Syrian Students in Public Schools | Syrian Students in TECs | Syrian Children Registered as Students | School-Aged Syrian Children in Turkey | School Enrolment of Syrian Children in Turkey (%) |
|---|---|---|---|---|---|
| 2014-2015 | 40,000 | 190,000 | 230,000 | 756,000 | 30 |
| 2015-2016 | 62,357 | 248,902 | 311,259 | 834,842 | 37 |
| 2016-2017 | 201,505 | 291,039 | 492,544 | 833,039 | 59 |
| 2017-2018 | 387,849 | 222,429 | 610,278 | 976,200 | 62.52 |

It should be noted that, between 2014 and 2018, enrolment in TECs has been decreasing from 82.61% to 36.45%, meanwhile enrolment at public schools have been increasing from only 17.39% to 63.55% as demonstrated in the graph below.[96] Enrolment in TECs has been reduced due to the risk of "creating a marginalised community as a result of parallel education systems". The Turkish government has considerably planned to assimilate Syrian children into the national structure by eliminating TECs, in that Syrians starting primary and pre-school cannot register in TECs, rather they can only attend public schools. Accordingly, TECs will be gradually ceased. Certainly, the government has responded to the fear of parents that their children will not develop proficiency in their mother-tongue and will have difficulties of reintegration into the Syrian school system upon return by "working on ways to enable the children to maintain their Arabic language with elective and extra-curricular classes in public schools".[97] Furthermore, the Turkish government encourages families to send their children to school by providing 'education cash grant' for each child attending school as an attempt to guarantee education for Syrian children and impede child labour since many families need their children to earn money for household.[98]

Regarding healthcare, on the one hand, Syrians with temporary protection status are entitled to access social support and medical care under the Law on Foreigners and International Protection (LFIP) and Temporary Protection Regulation (TPR). On the other hand, they may have access to healthcare only in the city where they are registered, though there are some suggestions that under specific conditions they may be able to use care services elsewhere. Healthcare services are provided by the Ministry of

---

Refugees", 2020, p. 1, https://www.unicef.org/turkey/en/media/9006/file (Access 30.05.2020).
[95] Ministry of National Education, 2018, Retrieved from Memişoğlu, op. cit, p. 25.
[96] Memişoğlu, op. cit, p. 25.
[97] Turkey's refugee crisis: The Politics of Permanence. Report No. 241. International Crisis Group, p. 6.
[98] **The Rising Costs of Turkey's Syrian Quagmire. Europe Report N°230.** International Crisis Group, 2014, p. 9, https://d2071andvip0wj.cloudfront.net/the-rising-costs-of-turkey-s-syrian-quagmire.pdf (Access 30.05.2020).
Turkey's refugee crisis: The Politics of Permanence. Report No. 241. International Crisis Group, pp. 6-7.

Health (MoH) for Syrians in TACs. Unregistered Syrians receive emergency and essential public healthcare services free of charge.[99] According to report published in 2018 by the Grand National Assembly of Turkey (TGNA), there had been ca. 20 million treatments in outpatient clinics, ca. 1 million in inpatient clinics and ca. 1 million surgeries for Syrian patients.[100]

**Figure 9.** Share (%) of Syrian students enrolment at public schools and in TECs (2014-2018)[101]

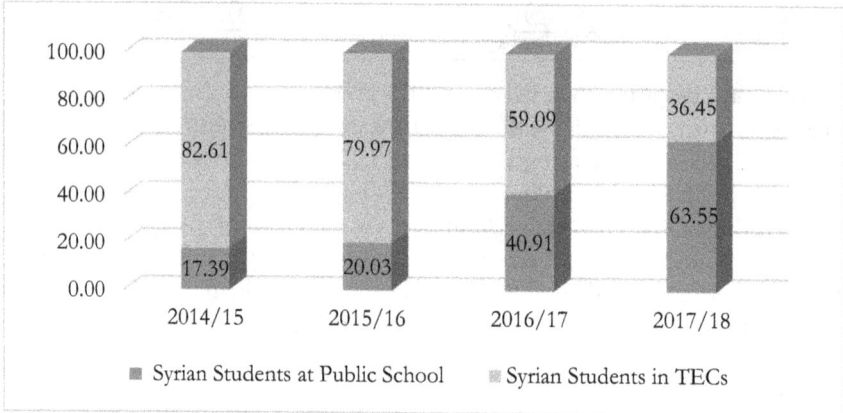

The MoH has managed to resolve the problems of overcrowding in public hospitals, particularly those in border provinces by establishing a new unit called the Department of Migration Health. Ca. 103 Migrant Health Centres (MHCs) have been established within the framework of the Sıhhat project, funded by €300 million under the EU Facility for Refugees in Turkey.[102] MHCs employ Syrian healthcare personnel to provide services to Syrians under temporary protection with supervision maintained by Turkish doctors. Ca. 764,000 consultations were provided, and ca. to 413,000 Syrian refugee children under the age of five had vaccinations in the MHCs in 2017. Additionally, ca. 2,200 Syrian doctors and nurses had training and certificates, of whom more than 780 work in MHCs by 2018. Furthermore, the EU has engaged in supporting 178 MHCs, as well as 10 community mental health centres for refugees.[103] According to a survey published by AFAD in 2013, Syrian migrants' satisfaction with the health services they received was 60%

[99] Memişoğlu, op. cit, p. 27.
[100] TGNA, "Türkiye Büyük Millet Meclisi, İnsan Haklarını İnceleme Komisyonu, Mülteci Hakları Alt Komisyonu, Göç ve Uyum Raporu [The Grand National Assembly of Turkey, Human Rights Inquiry Committee Migration and Integration Report]", 2018, p. 134, https://www.tbmm.gov.tr/komisyon/insanhaklari/docs/2018/goc_ve_uyum_raporu.pdf (01.06.2020).
[101] Ministry of National Education, 2018, Retrieved from Memişoğlu, op. cit, p. 25.
[102] Ibid., p. 257.
[103] Memişoğlu, op. cit, p. 28.

within the camps and 81.4% outside the camps.[104]

Overall, according to the Regional Refugee and Resilience Plan (3RP) annual report of 2017, Turkey achieved the optimum results among LJT. The out-reach of Turkey to Syrian refugees was the highest, in that 80% of the refugee population were assisted although Turkey in that year received only 45% of the required funding.[105]

## Challenges to the integration process and policy recommendations

It is evident that none of the durable solutions are currently in sight for the majority of Syrian refugees in LJT, particularly Lebanon. For that reason, firstly, it is crucial to ensure that non-refoulement is respected by all parties. Second, it is in the interest of LJT, especially Lebanon, to seek to reduce hostility and ameliorate livelihoods of both hosting and refugee communities, hence contributing to the economic development and stability of their countries.

Better access to employment by all refugees is a key factor to manage the refugee crisis, by increasing their self-reliance and feeling of security thereby ensuring their inclusion of into local communities and maintaining economic stability. For Lebanon, the government is entitled to grant a stable legal status to refugees as a first step to achieve this end. It should then adopt a fair and transparent system that permits all refugees to obtain legal residency without fees or sponsorship and to facilitate the granting of work permits and its process.

It is evident that economic and employment-related considerations are significant to the refugees' long-term presence in Lebanon and Jordan, with a difference of much higher ratio of Syrian refugees to the local population in Lebanon. The situation is similar in both countries; however, the Jordanian government has efficiently initiated the Jordan Compact which has been achieving effective results. In Lebanon, the generally held belief that Syrian refugees are forcing wages down, bringing about greater unemployment, and increasing the number of Lebanese living below the poverty line should be mitigated by government. Such a belief constitutes an enormous hurdle in front of refugees' access to employment and their fraternisation with local Lebanese communities. In contrast, the positive multiplier effect on the Lebanese economy due to the inflow of humanitarian aid should be

---

[104] AFAD, "Türkiye'deki Suriyeli Sığınmacılar, 2013 Saha Araştırması Sonuçları [Syrian refugees in Turkey: Results of 2013 survey]", 2013, p. 39, https://reliefweb.int/sites/reliefweb.int/files/resources/AFADSurveyonSyrianRefugeesinTurkey2013.pdf (Access 01.06.2020).

[105] UNHCR and UNDP, "Regional Refugee and Resilience Plan 2017-2018 in Response to the Syria Crisis: 2017 Report" 2018, p. 16, https://data2.unhcr.org/en/documents/download/63530 (Access 10.05.2018).

accentuated.[106]

Equally important, better access to education by all school-aged refugee children is another pivotal factor behind efficient handling of the crisis and effective integration of refugees into local communities. It should be noted that despite the increase in school enrolment, there are still many children out of school in LJT. In all three countries, only a fraction of the school-age children currently attend school regularly; for example, only a third of the 621,000 school-age Syrian refugee children are accessing school in Turkey. The situation in Lebanon and Jordan is not more advantageously, in that several challenges keep children from attending schools regularly, including economic difficulties, and the "negative coping mechanisms" adopted for maintaining a livelihood. For that reason, initiatives addressing barriers to education must be planned, particularly those addressing administrative and financial constraints, issues of child protection and safety concerns, the fact schools being too far from child's residence, and the provision of psychosocial support to children.

However, in this educational context, the process of inclusion is much easier in Lebanon and Jordan than in Turkey since they share a common language with Syria. In Turkey, the greatest challenge for Syrian refugees, unless they are Turcoman, is language, in that they encounter a completely different linguistic environment. The Turkish initiative to teach refugee children the Arabic language in extra-curricular classes in public schools has been a positive step to help the new generation retain their mother-tongue. Yet, such an approach will not disregard the difficult linguistic context experienced by refugees and the repercussions engendered by it. It should be noted that this challenge is faced also in Lebanon, in that the language of education is usually in French or English, with Arabic being taught in parallel. Nevertheless, it is advantageous that Lebanon introduced double shifts at schools to accommodate the children.

Addressing the problem of out-of-school children is a critical issue to restrain child labour and early marriage across the three host countries. Child labour is a serious concern usually condoned by households since children are less exposed to arrest for working illegally than are adult men and women. Additionally, early marriage is permitted and even encouraged by some Syrian households as a solution to their disadvantageous situations. There are even those who submit their daughters to polygamous marriages, a fact which represents a serious legal issue in Turkey, where marriage under the age of eighteen and polygamy are both outlawed.

Another key challenge is the absence of proactive initiatives by

---

[106] Ferris and Kirisci, op. cit, p. 60.

governments, particularly the GoL to enhance relations between Syrian refugees and the host communities. In Lebanon, according to a report published by Care International, this gap is "filled by other stakeholders" as a local NGO stressed "NGOs do the work that the national government should do to create a bridge between people and the municipality in which they live, and to link municipalities with each other". Syrian refugees and host communities quotidianly interact in shops and on the streets; yet, the level of meaningful interaction remains extremely low in general.[107] The situation in Turkey is not much better, particularly as both communities do not have commonalities as in Lebanon. Language barriers and inaccurate held beliefs are the main challenges faced to reduce tensions between communities. Regarding Jordan, the situation is less intensified due to the substantial cultural similarities coordinating Syrians and Jordanians.

Overall, for the three countries, consolidating social bonds is a compelling step to break down social barriers. A promising strategy is to bring communities together, create interaction and emphasise their commonalities. Equally crucial, ensuring aid transparency is efficiently convincing for host communities as an approach to excise erroneous held beliefs on government expenditure on refugees. It should be elucidated by policy makers that whether funds come from the governments or international donors, they are intended to benefit both communities and to ensure social stability.

Another pivotal challenge is the under-funding issue. It is evident that whatever the actual cost for Lebanon, Jordan, and Turkey, the financial assistance from the international community has inclined well downwards of what is needed. Turkey puts the direct cost of caring for the refugees at $7.6 to $8 billion, Jordan at $ 4.5 billion by 2016, and Lebanon at more than $4 billion so far.[108] It is conspicuous that the Syrian crisis has received a disproportionate share of global humanitarian funds.

To respond to these challenges and opportunities, some policy recommendations should be developed addressing the needs of both refugees and host countries. Accordingly, related studies should be conducted by mainly UNHCR, hosting governments, NGOs and international research centres in order to assess the development of the displacement situation in regional protection policies and evaluate the status quo, thereby suggest some policy options. These policy recommendations are to be suggested on the ground of desk research and consultations with stakeholders (government institutions, NGOs, chambers of commerce, UN agencies, donors). These policy recommendations are to be concentrated on crucial areas of work and policy options, which should be taken into account

---

[107] Care International, op. cit, pp. 9-10.
[108] Ferris and Kirisci, op. cit, p. 64.

from the time of first arrivals so as to best integrate development approaches.

## Conclusion

Owing to the present tenuous character of the two main prongs of durable solutions to Syrian refugees, that is repatriation and resettlement, local integration as the third prong has much endured the Syrian refugee crisis in LJT with different responses from the parts of governments and communities.

After scrutinising the status quo in Lebanon, it is possible to conclude that the prospect of social inclusion of Syrian refugees within the Lebanese communities is obstructed to a certain extent. The access of Syrians to labour market is restricted, in that scarce work permits are issued, and refugees are only employed in third sector jobs for the most part. Equally important, it appears that the access of Syrian refugee children to schools is one measure to prevent the setting up of refugee camps. Additionally, Syrian and Lebanese children generally still do not share the same classrooms owing to the instruction language, notwithstanding the increase of Syrian children enrolment. Healthcare access is also limited, in the sense that Syrian refugees are admitted only to certain primary healthcare centres and accepted only to public hospitals contracted with UNHCR. It is particularly significant to conclude that the absence of governmental initiatives to reduce hostility and strengthen social bonds between the Lebanese communities and Syrian refugees impedes any prospect of integration.

It should be stressed that Jordan has partly managed the crisis and developed its mechanisms to sustain the inclusion of Syrian refugees in the country due to its extended experience of hosting refugees. The GoJ provides access to labour market and grants work permits, albeit closed to self-employment. Equally crucial, Syrian refugee children have access to education and school enrolment has increased nonetheless the high percentage of out-of-school children. Access to both public and private healthcare institutions is also provided along with other subsidised health services. It is concluded that Jordan has remained steadfast in its humanitarian response to refugees and multiplied its efforts to include Syrians into the Jordanian society.

In reference to Turkey, it is observed that the GoT has focused on local integration beside return. Syrian refugees in Turkey have access to labour market and work permits, nonetheless the low number issued in comparison with the total working-age refugees. The GoT also provides access to education for Syrian refugee children and has implemented policies enhancing school enrolment nevertheless the high percentage of out-of-school children and the language barrier. Access to healthcare also is assured through governmental regulations along with subsidised healthcare services. The GoT has even granted citizenship to certain Syrian refugees. Hence, it is possible to conclude that Turkey has attempted to concentrate on local integration in the long term as a plan to damp down the refugee crisis.

Overall, the economic and political considerations make the prospects of enhancing the inclusion of Syrian refugees into mainstream Lebanese society an even greater challenge than in Jordan and Turkey. In addition, while considerable progress has been made in these two last countries concerning the local integration, several challenges remain overarching, particularly in Lebanon. Additionally, the process of social inclusion as a durable solution should concentrate on the extent to which integration indicators improve life standards of refugees. Including refugee perspectives is as crucial as integrating and assimilating refugees according to the mainstream social environment. Thus, donor governments, host governments and international organisations currently focusing on refugee compacts should focus on what refugees need and want in order to be wholesomely integrated and simultaneously be part of the host country.

Although the core of this essay is evidently related to local integration, as the third prong of durable solutions, it should be stressed that this approach can only be successful when exhaustively implemented within a more comprehensive global response which takes into consideration the other durable solutions of return and resettlement.

## Abbreviations

**3RP** Regional Refugee and Resilience Plan

**AFAD** Afet ve Acil Durum Yönetimi Başkanlığı (Disaster and Emergency Management Presidency)

**CBP** Community-Based Protection

**CCTE** Conditional Cash Transfer for Education

**DGMM** Directorate-General for Migration Management (Göç İdaresi Genel Müdürlüğü)

**GCR** Global Compact on Refugees

**GoJ** Government of Jordan

**GoL** Government of Lebanon

**GoT** Government of Turkey

**ILO** International Labour Organisation

**LFIP** Law on Foreigners and International Protection

**LJT** Lebanon, Jordan, and Turkey

**MHCs** Migrant Health Centres

**MoH** Ministry of Health

**MoI** the Ministry of Interior

**MoL** Ministry of Labour

**MoSA** Ministry of Social Affairs

**NGOs** Non-Governmental Organisations

**TACs** Temporary Accommodation Centres

**TECs** Temporary Education Centres

**TEPAV** Economic Policy Research Foundation of Turkey

**TGNA** Grand National Assembly of Turkey (Türkiye Büyük Millet Meclisi)

**TOBB** Union of Chambers and Commodity Exchanges of Turkey (Türkiye Odalar ve Borsalar Birliği)

**TPR** Temporary Protection Regulation

**UNDP** The United Nations Development Programme

**UNHCR** United Nations High Commissioner for Refugees

**UNICEF** United Nations Children's Fund

**UNRWA** The United Nations Relief and Works Agency for Palestine Refugees

**WFP** World Food Programme

www.ingramcontent.com/pod-product-compliance
Lightning Source LLC
Chambersburg PA
CBHW050343270326
41926CB00016B/3598